THE CAMBRIDGE LITURGICAL PSALTER

AQUILA

2013

First published by William Collins as
The Psalms: A New Translation for Worship
© 1976, 1977, inclusive language version 1994,
this version was used and bound up with
An Alternative Service 1980 as *The Liturgical
Psalter* and included in six national prayer books.

A new edition published in 2012 by Aquila Books,
26 Richmond Road, Cambridge CB4 3PU, U.K.
as a Kindle Book (ISBN 978-1-872897-11-0),
included for the first time notes on the text by the
Secretary of the Hebrew Panel. The same text is here
made available through Amazon CreateSpace as a
book-on-demand.

The cover of this edition derives from an icon
King David the Psalmist
by courtesy of Juliet Venter
© Juliet Venter 2010
www.juliet-icons.co.uk

ISBN 978-1-872897-12-7

CONTENTS

INTRODUCTION

THE PSALMS

Christians have used the Psalms in their praises of God, in their prayers and in their meditations since the earliest days of the Church. The Jews have used the Psalms for a much longer time, for they were composed for use in ancient Israel. The majority of the Psalms are hymns of praise and thanksgiving to God for what he is and for what he has done (e.g. Pss. 8, 104, 135), or prayers for help and laments because of the sufferings of an individual (e.g. Pss. 6, 22) or his anxieties (e.g. Ps.77), or because of some national disaster such as defeat in battle (e.g. Ps. 44) or the destruction of Jerusalem and its temple (e.g. Pss. 74, 79). There are also meditations on God's providence (e.g. Pss. 49, 73, 78) or on his commandments (e.g. Pss.1, 119). Other Psalms were composed for particular occasions in the nation's life: for the accession of a new king (Ps. 2), for a royal wedding (Ps. 45), or for a pilgrimage to Jerusalem to worship at the temple (e.g. Pss. 84, 122). The temple was the place where most Psalms were originally intended to be sung, but they also came to be used by Jewish congregations in their synagogues and by individuals in their private prayers.

The period in which the Psalms were composed in ancient Israel goes back as early as the time of King David (c. 1000 BC), though modern scholars have questioned the tradition that he was the author of a large number of the poems in our Psalter. Some Psalms were certainly written much later: Ps. 137, for instance, speaks of the exile of the Jews from Jerusalem to Babylon in the sixth century BC. Most of the Psalms, however, cannot be dated precisely and might have been written at almost any time within a period of several centuries. Nor do we know when the last poem in the Psalter was written, though it was probably not later than about 200 BC and may well have been much earlier. The Psalms thus reflect something like three quarters of a millennium in the life and worship of ancient Israel.

Jesus was born a Jew, and he was brought up to know the Psalms intimately and to ponder them. He quoted them in his teaching, and words from the Psalter were on his lips as he hung on the cross. The

Church learned from him, and from God's ancient people the Jews, to value the Psalms, and Christians have used them ever since.

When Christians read the Psalms, they meditate and share the thoughts and varied emotions of the people of God in the Old Testament, the people to whom God made himself known, and they share in Israel's experience of God. The God of the Psalms is the God and Father of our Lord Jesus Christ. The coming of Christ has, however, made a difference, and Christians cannot always think of God in exactly the same way as those who lived before the birth, and death, and resurrection of Jesus. Christians cannot make their own everything in the Psalter, at least not in its original sense. We cannot, for example, identify ourselves with the author of Ps. 137 when he blesses those who will dash Babylonian children against the rocks, however well we may understand the Psalmist's reaction to the murder by Babylonian soldiers of Jewish children. There are parts of the Psalter that Christians must read with detachment. Many Christians feel that they must go further and refrain from the use of such passages, at least in public worship. Nevertheless, although there are verses in the Psalter whose sentiments Christians must not share, there remains much more which they can wholeheartedly make their own.

Throughout the centuries, Christians of different persuasions have found the Psalms a means of prayer and worship that fulfilled their needs. In the future, as in the past, Christians will use the Psalms both in the public worship of the Church and in their private devotions, in meditation, in prayer, and, above all, in praise.

THE NEW TRANSLATION

This present translation was made primarily, though not exclusively, for public worship. Miles Coverdale's version of the Psalms in the Book of Common Prayer has been used for more than four hundred years, and it is well loved by many Anglicans (not least by the members of the translation panel). It will doubtless continue to be used. Yet there are two reasons why a new translation was necessary. First, the Psalms were written in Hebrew, and the study of the Hebrew language and the textual problems of the Old Testament has advanced considerably in the past century, and even in recent years.

More is known about the meanings of the Hebrew words and the history of the text of the Hebrew Bible, and techniques have been developed for dealing with obscure passages and verses where it is likely that mistakes were made by scribes copying the text by hand in ancient times. Second, there was need for a translation that would express the meaning clearly in modern English in a style suitable for use in public worship. There have been several new translations in recent years, but the present one is intended primarily for public speaking and singing.

In September 1970 the Church of England Liturgical Commission invited one of its members, Dr (now Professor) David Frost, to begin work on a liturgical Psalter suitable for use in the services in modern English that the Commission was in process of preparing. At that early stage it was hoped to produce such a Psalter by modestly revising Coverdale's version in the Book of Common Prayer by reference to other English versions (both old and new) and, where it was thought necessary, to the Hebrew Bible. A revision of the Coverdale version had, indeed, earlier been undertaken for the Church of England at the request of the then Archbishops of Canterbury and York and published by the S.P.C.K. in 1963 as *The Revised Psalter*. The members of the Commission who prepared it have been justifiably praised for their skill in removing many errors and obscurities without losing the familiar flavour of the English of the Prayer Book. Yet their very success in achieving their purpose meant that the revised translation did not meet the needs of services in modern English.

As the work proceeded, it became clear that the projected Psalter could not be produced satisfactorily except on the basis of a fresh translation of the Hebrew original. At the same time, increasing interest in the project in this country and abroad, not only from Anglicans but also from members of other Churches, was reported to the Commission. Therefore, with the approval of the Archbishops of Canterbury and York, the Regius Professor of Hebrew in the University of Cambridge was invited in 1972 to convene a panel of Hebrew scholars drawn from various Churches to cooperate with Dr Frost in preparing a new translation of the Psalter.

In the meantime, the work done between 1970 and 1972 was published in 1973 by the Church Information Office under the title

Twenty-Five Psalms from a Modern Liturgical Psalter, with the intention that critics should have an opportunity to judge what was now regarded as a pilot scheme of the project as a whole. The pilot scheme was the work of Dr David Frost in collaboration with the Rev. Andrew Macintosh. Their translation has been revised and incorporated in the present version of the Psalter.

The preparation of this new translation of the Psalter is thus part of the process of revising the services of the Church of England, but it is hoped that it will be found useful by other branches of the Anglican Communion and also by other Christians. The panel responsible for the translation included members of the Roman Catholic, Methodist, and United Reformed Churches, as well as Anglicans—and it may be added that the differences of Christian allegiance made no difference at all to the way in which the problems of translation were tackled. It is also hoped that the translation will be found useful for private prayer and study in addition to public worship.

The translation panel consisted of eight Hebrew and biblical scholars, whose task was to determine the meaning of the Hebrew text, and of Dr Frost, who was responsible for the English wording of the translation. Seven of the Hebrew scholars (of whom two are laymen) teach in universities, and the eighth is the vicar of a country parish.

The first step in preparing the translation was for one of the Hebrew scholars (not always the same one) to make a draft rendering of a Psalm, and for his draft to be discussed and revised by the others. The second draft thus reflected the judgement, not just of one scholar, but of a team of scholars with a specialised knowledge of Hebrew and the Old Testament—and experience showed how much more could be learned by working as a team. The aim at this stage was to produce a rendering that expressed the meaning as simply and clearly as possible, and no attempt was made to achieve an acceptable English style, let alone literary elegance. While the meaning of most parts of the Psalms is clear, there are some obscure passages (e.g. Ps. 87), and the panel did their best to find a meaningful translation. There are also places where good sense cannot be obtained from the Hebrew text, and where there is reason to believe that mistakes were made by scribes in ancient times. In such passages the panel felt free to make small corrections of the

iv

Hebrew text. However, they were reluctant to make changes except where there was no satisfactory alternative. They were also cautious about accepting many recent theories concerning new meanings of Hebrew words, which have not won general acceptance. A translation for use in church should display a cautious attitude both towards emendations of the text and towards new lexicographical theories.

The next stage was the responsibility of David Frost. He took the draft agreed by the Hebrew scholars and prepared a rendering in an English style and rhythm suitable for singing or reading aloud in church. His translation came back to the panel, who were free to criticise it if they believed it to misrepresent the meaning of the Hebrew, or if (which happened only very rarely) they were dissatisfied with the English wording. They did not themselves alter the translation, but asked David Frost to take it away and revise it himself and to bring the revision back to the panel. It was thus hoped, on the one hand, to gain the considered opinion of the team of Hebrew scholars and, on the other, to avoid the flatness of what has been described as 'committee English'.

Finally, a panel of musicians studied the translation and prepared the edition that is pointed for chanting. If the wording was, in their opinion, difficult to sing, they asked the translators to consider whether revision was possible.

This translation is a new rendering of the Hebrew into modern English, not a revision of an older version. However, novelty has not been sought for its own sake, and we have felt free to make use of many phrases from earlier translations. Further, we have followed the example of the great translators in the sixteenth and seventeenth centuries, in keeping close to the images and idioms of the original Hebrew. The English language has been regularly refreshed by the importation of elements from foreign cultures, not least from Hebraic culture through the wisdom of early translators of the Bible into English; and we have thought lively expressions modelled on the Hebrew to be poetically preferable to tired expressions and clichés drawn from the vernacular. Partly because it seems right that the Psalms in Christian worship should be recognised to be from ancient Israel, we have not avoided slight archaisms appropriate to the purposes of poetry. However, we have tested the intelligibility of our drafts, particularly on those who are unfamiliar with older English versions: if we have not attempted to speak in the tones of daily conversation we have made every effort to render the Psalms into language that the ordinary Christian can understand.

Because we have been creating a literary version for public recitation and singing, we have not felt ourselves bound in all places to the strict letter of the Hebrew text, though we have translated the meaning of the whole as well as we were able. On occasion, to give singers sufficient syllables to sing, we have added one or two words to a half-verse, but these have always been justifiable expansions of the meaning of the Hebrew. Again, we have at times put 'God' instead of 'the Lord', or expanded a phrase so that it flows more smoothly: for instance, instead of beginning a Psalm with 'O God' we may begin 'O Lord our God'. Where a Hebrew phrase was obscure if translated baldly we have sometimes added a explanatory word, or offered a paraphrase or a double translation to convey the full meaning in English. Throughout, we have felt free to renumber and redivide the verses where that seemed required by the structure of the verse in English translation, but we have kept to the parallelism of Hebrew poetry and observed most of those divisions into half-lines indicated by Jewish tradition.

Some verses in this translation of the Psalms are printed in square brackets, so that they may be omitted by those who believe their contents to be unsuitable for use in public worship. Most of the bracketed verses are those that were bracketed in the 1928 Prayer Book, but a few changes have been made.

THE TRANSLATORS

Hebrew Panel

Sebastian P. Brock, M.A., D.Phil., University Lecturer in Aramaic and Syriac, and Fellow of Wolfson College, Oxford. (Church of England)

The Rev. J. A. Emerton, M.A., D.D. *(Chairman)*, Regius Professor of Hebrew, and Fellow of St John's College, Cambridge. (Church of England)

The Rev. William Horbury, M.A., Ph.D., Vicar of Great Gransden; formerly Fellow of Clare College, Cambridge; Examining Chaplain to the Bishop of Peterborough. (Church of England)

The Rev. John F. McHugh, L.S.S., Ph.L., S.T.D., Lecturer in Theology, University of Durham; formerly Director of Studies and Lecturer in Sacred Scripture at Ushaw College, Durham. (Roman Catholic)

The Rev. A. A. Macintosh, M.A. *(Secretary)*, Fellow, Tutor and Assistant Dean of St John's College, Cambridge; Examining Chaplain to the Bishop of Carlisle. (Church of England)

The Rev. A. G. MacLeod, M.A., Principal of Westminster College, Cambridge; formerly Moderator of the Presbyterian Church of England. (United Reformed Church)

The Rev. Ernest W. Nicholson, M.A., B.D., Ph.D., University Lecturer in Divinity, and Fellow and Dean of Pembroke College, Cambridge. (Church of England)

John G. Snaith, M.A., B.D., University Lecturer in Hebrew and Aramaic, Cambridge; Member of the Faith and Order Committee of the Methodist Church; Local Preacher. (Methodist)

English

David L. Frost, M.A., Ph.D., Professor of English, University of Newcastle, New South Wales; formerly Fellow of St John's College, Cambridge; member of the Church of England Liturgical Commission. (Church of England)

A version of the Psalms for singing to Anglican chant was prepared by

Roy Massey, B.Mus., Organist and Master of the Choristers, Hereford Cathedral.

Lionel Dakers, B.Mus., Director of the Royal School of Church Music.

The Rev. Canon Cyril V. Taylor, M.A., formerly Precentor of Salisbury Cathedral.

PUBLISHING HISTORY

The Liturgical Psalter was first published in 1977 as *The Psalms: A New Translation for Worship* by William Collins, in cooperation with the Church Information Office. It was put out in two editions, one a plain text (as here), one pointed for singing to Anglican chant.

The text was excerpted in Church of England draft services before its publication and was used in the text of *The Alternative Service Book 1980*. As *The Liturgical Psalter*, the complete translation was bound up with most editions of *The Alternative Service Book 1980*.

The translation had been previously incorporated in *An Australian Prayer Book* (1978), and was subsequently included in *Alternative Prayer Book 1984* (Church of Ireland), and in *An Anglican Prayer Book* (Church of the Province of South Africa). It has been reprinted in a variety of publications in England and abroad, adopted for use by the Uniting Church in Australia and excerpted for the Methodist *Hymns and Psalms* (1983).

An adapted version was published by HarperCollins in 1995 as *The Psalms: The Liturgical Psalter (New Inclusive Language Version)* and in this form was incorporated into *A Prayer Book for Australia* (1995).

In 1996 *The Liturgical Psalter* was extensively excerpted in Donald Davie's edition for Penguin Classics, *The Psalms in English*, as one of two versions representative of the twentieth century.

The original 1977 'Liturgical Psalter' must be distinguished from a Roman Catholic version by the International Consultation on English in the Liturgy, published in 1995, that took the same name, but had its imprimatur revoked in 1998 because of 'concerns about the doctrinal accuracy of the translation'.

Since the original 'Liturgical Psalter' remains permitted for church use in the Anglican Church and elsewhere, the copyright holders have taken the opportunity to differentiate this first version by renaming it *The Cambridge Liturgical Psalter.*

COPYRIGHT PERMISSION

Psalm 1

1   Blessed is the man
who has not walked in the counsel of the ungodly:
nor followed the way of sinners,
nor taken his seat amongst the scornful.

2   But his delight is in the law of the Lord:
and on that law will he ponder day and night.

3   He is like a tree planted beside streams of water:
that yields its fruit in due season.

4   Its leaves also shall not wither:
and look, whatever he does, it shall prosper.

5   As for the ungodly, it is not so with them:
they are like the chaff which the wind scatters.

6   Therefore the ungodly
shall not stand up at the judgement:
nor sinners in the congregation of the righteous.

7   For the Lord cares for the way of the righteous:
but the way of the ungodly shall perish.

Psalm 2

1   Why are the nations in tumult:
and why do the peoples cherish a vain dream?

2   The kings of the earth rise up
and the rulers conspire together:
against the Lord and against his anointed, saying,

1

3   'Let us break their bonds asunder:
       let us throw off their chains from us.'

4   He that dwells in heaven shall laugh them to scorn:
       the Lord will hold them in derision.

5   Then will he speak to them in his wrath,
       and terrify them in his fury:
       'I, the Lord, have set up my king on Zion my holy hill.'

6   I will announce the Lord's decree,
       that which he has spoken:
       'You are my son, this day have I begotten you.

7   'Ask of me,
       and I will give you the nations for your inheritance:
       the uttermost parts of the earth for your possession.

8   'You shall break them with a rod of iron:
       and shatter them in pieces like a potter's vessel.'

9   Now therefore be wise, O kings:
       be advised, you that are judges of the earth.

10   Serve the Lord with awe,
        and govern yourselves in fear and trembling:
       lest he be angry, and you perish in your course.

11   For his wrath is quickly kindled:
       blessed are those that turn to him for refuge.

Psalm 3

1   Lord, how numerous are my enemies:
       many they are that rise against me.

2　　Many there are that talk of me and say:
　　　'There is no help for him in his God.'

3　　But you, Lord, are about me as a shield:
　　　you are my glory, and the lifter up of my head.

4　　I cry to the Lord with a loud voice:
　　　and he answers me from his holy hill.

5　　I lay myself down and sleep:
　　　I wake again, because the Lord sustains me.

6　　Therefore I will not be afraid
　　　of the multitudes of the nations:
　　　who have set themselves against me on every side.

7　　Arise, Lord, and deliver me, O my God:
　　　for you will strike all my enemies upon the cheek,
　　　you will break the teeth of the ungodly.

8　　Deliverance belongs to the Lord:
　　　O let your blessing be upon your people.

Psalm 4

1　　Answer me when I call, O God of my righteousness:
　　　when I was hard-pressed you set me free;
　　　be gracious to me now and hear my prayer.

2　　Sons of men,
　　　how long will you turn my glory to my shame:
　　　how long will you love what is worthless
　　　and seek after lies?

3　　Know that the Lord has shown me his wonderful kindness:
　　　when I call to the Lord he will hear me.

4   Tremble, and do no sin:
      commune with your own heart upon your bed
      and be still.

5   Offer the sacrifices that are right:
      and put your trust in the Lord.

6   There are many who say 'Who will show us any good?:
      the light of your countenance, O Lord, has gone from us.'

7   Yet you have given my heart more gladness:
      than they have when their corn, wine and oil increase.

8   In peace I will lie down and sleep:
      for you alone, Lord, make me dwell in safety.

Psalm 5

1   Hear my words, O Lord, give heed to my groaning:
      listen to my cry, you that are my king and my God.

2   In the morning when I pray to you,
      surely you will hear my voice:
      at daybreak I lay my prayers before you, and look up.

3   For you are not a God
      who takes pleasure in wickedness:
      nor can any evil dwell with you.

4   The boastful cannot stand in your sight:
      you hate all those that work mischief.

5   Those who speak lies you destroy:
      you abhor the treacherous, O Lord,
      and those that are stained with blood.

6   But because of your great goodness
I will come into your house:
I will bow down toward your holy temple
in awe and fear of you.

7   Lead me, O Lord, in your righteousness,
for my enemies lie in wait:
make straight your way before me.

8   For there is no truth in their mouth:
and within they are eaten up by malice.

9   Their throat is an open sepulchre:
and their tongue speaks smooth and flattering words.

10   Destroy them, O God,
let them fall by their own contriving:
cast them out for their many offences,
for they have rebelled against you.

11   But let all who put their trust in you rejoice:
let them shout with joy for ever.

12   Be the defender of those who love your name:
let them exult because of you.

13   For you will bless, O Lord, the man that is righteous:
you will cover him with your favour as with a shield.

Psalm 6

1   O Lord, rebuke me not in your indignation:
nor chasten me in your fierce displeasure.

2   Have mercy upon me, O Lord, for I am weak:
O Lord, heal me, for my very bones are afraid.

3   My soul also is greatly troubled:
and you, Lord – how long will you delay?

4   Turn again, O Lord, and deliver my soul:
O save me for your mercy's sake.

5   For in death no man remembers you:
and who can give you thanks from the grave?

6   I am wearied with my groaning:
every night I drown my bed with weeping,
and water my couch with my tears.

7   My eyes waste away for sorrow:
they grow dim because of all my enemies.

8   Away from me, all you that do evil:
for the Lord has heard the voice of my weeping.

9   The Lord has heard my supplication:
the Lord will receive my prayer.

10   All my enemies shall be put to shame
and greatly dismayed:
they shall turn back and be confounded in a moment.

Psalm 7

1   O Lord my God, to you have I come for shelter:
save me from all who pursue me, O save and deliver me,

2   Lest like lions they tear my throat:
lest they carry me off and none can save me.

3   O Lord my God, if I have done such a thing:
if there is any wickedness on my hands,

4 If I have repaid with evil him that was my friend:
  or plundered my enemy without just cause,

5 Then let the enemy pursue me and overtake me:
  let him trample my life to the ground,
  and lay my honour in the dust.

6 Arise, O Lord, in your anger:
  rise up in wrath against my adversaries.

7 Awake, my God, you that ordain justice:
  and let the assembly of the peoples gather about you;

8 Take your seat high above them:
  and sit in judgement, O Lord, over the nations.

9 Judge for me, O Lord, according to my righteousness:
  and as my integrity requires.

10 Let the wickedness of the ungodly cease,
  but establish the righteous:
  for you try the very hearts and minds of men,
  O righteous God.

11 God is my shield over me:
  he preserves the true of heart.

12 God is a righteous judge:
  and God condemns evil every day.

13 If a man does not turn, he whets his sword:
  he bends his bow and makes it ready;

14 He prepares the instruments of death:
  and makes his arrows darts of fire.

15 See how the ungodly conceives mischief:
  how he swells with wickedness and gives birth to lies.

16   He digs a pit and hollows it out:
      but falls himself into the trap he had made for others.

17   His mischief rebounds upon his own head:
      and his violence comes down on his own pate.

18   I will thank the Lord for his justice:
      I will sing praises to the Lord Most High.

Psalm 8

1   O Lord our Governor:
      how glorious is your name in all the earth!

2   Your majesty above the heavens is yet recounted:
      by the mouths of babes and sucklings.

3   You have founded a strong defence
      against your adversaries:
      to quell the enemy and the avenger.

4   When I consider your heavens, the work of your fingers:
      the moon and the stars which you have set in order,

5   What is man, that you should be mindful of him:
      or the son of man, that you should care for him?

6   Yet you have made him little less than a god:
      and have crowned him with glory and honour.

7   You have made him the master of your handiwork:
      and have put all things in subjection beneath his feet,

8   All sheep and oxen:
      and all the creatures of the field,

9   The birds of the air and the fish of the sea:
      and everything that moves
      in the pathways of the great waters.

10   O Lord our Governor:
      how glorious is your name in all the earth!

Psalm 9

1   I will give you thanks, O Lord, with my whole heart:
      I will tell of all the wonders you have done.

2   I will rejoice and be glad in you:
      I will make my songs to your name, O Most High.

3   For my enemies are driven back:
      they stumble and perish at your presence.

4   You have maintained my cause and my right:
      you sat enthroned as a righteous judge.

5   You rebuked the heathen nations,
      you brought the wicked to destruction:
      you blotted out their name for ever and ever.

6   The strongholds of the enemy
      are made a perpetual desolation:
      you plucked up their cities,
      and even their memory has perished.

7   The Lord confounds them; but the Lord endures for ever:
      he has set up his throne for judgement.

8   He shall judge the world with righteousness:
      and deal true justice to the peoples.

9   The Lord is a strong tower to him that is oppressed:
      he is a tower of strength in time of need.

10   All who heed your name will trust in you:
      for you have never forsaken those that seek you.

11   O sing praises to the Lord who dwells in Zion:
      tell among the peoples what great things he has done.

12   For he that avenges blood has remembered the poor:
      he has not forgotten their cry.

13   The Lord has been merciful toward me,
      he saw what I suffered from my foes:
      he raised me up again from the gates of death,

14   That I might tell all your praises in the gates of Zion:
      that I might rejoice in your deliverance.

15   The nations have sunk into the pit they dug for others:
      in the very snare they laid is their foot taken;

16   The Lord has declared himself and upheld the right:
      the wicked are trapped in the work of their own hands.

17   The wicked shall be given over to death:
      and all the nations that forget God.

18   For the needy shall not always be forgotten:
      nor shall the hope of the poor perish for ever.

19   Arise, Lord, let not man prevail:
      let the nations be judged before you.

20   Put them in fear, O Lord:
      and let the nations know that they are but men.

Psalm 10

1   Why do you stand far off, O Lord:
why do you hide your face in time of need?

2   The ungodly in their pride persecute the poor:
let them be caught in the schemes they have devised.

3   For the ungodly man boasts of his heart's desire:
he grasps at profit, he spurns and blasphemes the Lord.

4   He says in his arrogance 'God will not avenge':
'There is no God' is all his thought.

5   He is settled in all his ways:
your statutes, O Lord, are far above him,
and he does not see.

6   He snorts defiance at his enemies,
he says in his heart 'I shall never be shaken:
I shall walk secure from any man's curse'.

7   His mouth is full of oppression and deceit:
mischief and wickedness lie under his tongue.

8   He skulks about in the villages:
and secretly murders the innocent.

9   His eyes watch out for the helpless:
he lurks concealed like a lion in a thicket.

10   He lies in wait to seize upon the poor:
he lays hold on the poor man and drags him off in his net.

11   The upright are crushed and humbled before him:
and the helpless fall into his power.

12   He says in his heart 'God has forgotten:
          he has covered his face and sees nothing'.

13   Arise, O Lord God, lift up your hand:
          forget not the poor for ever.

14   Why should the wicked man spurn God:
          why should he say in his heart 'He will not avenge'?

15   Surely you see the trouble and the sorrow:
          you look on, and will take it into your own hands.

16   The helpless commits himself to you:
          for you are the helper of the fatherless.

17   Break the power of the ungodly:
          search out his wickedness till it is found no more.

18   The Lord is king for ever and ever:
          the heathen have perished from his land.

19   You have heard the longing of the meek, O Lord:
          you turned your ear to their hearts' desire,

20   To help the poor and fatherless to their right:
          that men may no more be terrified from their land.

Psalm 11

1   In the Lord I have found my refuge:
         how then can you say to me
         'Flee like a bird to the mountains;

2   'Look how the wicked bend their bows,
     and notch the arrow upon the string:
     to shoot from the darkness at the true of heart;

3   'If the foundations are destroyed:
     what can the just man do?'

4   The Lord is in his holy place,
     the Lord is enthroned in heaven:
     his eyes search out, his glance tries the children of men.

5   He tries the righteous and the wicked:
     and him that delights in violence his soul abhors.

6   He will rain down coals of fire and brimstone
     upon the wicked:
     a scorching wind shall be their cup to drink.

7   For the Lord is righteous and loves righteous acts:
     the upright shall see his face.

Psalm 12

1   Help, Lord, for there is not one godly man left:
     the faithful have vanished
     from among the children of men.

2   Everyone tells lies to his neighbour:
     they flatter with their lips, but speak from a double heart.

3   If only the Lord would cut off all flattering lips:
     and the tongue that speaks so proudly!

4   They say 'By our tongues we shall prevail:
     our lips are our servants – who is lord over us?'

5   Because of the oppression of the poor,
       because of the groaning of the needy:
       'I will arise', says the Lord,
       'and set them in safety from those that snarl after them.'

6   The words of the Lord are pure,
       as silver refined in a crucible:
       as gold that is seven times purified in the fire.

7   You will surely guard us, O Lord:
       and shield us for ever from this evil generation,

8   Though the ungodly strut on every side:
       though the vilest of men have mastery of mankind.

Psalm 13

1   How long, O Lord, will you so utterly forget me:
       how long will you hide your face from me?

2   How long must I suffer anguish in my soul,
       and be so grieved in my heart day and night:
       how long shall my enemy triumph over me?

3   Look upon me, O Lord my God, and answer me:
       lighten my eyes, lest I sleep in death;

4   Lest my enemy say 'I have prevailed against him':
       lest my foes exult at my overthrow.

5   Yet I put my trust in your unfailing love:
       O let my heart rejoice in your salvation.

6   And I will make my song to the Lord:
       because he deals so bountifully with me.

Psalm 14

1   The fool has said in his heart 'There is no God':
    they have all become vile and abominable in their doings,
    there is not one that does good.

2   The Lord looked down from heaven
    upon the children of men:
    to see if there were any who would act wisely
    and seek after God.

3   But they have all turned out of the way,
    they have all alike become corrupt:
    there is none that does good, no not one.

4   Are all the evildoers devoid of understanding:
    who eat up my people as men eat bread,
    and do not pray to the Lord?

5   They shall be struck with terror:
    for God is with the company of the righteous.

6   Though they frustrate the poor man in his hopes:
    surely the Lord is his refuge.

7   O that deliverance for Israel might come forth from Zion:
    when the Lord turns again the fortunes of his people,
    then shall Jacob rejoice and Israel be glad.

Psalm 15

1   Lord, who may abide in your tabernacle:
    or who may dwell upon your holy hill?

2   He that leads an uncorrupt life
      and does the thing which is right:
      who speaks the truth from his heart,
      and has not slandered with his tongue;

3   He that has done no evil to his fellow:
      nor vented abuse against his neighbour;

4   In whose eyes the worthless have no honour:
      but he makes much of those that fear the Lord;

5   He that has sworn to his neighbour:
      and will not go back on his oath;

6   He that has not put his money to usury:
      nor taken a bribe against the innocent.

7   He that does these things:
      shall never be overthrown.

Psalm 16

1   Preserve me, O God:
      for in you have I taken refuge.

2   I have said to the Lord, You are my lord:
      and all my good depends on you.

3   As for those who are held holy on the earth:
      the other gods in whom men delight,

4   Though the idols are many that men run after:
      their offerings of blood I will not offer,
      nor take their name upon my lips.

5   The Lord is my appointed portion and my cup:
        you hold my lot in your hands.

6   The share that has fallen to me is in pleasant places:
        and a fair land is my possession.

7   I will bless the Lord who has given me counsel:
        at night also he has instructed my heart.

8   I have set the Lord always before me:
        he is at my right hand, and I shall not fall.

9   Therefore my heart is glad and my spirit rejoices:
        my flesh also shall rest secure.

10   For you will not give me over to the power of death:
        nor suffer your faithful one to see the Pit.

11   You will show me the path of life:
        in your presence is the fulness of joy,
        and from your right hand flow delights for evermore.

Psalm 17

1   Hear my just cause, O Lord, give heed to my cry:
        listen to my prayer, that comes from no lying lips.

2   Let judgement for me come forth from your presence:
        and let your eyes discern the right.

3   Though you search my heart,
        and visit me in the night-time:
        though you try me by fire,
        you will find no wickedness in me.

4 My mouth does not transgress, like the mouth of others:
for I have kept the word of your lips.

5 My steps have held firm in the way of your commands:
and my feet have not stumbled from your paths.

6 I call upon you, O God, for you will surely answer:
incline your ear to me, and hear my words.

7 Show me the wonders of your steadfast love,
O saviour of those who come to you for refuge:
who by your right hand deliver them
from those that rise up against them.

8 Keep me as the apple of your eye:
hide me under the shadow of your wings,

9 From the onslaught of the wicked:
from my enemies that encircle me to take my life.

10 They have closed their hearts to pity:
and their mouths speak proud things.

11 They advance upon me, they surround me on every side:
watching how they may bring me to the ground,

12 Like a lion that is greedy for its prey:
like a lion's whelp lurking in hidden places.

13 Arise, O Lord, stand in their way and cast them down:
deliver me from the wicked by your sword.

[14 Slay them by your hand, O Lord, slay them,
so that they perish from the earth:
destroy them from among the living.]

15   But as for your cherished ones,
     let their bellies be filled and let their sons be satisfied:
     let them pass on their wealth to their children.

16   And I also shall see your face, because my cause is just:
     when I awake and see you as you are, I shall be satisfied.

Psalm 18

1   I love you, O Lord my strength:
     O Lord my crag, my fortress and my deliverer,

2   My God, the rock to which I come for refuge:
     my shield, my mighty saviour, and my high defence.

3   I called to the Lord with loud lamentation:
     and I was rescued from my enemies.

4   The waves of death encompassed me:
     and the floods of chaos overwhelmed me;

5   The cords of the grave tightened about me:
     and the snares of death lay in my path.

6   In my anguish I called to the Lord:
     I cried for help to my God.

7   From his temple he heard my voice:
     and my cry came even to his ears.

8   The earth heaved and quaked,
     the foundations of the hills were shaken:
     they trembled because he was angry.

9   Smoke went out from his nostrils:
     and a consuming fire from his mouth.

10   He parted the heavens and came down:
and there was darkness under his feet.

11   He rode upon the cherubim and flew:
he came swooping upon the wings of the wind.

12   He made the darkness his covering:
and his canopy was thick cloud and watery darkness.

13   Out of his clouds, from the brightness before him:
broke hailstones and coals of fire.

14   The Lord thundered in the heavens:
the Most High uttered his voice.

15   He let loose his arrows, he scattered them on every side:
he hurled down lightnings
with the roar of the thunderbolt.

16   The springs of the sea were uncovered:
and the foundations of the world laid bare,

17   At your rebuke, O Lord:
at the blast of the breath of your displeasure.

18   He reached down from on high and took me:
he drew me out of the great waters.

19   He delivered me from my strongest enemy:
from my foes that were mightier than I.

20   They confronted me in the day of my calamity:
but the Lord was my upholder.

21   He brought me out into a place of liberty:
and rescued me because I delighted his heart.

22 The Lord rewarded me for my righteous dealing:
   he recompensed me
   according to the cleanness of my hands,

23 Because I had kept to the ways of the Lord:
   and had not turned from my God to do evil.

24 For I had an eye to all his laws:
   and did not put his commandments from me.

25 I was also blameless before him:
   and I kept myself from wrongdoing.

26 Therefore the Lord rewarded my innocence:
   because my hands were undefiled in his sight.

27 With the faithful you show yourself faithful:
   with the blameless you show yourself blameless;

28 With the pure you are pure:
   but with the crooked you show yourself perverse.

29 For you will save a humble people:
   but you bring down the high looks of the proud.

30 You light my lamp, O Lord my God:
   you make my darkness to be bright.

31 For with your help I can charge a troop of men:
   with the help of my God I can leap a city wall.

32 The way of our God is perfect,
   the word of the Lord has been tried in the fire:
   he is a shield to all that trust in him.

33 For who is God but the Lord:
   or who is our rock but our God?

34   It is God that girded me with strength:
       that made my way perfect.

35   He made my feet like the feet of a hind:
       and set me surefooted upon the mountains.

36   He taught my hands to fight:
       and my arms to aim an arrow of bronze.

37   You gave me the shield of your salvation:
       your right hand upheld me,
       and your swift response has made me great.

38   You lengthened my stride beneath me:
       and my ankles did not slip.

39   I pursued my enemies and overtook them:
       nor did I turn again till I had made an end of them.

40   I smote them, till they could rise no more:
       and they fell beneath my feet.

41   You girded me with strength for the battle:
       you threw down my adversaries under me.

42   You caused my enemies to show their backs:
       and I destroyed those that hated me.

43   They cried for help, but there was none to save them:
       they cried to the Lord, but he would not answer.

44   I pounded them fine as dust before the wind:
       I trod them under like the mire of the streets.

45   You delivered me from the strife of the peoples,
       you made me the head of the nations:
       a people that I had not known became my servants.

46   As soon as they heard me they obeyed me:
and aliens humbled themselves before me.

47   The strength of the aliens withered away:
they came faltering from their strongholds.

48   The Lord lives, and blessed be my rock:
exalted be the God of my salvation,

49   The God who sees to it that I am avenged:
who subdues the peoples under me.

50   You set me free from my enemies,
you put me out of reach of my attackers:
you delivered me from violent men.

51   For this will I give you thanks among the nations, O Lord:
and sing praises to your name,

52   To him that gives great triumphs to his king:
that deals so faithfully with his anointed;
with David and with his seed for ever.

Psalm 19

1   The heavens declare the glory of God:
and the firmament proclaims his handiwork;

2   One day tells it to another:
and night to night communicates knowledge.

3   There is no speech or language:
nor are their voices heard;

4 Yet their sound has gone out through all the world:
  and their words to the ends of the earth.

5 There he has pitched a tent for the sun:
  which comes out as a bridegroom from his chamber,
  and rejoices like a strong man to run his course.

6 Its rising is at one end of the heavens,
  and its circuit to their farthest bound:
  and nothing is hidden from its heat.

7 The law of the Lord is perfect, reviving the soul:
  the command of the Lord is true,
  and makes wise the simple.

8 The precepts of the Lord are right, and rejoice the heart:
  the commandment of the Lord is pure,
  and gives light to the eyes.

9 The fear of the Lord is clean, and endures for ever:
  the judgements of the Lord are unchanging,
  and righteous every one.

10 More to be desired are they than gold,
  even much fine gold:
  sweeter also than honey,
  than the honey that drips from the comb.

11 Moreover, by them is your servant taught:
  and in keeping them there is great reward.

12 Who can know his own unwitting sins?:
  O cleanse me from my secret faults.

13 Keep your servant also from presumptuous sins,
  lest they get the mastery over me:
  so I shall be clean, and innocent of great offence.

14   May the words of my mouth
and the meditation of my heart
be acceptable in your sight:
O Lord, my strength and my redeemer.

Psalm 20

1   May the Lord hear you in the day of trouble:
the God of Jacob lift you up to safety.

2   May he send you his help from the sanctuary:
and be your strong support from Zion.

3   May he remember all your offerings:
and accept with favour your burnt sacrifices,

4   Grant you your heart's desire:
and fulfil all your purposes.

5   May we also rejoice in your victory
and triumph in the name of our God:
the Lord perform all your petitions.

6   Now I know that the Lord will save his anointed:
that he will answer him from his holy heaven
with the victorious strength of his right hand.

7   Some put their trust in chariots and some in horses:
but we will trust in the name of the Lord our God.

8   They are brought down and fallen:
but we are made strong and stand upright.

9   O Lord, save the king:
and hear us when we call upon you.

Psalm 21

1   The king shall rejoice in your strength, O Lord:
     he shall exult in your salvation.

2   You have given him his heart's desire:
     you have not denied him the request of his lips.

3   For you came to meet him with the blessings of success:
     and placed a crown of gold upon his head.

4   He asked you for life and you gave it him:
     length of days for ever and ever.

5   Great is his glory because of your salvation:
     you have clothed him with honour and majesty.

6   You have given him everlasting felicity:
     and made him glad with the joy of your presence.

7   For the king puts his trust in the Lord:
     and through the tender mercy of the Most High
     he shall never be moved.

8   Your hand shall light upon your enemies:
     and your right hand shall find out all who hate you.

9   You will make them like a blazing furnace
     in the day of your coming:
     the Lord will overwhelm them in his wrath,
     and fire shall consume them.

10   You will root out their offspring from the earth:
     and their seed from among the children of men;

11   Because they have stirred up evil against you:
     and plotted mischief, which they cannot perform.

12   Therefore will you set your shoulder toward them:
        and draw the string of the bow to strike at their faces.

13   Arise, O Lord, in your great strength:
        and we will sing and praise your power.

Psalm 22

1   My God, my God, why have you forsaken me:
        why are you so far from helping me
        and from the words of my groaning?

2   My God, I cry to you by day, but you do not answer:
        and by night also I take no rest.

3   But you continue holy:
        you that are the praise of Israel.

4   In you our fathers trusted:
        they trusted, and you delivered them;

5   To you they cried and they were saved:
        they put their trust in you and were not confounded.

6   But as for me, I am a worm and no man:
        the scorn of men and despised by the people.

7   All those that see me laugh me to scorn:
        they shoot out their lips at me and wag their heads, saying,

8   'He trusted in the Lord – let him deliver him:
        let him deliver him, if he delights in him.'

9   But you are he that took me out of the womb:
        that brought me to lie at peace on my mother's breast.

10   On you have I been cast since my birth:
you are my God, even from my mother's womb.

11   O go not from me, for trouble is hard at hand:
and there is none to help.

12   Many oxen surround me:
fat bulls of Bashan close me in on every side.

13   They gape wide their mouths at me:
like lions that roar and rend.

14   I am poured out like water,
and all my bones are out of joint:
my heart within my breast is like melting wax.

15   My mouth is dried up like a potsherd:
and my tongue clings to my gums.

16   My hands and my feet are withered:
and you lay me in the dust of death.

17   For many dogs are come about me:
and a band of evildoers hem me in.

18   I can count all my bones:
they stand staring and gazing upon me.

19   They part my garments among them:
and cast lots for my clothing.

20   O Lord, do not stand far off:
you are my helper, hasten to my aid.

21   Deliver my body from the sword:
my life from the power of the dogs;

22   O save me from the lion's mouth:
and my afflicted soul from the horns of the wild oxen.

23   I will tell of your name to my brethren:
            in the midst of the congregation will I praise you.

24   O praise the Lord, all you that fear him:
            hold him in honour, O seed of Jacob,
            and let the seed of Israel stand in awe of him.

25   For he has not despised nor abhorred the poor man
            in his misery:
            nor did he hide his face from him,
            but heard him when he cried.

26   From you springs my praise in the great congregation:
            I will pay my vows in the sight of all that fear you;

27   The meek shall eat of the sacrifice and be satisfied:
            and those who seek the Lord shall praise him
            – may their hearts rejoice for ever!

28   Let all the ends of the earth remember
            and turn to the Lord:
            and let all the families of the nations worship before him.

29   For the kingdom is the Lord's:
            and he shall be ruler over the nations.

30   How can those who sleep in the earth do him homage:
            or those that descend to the dust bow down before him?

31   But he has saved my life for himself:
            and my posterity shall serve him.

32   This shall be told of my Lord to a future generation:
            and his righteousness declared to a people yet unborn,
            that he has done it.

Psalm 23

1   The Lord is my shepherd:
     therefore can I lack nothing.

2   He will make me lie down in green pastures:
     and lead me beside still waters.

3   He will refresh my soul:
     and guide me in right pathways for his name's sake.

4   Though I walk through the valley of the shadow of death,
     I will fear no evil:
     for you are with me, your rod and your staff comfort me.

5   You spread a table before me
     in the face of those who trouble me:
     you have anointed my head with oil,
     and my cup will be full.

6   Surely your goodness and loving-kindness
     will follow me all the days of my life:
     and I shall dwell in the house of the Lord for ever.

Psalm 24

1   The earth is the Lord's and all that is in it:
     the compass of the world and those who dwell therein.

2   For he has founded it upon the seas:
     and established it upon the waters.

3   Who shall ascend the hill of the Lord:
     or who shall stand in his holy place?

4   He that has clean hands and a pure heart:
who has not set his soul upon idols,
nor sworn his oath to a lie.

5   He shall receive blessing from the Lord:
and recompense from the God of his salvation.

6   Of such a kind as this are those who seek him:
those who seek your face, O God of Jacob.

7   Lift up your heads, O you gates,
and be lifted up, you everlasting doors:
and the King of glory shall come in.

8   Who is the King of glory?:
the Lord, strong and mighty, the Lord mighty in battle.

9   Lift up your heads, O you gates,
and be lifted up, you everlasting doors:
and the King of glory shall come in.

10   Who is the King of glory?:
the Lord of hosts, he is the King of glory.

Psalm 25

1   In you, O Lord my God, have I put my hope:
in you have I trusted, let me not be ashamed,
nor let my enemies triumph over me.

2   Let none who wait for you be put to shame:
but let those that break faith be confounded
and gain nothing.

3   Show me your ways, O Lord:
and teach me your paths.

4   Lead me in the ways of your truth, and teach me:
for you are the God of my salvation.

5   In you have I hoped all the day long:
because of your goodness, O Lord.

6   Call to mind your compassion
and your loving-kindness:
for they are from of old.

7   Remember not the sins of my youth,
nor my transgressions:
but according to your mercy think on me.

8   Good and upright is the Lord:
therefore will he direct sinners in the way.

9   The meek he will guide in the path of justice:
and teach the humble his ways.

10   All the paths of the Lord are faithful and true:
for those who keep his covenant
and his commandments.

11   For your name's sake, O Lord:
be merciful to my sin, though it is great.

12   Who is he that fears the Lord?:
him will the Lord direct in the way that he should choose.

13   His soul shall dwell at ease:
and his children shall inherit the land.

14   The confidences of God belong to those that fear him:
and his covenant shall give them understanding.

15   My eyes are ever looking to the Lord:
for he will bring my feet out of the net.

| 16 | Turn your face toward me and be gracious: |
| | for I am alone and in misery. |

| 17 | O free my heart from pain: |
| | and bring me out of my distress. |

| 18 | Give heed to my affliction and adversity: |
| | and forgive me all my sins. |

| 19 | Consider my enemies, how many they are: |
| | and they bear a violent hate against me. |

| 20 | O keep my life, and deliver me: |
| | put me not to shame, for I come to you for refuge. |

| 21 | Let innocence and integrity be my guard: |
| | for in you have I hoped. |

| 22 | O God, deliver Israel: |
| | out of all his tribulation. |

Psalm 26

1	Give judgement for me, O Lord,
	for I have walked in my integrity:
	I have trusted in the Lord and not wavered.

| 2 | Put me to the test, O Lord, and prove me: |
| | try my mind and my heart. |

| 3 | For your steadfast love has been ever before my eyes: |
| | and I have walked in your truth. |

| 4 | I have not sat with deceivers: |
| | nor consorted with the hypocrites; |

5   I hate the assembly of the wicked:
          I will not sit with the ungodly.

6   I wash my hands in innocence, O Lord:
          that I may go about your altar,

7   And lift up the voice of thanksgiving:
          to tell of all your marvellous works.

8   Lord, I love the house of your habitation:
          and the place where your glory dwells.

9   Do not sweep me away with sinners:
          nor my life with men of blood,

10   In whose hand is abomination:
          and their right hand is full of bribes.

11   As for me, I walk in my integrity:
          O ransom me and be favourable toward me.

12   My foot stands on an even path:
          I will bless the Lord in the great congregation.

Psalm 27

1   The Lord is my light and my salvation;
          whom then shall I fear?:
          the Lord is the stronghold of my life;
          of whom shall I be afraid?

2   When the wicked, even my enemies and my foes,
          come upon me to devour me:
          they shall stumble and fall.

3   If an army encamp against me,
my heart shall not be afraid:
and if war should rise against me, yet will I trust.

4   One thing I have asked from the Lord, which I will require:
that I may dwell in the house of the Lord
all the days of my life,

5   To see the fair beauty of the Lord:
and to seek his will in his temple.

6   For he will hide me under his shelter in the day of trouble:
and conceal me in the shadow of his tent,
and set me high upon a rock.

7   And now he will lift up my head:
above my enemies round about me.

8   And I will offer sacrifices in his sanctuary with exultation:
I will sing, I will sing praises to the Lord.

9   O Lord, hear my voice when I cry:
have mercy upon me and answer me.

10   My heart has said of you, 'Seek his face':
your face, Lord, I will seek.

11   Do not hide your face from me:
or thrust your servant aside in displeasure;

12   For you have been my helper:
do not cast me away or forsake me,
O God of my salvation.

13   Though my father and my mother forsake me:
the Lord will take me up.

14   Teach me your way, O Lord:
and lead me in an even path, for they lie in wait for me.

15   Do not give me over to the will of my enemies:
for false witnesses have risen against me,
and those who breathe out violence.

16   But I believe that I shall surely see
the goodness of the Lord:
in the land of the living.

17   O wait for the Lord;
stand firm and he will strengthen your heart:
and wait, I say, for the Lord.

Psalm 28

1   To you will I cry, O Lord my Rock,
be not deaf to my prayer:
lest, if you turn away silent,
I become like those that go down to the grave.

2   Hear the voice of my supplication
when I cry to you for help:
when I lift up my hands
toward the holiest place of your sanctuary.

3   Do not snatch me away with the ungodly,
with the evildoers:
who speak peace to their neighbours,
but nourish malice in their hearts.

4   Repay them according to their deeds:
and according to the wickedness of their endeavours;

5   Requite them for the work of their hands:
and give them their deserts.

6   For they pay no heed to the Lord's acts,
nor to the operation of his hands:
therefore shall he break them down
and not build them up.

7   Let the Lord's name be praised:
for he has heard the voice of my supplication.

8   The Lord is my strength and my shield,
in him my heart trusts and I am helped:
therefore my heart dances for joy,
and in my song will I praise him.

9   The Lord is the strength of his people:
and a sure refuge for his anointed king.

10   O save your people
and give your blessing to your own:
be their shepherd, and bear them up for ever.

Psalm 29

1   Ascribe to the Lord, you sons of heaven:
ascribe to the Lord glory and might.

2   Ascribe to the Lord the honour due to his name:
O worship the Lord in the beauty of his holiness.

3   The voice of the Lord is upon the waters:
the God of glory thunders, the Lord upon the great waters.

4   The voice of the Lord is mighty in operation:
the voice of the Lord is a glorious voice.

5   The voice of the Lord breaks the cedar-trees:
       the Lord breaks in pieces the cedars of Lebanon.

6   He makes them skip like a calf:
       Lebanon and Sirion like a young wild ox.

7   The voice of the Lord divides the lightning-flash:
       the voice of the Lord whirls the sands of the desert,
       the Lord whirls the desert of Kadesh.

8   The voice of the Lord rends the terebinth trees,
       and strips bare the forests:
       in his temple all cry 'Glory'.

9   The Lord sits enthroned above the water-flood:
       the Lord sits enthroned as a king for ever.

10   The Lord will give strength to his people:
       the Lord will give to his people the blessing of peace.

Psalm 30

1   I will exalt you, O Lord,
       for you have drawn me up from the depths:
       and have not suffered my foes to triumph over me.

2   O Lord my God, I cried to you:
       and you have made me whole.

3   You brought me back, O Lord,
       from the land of silence:
       you saved my life
       from among those that go down to the Pit.

4   Sing praises to the Lord, all you his faithful ones:
       and give thanks to his holy name.

5   For if in his anger is havoc, in his good favour is life:
heaviness may endure for a night,
but joy comes in the morning.

6   In my prosperity I said 'I shall never be moved:
your goodness, O Lord, has set me on so firm a hill.'

7   Then you hid your face from me:
and I was greatly dismayed.

8   I cried to you, O God:
and made my petition humbly to my Lord.

9   'What profit is there in my blood, if I go down to the Pit:
can the dust give you thanks, or declare your faithfulness?

10   'Hear, O Lord, and be merciful:
O Lord, be my helper.'

11   You have turned my lamentation into dancing:
you have put off my sackcloth and girded me with joy,

12   That my heart may sing your praise and never be silent:
O Lord my God, I will give you thanks for ever.

Psalm 31

1   To you, Lord, have I come for shelter:
let me never be put to shame.

2   O deliver me in your righteousness:
incline your ear to me and be swift to save me.

3   Be for me a rock of refuge, a fortress to defend me:
for you are my high rock and my stronghold.

4   Lead me and guide me for your name's sake:
bring me out of the net that they have secretly laid for me,
for you are my strength.

5   Into your hands I commit my spirit:
you will redeem me, O Lord God of truth.

6   I hate those that clutch vain idols:
but my trust is in the Lord.

7   I will rejoice and be glad in your loving-kindness:
for you have looked on my distress
and known me in adversity.

8   You have not given me over to the power of the enemy:
you have set my feet where I may walk at liberty.

9   Have mercy upon me, O Lord, for I am in trouble:
my eye wastes away for grief,
my throat also and my inward parts.

10   For my life wears out in sorrow,
and my years with sighing:
my strength fails me in my affliction,
and my bones are consumed.

11   I am become the scorn of all my enemies:
and my neighbours wag their heads in derision.

12   I am a thing of horror to my friends:
and those that see me in the street shrink from me.

13   I am forgotten like a dead man out of mind:
I have become like a broken vessel.

14   For I hear the whispering of many:
and fear is on every side;

15   While they plot together against me:
    and scheme to take away my life.

16   But in you, Lord, have I put my trust:
    I have said 'You are my God'.

17   All my days are in your hand:
    O deliver me from the power of my enemies
    and from my persecutors.

18   Make your face to shine upon your servant:
    and save me for your mercy's sake.

19   O Lord, let me not be confounded,
    for I have called upon you:
    but let the wicked be put to shame
    and brought to silence in the grave.

20   Let the lying lips be dumb:
    that in pride and contempt
    speak such insolence against the just.

21   O how plentiful is your goodness,
    stored up for those that fear you:
    and prepared in the sight of men
    for all who come to you for refuge.

22   You will hide them in the cover of your presence
    from the plots of men:
    you will shelter them in your refuge
    from the strife of tongues.

23   Blessed be the Lord our God:
    for he has wonderfully shown me his steadfast love,
    when I was as a city besieged.

24   When I was afraid, I said in my haste:
    'I am cut off from your sight'.

25   But you heard the voice of my supplication:
           when I cried to you for help.

26   Love the Lord, all you his faithful ones:
           for the Lord guards the true, but fully requites the proud.

27   Be strong, and let your heart take courage:
           all you that hope in the Lord.

Psalm 32

1   Blessed is he whose sin is forgiven:
           whose iniquity is put away.

2   Blessed is the man to whom the Lord imputes no blame:
           and in whose spirit there is no guile.

3   For whilst I held my tongue:
           my bones wasted away with my daily complaining.

4   Your hand was heavy upon me day and night:
           and my moisture was dried up like a drought in summer.

5   Then I acknowledged my sin to you:
           and my iniquity I did not hide;

6   I said 'I will confess my transgressions to the Lord':
           and so you forgave the wickedness of my sin.

7   For this cause shall everyone that is faithful
           make his prayer to you in the day of trouble:
           and in the time of the great water-floods,
           they shall not come near him.

8   You are a place to hide me in,
          you will preserve me from trouble:
          you will surround me with deliverance on every side.

9   'I will instruct you,
          and direct you in the way that you should go:
          I will fasten my eye upon you, and give you counsel.

10   'Be not like horse or mule, that have no understanding:
          whose forward course must be curbed with bit and bridle.'

11   Great tribulations remain for the ungodly:
          but whoever puts his trust in the Lord,
          mercy embraces him on every side.

12   Rejoice in the Lord, you righteous, and be glad:
          and shout for joy, all you that are true of heart.

Psalm 33

1   Rejoice in the Lord, you righteous:
          for it befits the just to praise him.

2   Give the Lord thanks upon the harp:
          and sing his praise to the lute of ten strings.

3   O sing him a new song:
          make sweetest melody, with shouts of praise.

4   For the word of the Lord is true:
          and all his works are faithful.

5   He loves righteousness and justice:
          the earth is filled with the loving-kindness of the Lord.

6 By the word of the Lord were the heavens made:
   and their numberless stars by the breath of his mouth.

7 He gathered the waters of the sea as in a water-skin:
   and laid up the deep in his treasuries.

8 Let the whole earth fear the Lord:
   and let all the inhabitants of the world stand in awe of him.

9 For he spoke, and it was done:
   he commanded, and it stood fast.

10 The Lord frustrates the counsels of the nations:
   he brings to nothing the devices of the peoples.

11 But the counsels of the Lord shall endure for ever:
   the purposes of his heart from generation to generation.

12 Blessed is that nation whose God is the Lord:
   the people he chose to be his own possession.

13 The Lord looks down from heaven
   and surveys all the children of men:
   he considers from his dwelling-place
   all the inhabitants of the earth;

14 He who fashioned the hearts of them all:
   and comprehends all that they do.

15 A king is not saved by a mighty army:
   nor is a warrior delivered by much strength;

16 A horse is a vain hope to save a man:
   nor can he rescue any by his great power.

17 But the eye of the Lord is on those that fear him:
   on those that trust in his unfailing love,

18 To deliver them from death:
    and to feed them in the time of dearth.

19 We have waited eagerly for the Lord:
    for he is our help and our shield.

20 Surely our hearts shall rejoice in him:
    for we have trusted in his holy name.

21 Let your merciful kindness be upon us, O Lord:
    even as our hope is in you.

Psalm 34

1   I will bless the Lord continually:
    his praise shall be always in my mouth.

2   Let my soul boast of the Lord:
    the humble shall hear it and rejoice.

3   O praise the Lord with me:
    let us exalt his name together.

4   For I sought the Lord's help and he answered:
    and he freed me from all my fears.

5   Look towards him and be bright with joy:
    your faces shall not be ashamed.

6   Here is a wretch who cried, and the Lord heard him:
    and saved him from all his troubles.

7   The angel of the Lord encamps round those who fear him:
    and delivers them in their need.

8   O taste and see that the Lord is good:
    happy the man who hides in him!

9   Fear the Lord, all you his holy ones:
          for those who fear him never lack.

10   Lions may suffer want and go hungry:
          but those who seek the Lord lack nothing good.

11   Come, my children, listen to me:
          and I will teach you the fear of the Lord.

12   Which of you relishes life:
          wants time to enjoy good things?

13   Keep your tongue from evil:
          and your lips from telling lies.

14   Turn from evil and do good:
          seek peace and pursue it.

15   The eyes of God are on the righteous:
          and his ears towards their cry.

16   The Lord sets his face against wrongdoers:
          to root out their memory from the earth.

17   The righteous cry; the Lord hears it:
          and frees them from all their afflictions.

18   The Lord is close to those who are broken-hearted:
          and the crushed in spirit he saves.

19   The trials of the righteous are many:
          but our God delivers him from them all.

20   He guards all his bones:
          so that not one is broken.

21   Evil will slay the wicked:
          and those who hate the righteous will be destroyed.

22   The Lord ransoms the lives of his servants:
and none who hide in him will be destroyed.

Psalm 35

1   Contend, O Lord, with those who contend with me:
fight against those that fight against me.

2   Take up shield and buckler:
and arise, arise to help me.

3   Draw the spear
and bar the way against those that pursue me:
say to me 'I am your deliverer'.

4   Let those that seek my life be put to shame and disgraced:
let those that plot my destruction
be turned back and confounded.

5   Let them be like chaff before the wind:
with the angel of the Lord driving them;

6   Let their way be dark and slippery:
with the angel of the Lord pursuing.

7   For without cause they have secretly spread a net for me:
without cause they have dug a pit to entrap me.

8   Let sudden disaster strike them:
let the net that they have hidden catch them,
let them fall to their destruction.

9   Then shall my soul be joyful in the Lord:
and I will rejoice in his deliverance.

10   All my bones shall say 'Lord, who is like you?:
        for you deliver the poor man
        from him that is too strong for him,
        the poor and needy
        from him that would despoil them'.

11   Malicious witnesses rise up against me:
        I am questioned about things of which I know nothing.

12   They repay me evil for good:
        I am as one bereaved of his children.

13   Yet when they were sick, I put on sackcloth:
        I afflicted myself with fasting.

14   And if my prayer returned unanswered to my bosom:
        I went about mourning
        as though for a brother or a companion;

15   I was bowed down with grief:
        as though for my own mother.

16   But when I stumbled, they rejoiced and gathered together,
        they gathered together against me:
        as though they were strangers I never knew,
        they tore at me without ceasing.

17   When I slipped, they mocked me:
        and gnashed at me with their teeth.

18   Lord, how long will you look on?:
        take me from the evil they intend,
        take me from amidst the lions.

19   And I will give you thanks in the great congregation:
        I will praise you in the throng of the people.

20   Let not those that wrongfully are my enemies
triumph over me:
let not those that hate me without cause
mock me with their eyes.

21   For they speak words that do not make for peace:
they invent lies against those that are quiet in the land.

22   They stretch their mouths to jeer at me, and say:
'Aha, aha! We have seen all that we wish!'

23   And you also have seen, O Lord; do not be silent:
O God, go not far from me.

24   Bestir yourself, awake to do me right:
to plead my cause, O Lord my God.

25   Judge me, O Lord my God,
according to your righteousness:
and let them not rejoice over me.

26   Let them not say in their hearts 'We have our wish':
let them not say 'We have destroyed him'.

27   Let those that rejoice at my hurt
be disgraced and confounded altogether:
let those that lord it over me
be clothed in shame and dishonour.

28   But let those that long for my vindication
shout for joy and rejoice:
let them say always that the Lord is great,
who takes such delight in his servant's good.

29   And my tongue shall speak of your righteousness:
and of your praise all the day long.

Psalm 36

1 The transgressor speaks
 from the wickedness in his own heart:
 there is no fear of God before his eyes.

2 For he flatters himself in his own sight:
 he hates his iniquity to be found out.

3 The words of his mouth are wickedness and deceit:
 he has ceased to act wisely and do good.

4 He plots mischief as he lies upon his bed:
 he has set himself on a path that is not good,
 he does not spurn evil.

5 Your unfailing kindness, O Lord, is in the heavens:
 and your faithfulness reaches to the clouds.

6 Your righteousness is like the strong mountains:
 and your justice as the great deep;
 you, O Lord, save both man and beast.

7 How precious, O God, is your enduring kindness:
 the children of men shall take refuge
 under the shadow of your wings.

8 They shall be satisfied with the good things of your house:
 and you will give them drink
 from the river of your delights.

9 For with you is the well of life:
 and in your light shall we see light.

10 O continue your merciful kindness
 toward those who know you:
 and your righteous dealing to those that are true of heart.

11   Let not the foot of the proud come against me:
       nor the hand of the ungodly drive me away.

12   There are they fallen, those who do evil:
       they are thrust down, and shall not rise again.

Psalm 37

1   Do not vie with the wicked:
       or envy those that do wrong;

2   For they will soon wither like the grass:
       and fade away like the green leaf.

3   Trust in the Lord and do good:
       and you shall dwell in the land
       and feed in safe pastures.

4   Let the Lord be your delight:
       and he will grant you your heart's desire.

5   Commit your way to the Lord:
       trust him, and he will act.

6   He will make your righteousness
       shine as clear as the light:
       and your innocence as the noonday.

7   Be still before the Lord, and wait patiently for him:
       do not be vexed when a man prospers,
       when he puts his evil purposes to work.

8   Let go of anger and abandon wrath:
       let not envy move you to do evil.

9   For the wicked shall be cut down:
    but those who wait for the Lord shall possess the land.

10 In a little while the ungodly shall be no more:
    you will look for him in his place,
    but he will not be found.

11 But the meek shall possess the land:
    and enjoy the abundance of peace.

12 The ungodly man plots against the righteous:
    and gnashes at him with his teeth.

13 But the Lord shall laugh him to scorn:
    for he sees that the day for his overthrow is near.

14 The ungodly have drawn the sword and strung the bow:
    to strike down the poor and needy,
    to slaughter those that walk in innocence.

15 Their swords shall pierce their own hearts:
    and their bows shall be broken.

16 Though the righteous man has but a little:
    it is better than the great wealth of the ungodly.

17 For the strong arm of the ungodly shall be broken:
    but the Lord upholds the righteous.

18 The Lord cares for the lives of the innocent:
    and their heritage shall be theirs for ever.

19 They shall not be put to shame in the evil days:
    but in time of famine they shall eat their fill.

20 As for the ungodly, they shall perish,
    they are the enemies of the Lord:
    like fuel in a furnace they shall vanish away in smoke.

21   The ungodly man borrows but does not repay:
       but the righteous is gracious, and gives.

22   Those who are blessed by God shall possess the land:
       but those whom he has cursed shall be cut down.

23   If a man's steps are guided by the Lord:
       and he delights in his way,

24   Though he stumble, he shall not fall headlong:
       for the Lord holds him by the hand.

25   I have been young and now am old:
       but I never saw the righteous man forsaken,
       or his children begging their bread.

26   He is ever gracious, and lends:
       and his children shall be blessed.

27   Turn from evil and do good:
       and you shall dwell in the land for ever.

28   For the Lord loves justice:
       he will not forsake his faithful ones.

29   But the unjust shall be destroyed for ever:
       and the children of the ungodly shall be cut down.

30   The just shall possess the land:
       and they shall dwell in it for ever.

31   The mouth of the righteous man utters wisdom:
       and his tongue speaks what is right.

32   The law of his God is in his heart:
       and his footsteps will not slip.

33   The ungodly man watches out for the righteous:
      and seeks occasion to slay him.

34   But the Lord will not abandon him to his power.
      nor let him be condemned when he is judged.

35   Wait for the Lord, and hold to his way:
      and he will raise you up to possess the land,
      to see the ungodly when they are destroyed.

36   I have seen the ungodly in terrifying power:
      spreading himself like a luxuriant tree;

37   I passed by again, and he was gone:
      I searched for him, but he could not be found.

38   Observe the blameless man and consider the upright:
      for the man of peace shall have posterity.

39   But transgressors shall be destroyed altogether:
      and the posterity of the wicked shall be cut down.

40   Deliverance for the righteous shall come from the Lord:
      he is their strength in time of trouble.

41   The Lord will help them and deliver them:
      he will save them from the ungodly and deliver them,
      because they come to him for refuge.

Psalm 38

1   O Lord, rebuke me not in your anger:
      nor chasten me in your fierce displeasure.

2   For your arrows have been aimed against me:
      and your hand has come down heavy upon me.

3   There is no health in my flesh
because of your indignation:
nor soundness in my bones, by reason of my sin.

4   The tide of my iniquities has gone over my head:
their weight is a burden too heavy for me to bear.

5   My wounds stink and fester:
because of my foolishness.

6   I am bowed down and brought so low:
that I go mourning all the day long.

7   For my loins are filled with a burning pain:
and there is no sound part in all my body.

8   I am numbed and stricken to the ground:
I cry aloud in the yearning of my heart.

9   O Lord, all I long for is before you:
and my deep sighing is not hidden from you.

10   My heart is in tumult, my strength fails me:
and even the light of my eyes has gone from me.

11   My friends and my companions
hold aloof from my affliction:
and my kinsmen stand far off.

12   Those who seek my life strike at me:
and those that desire my hurt spread evil tales,
and murmur slanders all the day.

13   But I am like a deaf man and hear nothing:
like one that is dumb, who does not open his mouth.

14   So I have become as one who cannot hear:
in whose mouth there is no retort.

15   For in you, Lord, have I put my trust:
         and you will answer me, O Lord my God.

16   For I prayed 'Let them never exult over me:
         those who turn arrogant when my foot slips'.

17   Truly, I am ready to fall:
         and my pain is with me continually.

18   But I acknowledge my wickedness:
         and I am filled with sorrow at my sin.

19   Those that are my enemies without cause
         are great in number:
         and those who hate me wrongfully are many.

20   Those also who repay evil for good are against me:
         because I seek after good.

21   Forsake me not, O Lord, go not far from me, my God:
         hasten to my help, O Lord my salvation.

Psalm 39

1   I said 'I will keep watch over my ways,
         lest I sin with my tongue:
         I will keep a guard on my mouth
         while the wicked are in my sight'.

2   I held my tongue and said nothing:
         I kept silent, but found no comfort.

3   My pain was increased, my heart grew hot within me:
         while I mused, the fire blazed,
         and I spoke with my tongue;

4   'Lord, let me know my end:
    and the number of my days,

5   'That I may know how short my time is:
    for you have made my days but a handsbreadth
    and my whole span is as nothing before you.'

6   Surely every man, though he stand secure, is but breath:
    man lives as a passing shadow.

7   The riches he heaps are but a puff of wind:
    and he cannot tell who will gather them.

8   And now, Lord, what is my hope?:
    truly my hope is in you.

9   O deliver me from all my transgressions:
    do not make me the butt of fools.

10 I was dumb, I did not open my mouth:
    for surely it was your doing.

11 Take away your plague from me:
    I am brought to an end by the blows of your hand.

12 When with rebukes you chastise a man for sin:
    you cause his fair looks to dissolve in putrefaction
    – surely every man is but breath.

13 Hear my prayer, O Lord, and give ear to my cry:
    be not silent at my tears.

14 For I am but a stranger with you:
    a passing guest as all my fathers were.

15 Turn your eye from me, that I may smile again:
    before I go hence and am no more.

Psalm 40

1   I waited patiently for the Lord:
    and he inclined to me and heard my cry.

2   He brought me up from the pit of roaring waters,
    out of the mire and clay:
    and set my feet upon a rock, and made firm my foothold.

3   And he has put a new song in my mouth:
    even a song of thanksgiving to our God.

4   Many shall see it and fear:
    and shall put their trust in the Lord.

5   Blessed is the man who has made the Lord his hope:
    who has not turned to the proud,
    or to those who wander in deceit.

6   O Lord my God,
    great are the wonderful things which you have done,
    and your thoughts which are towards us:
    there is none to be compared with you;

7   Were I to declare them and speak of them:
    they are more than I am able to express.

8   Sacrifice and offering you do not desire:
    but my ears you have marked for obedience;

9   Burnt-offering and sin-offering you have not required:
    then said I, Lo, I come.

10   In the scroll of the book it is written of me,
    that I should do your will:
    O my God, I long to do it, your law delights my heart.

11 I have declared your righteousness
    in the great congregation:
    I have not restrained my lips, O Lord, and that you know.

12 I have not hidden your righteousness in my heart:
    I have spoken of your faithfulness and of your salvation.

13 I have not kept back your loving-kindness and your truth:
    from the great congregation.

14 O Lord, do not withhold your mercy from me:
    let your loving-kindness and your truth ever preserve me.

15 For innumerable troubles have come upon me:
    my sins have overtaken me, and I cannot see.

16 They are more in number than the hairs of my head:
    therefore my heart fails me.

17 Be pleased, O Lord, to deliver me:
    O Lord, make haste to help me.

18 Let those who seek my life to take it away:
    be put to shame and confounded altogether.

19 Let them be turned back and disgraced who wish me evil:
    let them be aghast for shame who say to me 'Aha, aha!'

20 Let all who seek you be joyful and glad because of you:
    let those who love your salvation
    say always 'The Lord is great'.

21 As for me, I am poor and needy:
    but the Lord will care for me.

22 You are my helper and my deliverer:
    make no long delay, O Lord my God.

Psalm 41

1   Blessed is he that considers the poor and helpless:
    the Lord will deliver him in the day of trouble.

2   The Lord will guard him and preserve his life,
    he shall be counted happy in the land:
    you will not give him over to the will of his enemies.

3   And if he lies sick on his bed, the Lord will sustain him:
    if illness lays him low, you will overthrow it.

4   I said 'O Lord, be merciful toward me:
    heal me, for I have sinned against you.'

5   My enemies speak evil of me, saying:
    'When will he die, and his name perish for ever?'

6   And if one should come to see me,
    he mouths empty words:
    while his heart gathers mischief,
    and when he goes out, he vents it.

7   All those that hate me whisper together against me:
    they devise plots against me.

8   They say 'A deadly thing has got hold of him:
    he will not get up again from where he lies'.

9   Even my bosom friend in whom I trusted:
    who shared my bread, has lifted his heel against me.

10   But you, O Lord, be gracious and raise me up:
    and I will repay them what they have deserved.

11   By this will I know that you favour me:
    That my enemy shall not triumph over me.

12   Because of my innocence you hold me fast:
        you have set me before your face for ever.

13   Blessed be the Lord, the God of Israel:
        from everlasting to everlasting.
        Amen, amen.

Psalm 42

1   As a deer longs for the running brooks:
        so longs my soul for you, O God.

2   My soul is thirsty for God,
        thirsty for the living God:
        when shall I come and see his face?

3   My tears have been my food day and night:
        while they ask me all day long
        'Where now is your God?'

4   As I pour out my soul by myself, I remember this:
        how I went to the house of the Mighty One,
        into the temple of God,

5   To the shouts and songs of thanksgiving:
        a multitude keeping high festival.

6   *Why are you so full of heaviness, my soul:*
        and why so unquiet within me?

7   *O put your trust in God:*
        for I will praise him yet,
        who is my deliverer and my God.

8 My soul is heavy within me:
  therefore I will remember you from the land of Jordan,
  from Mizar among the hills of Hermon.

9 Deep calls to deep in the roar of your waters:
  all your waves and breakers have gone over me.

10 Surely the Lord will grant his loving mercy
  in the day-time:
  and in the night his song will be with me,
  a prayer to the God of my life.

11 I will say to God, my rock,
  'Why have you forgotten me:
  why must I go like a mourner
  because the enemy oppresses me?'

12 Like a sword through my bones,
  my enemies have mocked me:
  while they ask me all day long
  'Where now is your God?'

13 *Why are you so full of heaviness, my soul:*
  and why so unquiet within me?

14 *O put your trust in God:*
  for I will praise him yet,
  who is my deliverer and my God.

Psalm 43

1 Give judgement for me, O God,
  take up my cause against an ungodly people:
  deliver me from deceitful and wicked men.

2   For you are God my refuge
why have you turned me away:
why must I go like a mourner
because the enemy oppresses me?

3   O send out your light and your truth, and let them lead me:
let them guide me to your holy hill and to your dwelling.

4   Then I shall go to the altar of God,
to God my joy and my delight:
and to the harp I shall sing your praises,
O God, my God.

5   *Why are you so full of heaviness, my soul:*
and why so unquiet within me?

6   *O put your trust in God:*
for I will praise him yet,
who is my deliverer and my God.

Psalm 44

1   We have heard with our ears, O God,
our fathers have told us:
what things you did in their time,
in the days of old;

2   How by your own hand you drove out the nations,
and planted us in:
how you crushed the peoples,
but caused us to root and grow.

3   For it was not by their swords
that our fathers took possession of the land:
nor did their own arm get them the victory,

4   But your right hand, your arm,
          and the light of your countenance:
          because you delighted in them.

5   You are my king and my God:
          who ordained victory for Jacob.

6   By your power we struck our enemies through:
          in your name we trod down those that rose against us.

7   For I did not trust in my bow:
          nor could my sword save me;

8   But it was you that delivered us from our enemies:
          and put our adversaries to confusion.

9   In God we made our boast all the day long:
          we gave thanks to your name without ceasing.

10   But now you have cast us off and brought us to shame:
          you go not out with our armies.

11   You have caused us to show our backs to the enemy:
          so that our foes plunder us at will.

12   You have given us like sheep to be butchered:
          you have scattered us among the nations.

13   You have sold your people for nothing:
          and made a profitless bargain.

14   You have made us a laughing-stock to our neighbours:
          mocked and held in derision by those about us.

15   You have made us a byword among the nations:
          so that the peoples toss their heads in scorn.

16   My disgrace is before me all the day:
        and shame has covered my face,

17   At the voice of the slanderer and reviler:
        at the sight of the enemy and avenger.

18   All this has come upon us,
        though we have not forgotten you:
        we have not betrayed your covenant.

19   Our hearts have not turned back:
        nor have our steps strayed from your paths.

20   And yet you have crushed us in the haunt of jackals:
        and covered us with the shadow of death.

21   If we had forgotten the name of our God:
        or stretched out our hands in prayer
        to some strange god,

22   Would not God search it out?:
        for he knows the very secrets of the heart.

23   But for your sake are we killed all the day long:
        we are counted as sheep for the slaughter.

24   Rouse yourself, O Lord, why do you sleep?:
        awake, do not cast us off for ever.

25   Why do you hide your face:
        and forget our misery and our affliction?

26   Our souls are bowed to the dust:
        our bellies cleave to the ground.

27   Arise, O Lord, to help us:
        and redeem us for your mercy's sake.

Psalm 45

1   My heart is astir with fine phrases,
     I make my song for a king:
     my tongue is the pen of a ready writer.

2   You are the fairest of the sons of men,
     grace flows from your lips:
     therefore has God blessed you for ever and ever.

3   Gird your sword upon your thigh, O mighty warrior:
     in glory and majesty tread down your foes, and triumph!

4   Ride on in the cause of truth:
     and for the sake of justice.

5   Your right hand shall teach a terrible instruction:
     peoples shall fall beneath you,
     your arrows shall be sharp
     in the hearts of the king's enemies.

6   Your throne is the throne of God, it endures for ever:
     and the sceptre of your kingdom is a righteous sceptre.

7   You have loved righteousness and hated evil:
     therefore God, your God, has anointed you
     with the oil of gladness above your fellows.

8   All your garments are fragrant
     with myrrh, aloes and cassia:
     music from ivory palaces makes you glad.

9   Kings' daughters are among your noble women:
     the queen is at your right hand in gold of Ophir.

10   Hear, O daughter, consider and incline your ear:
     forget your own people and your father's house.

11   The king desires your beauty:
he is your lord, therefore bow down before him.

12   The richest among the people, O daughter of Tyre:
shall entreat your favour with gifts.

13   The king's daughter is all glorious within:
her clothing is embroidered cloth-of-gold.

14   In robes of many colours she is led to you, O king:
and, after her, the virgins that are with her.

15   They are led with gladness and rejoicing:
they enter the palace of the king.

16   In place of your fathers you shall have sons:
and make them princes over all the land.

17   And I will make known your name to every generation:
therefore the peoples shall give you praise for ever.

Psalm 46

1   God is our refuge and strength:
a very present help in trouble.

2   Therefore we will not fear, though the earth be moved:
and though the mountains are shaken
in the midst of the sea;

3   Though the waters rage and foam:
and though the mountains quake at the rising of the sea.

4   There is a river whose streams make glad the city of God:
the holy dwelling-place of the Most High.

5   God is in the midst of her,
therefore she shall not be moved:
God will help her, and at break of day.

6   The nations make uproar, and the kingdoms are shaken:
but God has lifted his voice, and the earth shall tremble.

7   *The Lord of hosts is with us:*
the God of Jacob is our stronghold.

8   Come then and see what the Lord has done:
what destruction he has brought upon the earth.

9   He makes wars to cease in all the world:
he breaks the bow and shatters the spear,
and burns the chariots in the fire.

10   'Be still, and know that I am God:
I will be exalted among the nations,
I will be exalted upon the earth.'

11   *The Lord of hosts is with us:*
the God of Jacob is our stronghold.

Psalm 47

1   O clap your hands, all you peoples:
and cry aloud to God with shouts of joy.

2   For the Lord Most High is to be feared:
he is a great King over all the earth.

3   He cast down peoples under us:
and the nations beneath our feet.

4   He chose us a land for our possession:
that was the pride of Jacob, whom he loved.

5   God has gone up with the sound of rejoicing:
and the Lord to the blast of the horn.

6   O sing praises, sing praises to God:
O sing praises, sing praises to our King.

7   For God is the King of all the earth:
O praise him in a well-wrought psalm.

8   God has become the King of the nations:
he has taken his seat upon his holy throne.

9   The princes of the peoples are gathered together:
with the people of the God of Abraham.

10   For the mighty ones of the earth
are become the servants of God:
and he is greatly exalted.

Psalm 48

1   Great is the Lord and greatly to be praised:
in the city of our God.

2   High and beautiful is his holy hill:
it is the joy of all the earth.

3   On Mount Zion, where godhead truly dwells,
stands the city of the Great King:
God is well known in her palaces as a sure defence.

4   For the kings of the earth assembled:
      they gathered together and came on;

5   They saw, they were struck dumb:
      they were astonished and fled in terror.

6   Trembling took hold on them, and anguish:
      as on a woman in her travail;

7   Like the breath of the east wind:
      that shatters the ships of Tarshish.

8   As we have heard,
      so have we seen in the city of the Lord of hosts:
      in the city of our God, which God has established for ever.

9   We have called to mind your loving-kindness, O God:
      in the midst of your temple.

10   As your name is great, O God, so also is your praise:
      even to the ends of the earth.

11   Your right hand is full of victory – let Zion's hill rejoice:
      let the daughters of Judah be glad,
      because of your judgements.

12   Walk about Zion, go round about her,
      and count all her towers:
      consider well her ramparts, pass through her palaces;

13   That you may tell those who come after that such is God:
      our God for ever and ever, and he will guide us eternally.

Psalm 49

1   O hear this, all you peoples:
       give ear, all you inhabitants of the world,

2   All children of men and sons of Adam:
       both rich and poor alike.

3   For my mouth shall speak wisdom:
       and the thoughts of my heart
       shall be full of understanding.

4   I will incline my ear to a riddle:
       and unfold the mystery to the sounds of the harp.

5   Why should I fear in the evil days:
       when the wickedness of my deceivers surrounds me,

6   Though they trust to their great wealth:
       and boast of the abundance of their riches?

7   No man may ransom his brother:
       or give God a price for him,

8   So that he may live for ever:
       and never see the grave;

9   For to ransom men's lives is so costly:
       that he must abandon it for ever.

10   For we see that wise men die:
       and perish with the foolish and the ignorant,
       leaving their wealth to others.

11   The tomb is their home for ever,
       their dwelling-place throughout all generations:
       though they called estates after their own names.

12   A rich man without understanding:
        is like the beasts that perish.

13   This is the lot of the foolish:
        the end of those who are pleased with their own words.

14   They are driven like sheep into the grave,
        and death is their shepherd:
        they slip down easily into the tomb.

15   Their bright forms shall wear away in the grave:
        and lose their former glory.

16   But God will ransom my life:
        he will take me from the power of the grave.

17   Do not fear when a man grows rich:
        when the wealth of his household increases,

18   For he will take nothing away when he dies:
        nor will his wealth go down after him.

19   Though he counts himself happy while he lives:
        and praises you also when you prosper,

20   He will go to the company of his fathers:
        who will never see the light.

21   A rich man without understanding:
        is like the beasts that perish.

Psalm 50

1   The Lord our God, the Mighty One, has spoken:
        and summoned the earth, from the rising of the sun
        to its setting in the west.

2   From Zion, perfect in beauty:
      God has shone out in glory.

3   Our God is coming, he will not keep silent:
      before him is devouring fire,
      and tempest whirls about him.

4   He calls to the heavens above:
      and to the earth, so he may judge his people.

5   'Gather to me my faithful ones:
      those who by sacrifice made a covenant with me.'

6   The heavens shall proclaim his righteousness:
      for God himself is judge.

7   'Listen my people, and I will speak:
      O Israel, I am God your God,
      and I will give my testimony.

8   'It is not for your sacrifices that I reprove you:
      for your burnt-offerings are always before me.

9   'I will take no bull from your farms:
      or he-goat from your pens.

10   'For all the beasts of the forest belong to me:
      and so do the cattle upon the mountains.

11   'I know all the birds of the air:
      and the grasshoppers of the field are in my sight.

12   'If I were hungry, I would not tell you:
      for the whole world is mine, and all that is in it.

13   'Do I eat the flesh of bulls:
      or drink the blood of goats?

14   'Offer to God a sacrifice of thanksgiving:
          and pay your vows to the Most High.

15   'Call upon me in the day of trouble:
          I will bring you out, and you shall glorify me.'

16   But God says to the wicked:
          'What have you to do with reciting my laws,
          or taking my covenant on your lips,

17   'Seeing you loathe discipline:
          and have tossed my words behind you?

18   'When you saw a thief, you went along with him:
          and you threw in your lot with adulterers.

19   'You have loosed your mouth in evil:
          and your tongue strings lies together.

20   'You sit and speak against your brother:
          and slander your own mother's son.

21   'These things you have done, and I held my tongue:
          and you thought I was just such another as yourself.

22   `But I will convict you:
          and set before your eyes what you have done.

23   'O consider this, you who forget God:
          lest I tear you in pieces, and there be no one to save you.

24   'He honours me who brings sacrifice of thanksgiving:
          and to him who keeps to my way
          I will show the salvation of God.'

Psalm 51

1   Have mercy on me, O God, in your enduring goodness:
     according to the fulness of your compassion
     blot out my offences.

2   Wash me thoroughly from my wickedness:
     and cleanse me from my sin.

3   For I acknowledge my rebellion:
     and my sin is ever before me.

4   Against you only have I sinned
     and done what is evil in your eyes:
     so you will be just in your sentence
     and blameless in your judging.

5   Surely in wickedness I was brought to birth:
     and in sin my mother conceived me.

6   You that desire truth in the inward parts:
     O teach me wisdom in the secret places of the heart.

7   Purge me with hyssop, and I shall be clean:
     wash me, and I shall be whiter than snow.

8   Make me hear of joy and gladness:
     let the bones which you have broken rejoice.

9   Hide your face from my sins:
     and blot out all my iniquities.

10   Create in me a clean heart, O God:
     and renew a right spirit within me.

11   Do not cast me out from your presence:
     do not take your holy spirit from me.

12 O give me the gladness of your help again:
  and support me with a willing spirit.

13 Then will I teach transgressors your ways:
  and sinners shall turn to you again.

14 O Lord God of my salvation,
  deliver me from bloodshed:
  and my tongue shall sing of your righteousness.

15 O Lord, open my lips:
  and my mouth shall proclaim your praise.

16 You take no pleasure in sacrifice, or I would give it:
  burnt-offerings you do not want.

17 The sacrifice of God is a broken spirit:
  a broken and contrite heart, O God,
  you will not despise.

18 In your graciousness do good to Zion:
  rebuild the walls of Jerusalem.

19 Then will you delight in right sacrifices,
  in burnt-offerings and oblations:
  then will they offer young bulls upon your altar.

Psalm 52

1 Why, O man of power, do you boast all the day long:
  of mischief done to him that is faithful to God?

2 You contrive destroying slanders:
  your tongue is like a sharpened razor, it cuts deceitfully.

3   You have loved evil, and not good:
to tell lies, rather than to speak the truth.

4   You love all words that may do hurt:
and every deceit of the tongue.

5   But God will destroy you utterly:
he will snatch you away
and pluck you out of your dwelling,
he will uproot you from the land of the living.

6   The righteous shall see it, and fear:
they shall laugh you to scorn, and say,

7   'Behold, this is the man
who did not take God for his strength:
but trusted in the abundance of his riches,
and found his strength in slander.'

8   As for me, I am like a green olive tree in the house of God:
I will trust in the goodness of God for ever and ever.

9   I will always give you thanks, for this was your doing:
I will glorify your name before the faithful,
for it is good to praise you.

Psalm 53

1   The fool has said in his heart 'There is no God':
they have all become vile and abominable
in their wickedness,
there is not one that does good.

2   God looked down from heaven upon the children of men:
to see if there were any who would act wisely
and seek after God.

3 But they have all turned aside,
they have all alike become corrupt:
there is none that does good, no not one.

4 Are all the evildoers devoid of understanding:
who eat up my people as men eat bread,
and do not pray to God?

5 They shall be struck with terror:
for God will scatter the bones of the ungodly.

6 They shall be put to confusion:
because God has rejected them.

7 O that deliverance for Israel might come forth from Zion:
when the Lord turns again the fortunes of his people,
then shall Jacob rejoice and Israel be glad.

Psalm 54

1 Save me, O God, by the power of your name:
and vindicate me by your might.

2 Hear my prayer, O God:
and listen to the words of my mouth.

3 For the insolent have risen against me:
ruthless men, who have not set God before them,
seek my life.

4 But surely God is my helper:
the Lord is the upholder of my life.

[5 Let evil recoil on those that would waylay me:
O destroy them in your faithfulness!]

6   Then will I offer you sacrifice with a willing heart:
         I will praise your name, O Lord, for it is good.

7   For you will deliver me from every trouble:
         my eyes shall see the downfall of my enemies.

Psalm 55

1   Hear my prayer, O God:
         and do not hide yourself from my petition.

2   Give heed to me, and answer me:
         I am restless in my complaining.

3   I am in turmoil at the voice of the enemy:
         at the onslaught of the wicked.

4   For they bring down disaster upon me:
         they persecute me with bitter fury.

5   My heart writhes within me:
         and the terrors of death have fallen upon me.

6   Fear and trembling come upon me:
         and horror overwhelms me.

7   And I said 'O for the wings of a dove:
         that I might fly away and find rest.

8   'Then I would flee far off:
         and make my lodging in the wilderness.

9   'I would hasten to find me a refuge:
         out of the blast of slander,

10   'Out of the tempest of their calumny, O Lord:
      and far from their double tongues.'

11   For I have seen violence and strife in the city:
      day and night they go round it upon its walls.

12   Evil and wickedness are within it:
      iniquity is within it,
      oppression and fraud do not depart from its streets.

13   It was not an enemy that reviled me,
      or I might have borne it:
      it was not my foe that dealt so insolently with me,
      or I might have hidden myself from him;

14   But it was you, a man like myself:
      my companion and my familiar friend.

15   Together we enjoyed sweet fellowship:
      in the house of our God.

[16   Let them pass away in confusion:
      let death carry them to destruction;

17   Let them go down alive to Sheol:
      for evil is among them in their dwellings.]

18   But I will call to God:
      and the Lord my God will save me.

19   At evening, at morning, and at noon-day:
      I complain and groan aloud.

20   And he will hear my voice:
      and ransom my soul in peace,

21   From those that bear down upon me:
      for there are many against me.

22   God will hear and bring them low:
he that is enthroned for ever.

23   For they do not keep their word:
and they have no fear of God.

24   They lay violent hands
on those that are at peace with them:
they break solemn covenants.

25   Their mouths are smooth as butter,
but war is in their hearts:
their words are softer than oil,
yet they are drawn swords.

26   Cast your burden on the Lord, and he will sustain you:
he will never suffer the righteous man to stumble.

27   But as for them, you will bring them down, O God:
even to the depths of the Pit.

28   Bloodthirsty and deceitful men
shall not live out half their days:
but I will trust in you.

Psalm 56

1   Be merciful to me, O God, for men are treading me down:
all day long my adversary presses upon me.

2   My enemies tread me down all the day:
for there are many that arrogantly fight against me.

3   In the hour of fear:
I will put my trust in you.

4   In God, whose word I praise, in God I trust and fear not:
what can flesh do to me?

5   All day long they afflict me with their words:
And every thought is how to do me evil.

6   They stir up hatred and conceal themselves:
they watch my steps, while they lie in wait for my life.

7   Let there be no escape for them:
bring down the peoples in your wrath, O God.

8   You have counted my anxious tossings;
put my tears in your bottle:
are not these things noted in your book?

9   In the day that I call to you, my enemies shall turn back:
this I know, for God is with me.

10   In God, whose word I praise, in God I trust and fear not:
what can man do to me?

11   To you, O God, must I perform my vows:
I will pay the thank-offering that is due.

12   For you will deliver my soul from death,
and my feet from falling:
that I may walk before God in the light of the living.

Psalm 57

1   Be merciful to me, O God, be merciful:
for I come to you for shelter;

2   And in the shadow of your wings will I take refuge:
until these troubles are over-past.

3 I will call to God Most High:
to the God who will fulfil his purpose for me.

4 He will send from heaven and save me:
he will send forth his faithfulness and his loving-kindness,
and rebuke those that would trample me down.

5 For I lie amidst ravening lions:
men whose teeth are spears and arrows,
and their tongue a sharpened sword.

6 *Be exalted, O God, above the heavens:*
and let your glory be over all the earth.

7 They have set a net for my feet, and I am brought low:
they have dug a pit before me,
but shall fall into it themselves.

8 My heart is fixed, O God, my heart is fixed:
I will sing and make melody.

9 Awake my soul, awake lute and harp:
for I will awaken the morning.

10 I will give you thanks, O Lord, among the peoples:
I will sing your praise among the nations.

11 For the greatness of your mercy reaches to the heavens:
and your faithfulness to the clouds.

12 *Be exalted, O God, above the heavens:*
and let your glory be over all the earth.

Psalm 58

1   [I Do you indeed decree what is just, O rulers:
do you with uprightness judge the children of men?

2   No, you work in the land with evil heart:
you look on the violence that your hands have wrought.

3   The wicked are estranged, even from the womb:
they are liars that go astray from their birth.

4   They are venomous with the venom of serpents:
like the deaf asp that stops its ears,

5   And will not heed the voice of the charmers:
though the binder of spells be skilful.

6   Break their teeth, O God, in their mouths:
shatter the jaws of the young lions, O Lord.

7   Let them dissolve, and drain away like water:
let them be trodden down, let them wither like grass,

8   Like a woman's miscarriage that melts and passes away:
like an abortive birth that has not seen the sun.

9   Before they know it, let them be cut down like thorns:
like brambles which a man sweeps angrily aside.

10   The righteous shall rejoice when he sees the vengeance:
he will wash his feet in the blood of the ungodly.

11   And men will say 'There is reward for the righteous:
there is indeed a God who judges on earth'.]

Psalm 59

1   Deliver me from my enemies, O God:
    lift me to safety from those that rise against me;

2   O deliver me from the evildoers:
    and save me from bloodthirsty men.

3   For they lie in wait for my life:
    savage men stir up violence against me.

4   Not for my sin or my transgression, O Lord,
    not for any evil I have done:
    do they run and take up position against me.

5   Arise to meet me, and see:
    you that are Lord of hosts and God of Israel.

[6   Awake to punish all the nations:
    have no mercy on those that so treacherously do wrong.]

7   They return every evening, they howl like dogs:
    they prowl around the city.

8   Look how their mouths slaver:
    swords strike from their lips, for they say
    'Who will hear it?'

9   But you, O Lord, will laugh them to scorn:
    you will deride all the nations.

10   I will look to you, O my strength:
    for God is my strong tower.

11   My God in his steadfastness will come to meet me:
    God will show me the downfall of my enemies.

12   Slay them not, O Lord, lest my people forget:
    but make them stagger by your power,
    and bring them down.

13   Give them over to punishment
    for the sin of their mouths,
    for the words of their lips:
    let them be taken in their pride.

[14   For the curses and lies that they have uttered,
    O consume them in your wrath:
    consume them, till they are no more;]

15   That men may know that God rules over Jacob:
    even to the ends of the earth.

16   They return every evening, they howl like dogs:
    they prowl around the city.

17   They roam here and there looking for food:
    and growl if they are not filled.

18   But I will sing of your might:
    I will sing aloud each morning of your goodness.

19   For you have been my strong tower:
    and a sure refuge in the day of my distress.

20   I will sing your praises, O my strength:
    for God is my strong tower.

Psalm 60

1   O God, you have cast us off and broken us:
    you were enraged against us – O restore us again!

2   You have caused the land to quake, you have rent it open:
     heal the rifts, for the earth quivers and breaks.

3   You have steeped your people in a bitter draught:
     you have given them a wine to make them stagger.

4   You have caused those that fear you to take flight:
     so that they run from the bow.

5   O save us by your right hand, and answer us:
     that those whom you love may be delivered.

6   God has said in his holy place:
     'I will exult and divide Shechem,
     I will parcel out the valley of Succoth.

7   'Gilead is mine, and Manasseh is mine:
     Ephraim is my helmet, and Judah my rod of command.

8   'Moab is my wash-bowl, over Edom will I cast my shoe:
     against Philistia will I shout in triumph.'

9   Who will lead me into the fortified city:
     who will bring me into Edom?

10   Have you not cast us off, O God?:
     you go not out with our armies.

11   Give us your help against the enemy:
     for vain is the help of man.

12   By the power of our God we shall do valiantly:
     for it is he that will tread down our enemies.

Psalm 61

1   Hear my loud crying, O God:
       and give heed to my prayer.

2   From the ends of the earth I call to you
       when my heart faints:
       O set me on the rock that is higher than I.

3   For you have been my refuge:
       and my strong tower against the enemy.

4   I will dwell in your tent for ever:
       and find shelter in the covering of your wings.

5   For you have heard my vows, O God:
       you have granted the desire of those that fear your name.

6   You will give the king long life:
       and his years shall endure through many generations.

7   He shall dwell before God for ever:
       loving-kindness and truth shall be his guard.

8   So will I ever sing praises to your name:
       while I daily perform my vows.

Psalm 62

1   My soul waits in silence for God:
       for from him comes my salvation.

2   He only is my rock and my salvation:
       my strong tower, so that I shall never be moved.

3   How long will you all plot against a man to destroy him:
       as though he were a leaning fence or a buckling wall?

4 Their design is to thrust him from his height,
  and their delight is in lies:
  they bless with their lips, but inwardly they curse.

5 Nevertheless, my soul, wait in silence for God:
  for from him comes my hope.

6 He only is my rock and my salvation:
  my strong tower, so that I shall not be moved.

7 In God is my deliverance and my glory:
  God is my strong rock and my shelter.

8 Trust in him at all times, O my people:
  pour out your hearts before him, for God is our refuge.

9 The children of men are but breath,
  the children of men are a lie:
  place them in the scales and they fly upward,
  they are as light as air.

10 Put no trust in extortion,
  do not grow worthless by robbery:
  if riches increase, set not your heart upon them.

11 God has spoken once, twice have I heard him say:
  that power belongs to God,

12 That to the Lord belongs a constant goodness:
  for you reward a man according to his works.

Psalm 63

1   O God, you are my God:
     eagerly will I seek you.

2   My soul thirsts for you, my flesh longs for you:
     as a dry and thirsty land where no water is.

3   So it was when I beheld you in the sanctuary:
     and saw your power and your glory.

4   For your unchanging goodness is better than life:
     therefore my lips shall praise you.

5   And so I will bless you as long as I live:
     and in your name will I lift my hands on high.

6   My longing shall be satisfied as with marrow and fatness:
     my mouth shall praise you with exultant lips.

7   When I remember you upon my bed:
     when I meditate upon you in the night watches,

8   How you have been my helper:
     then I sing for joy in the shadow of your wings,

9   Then my soul clings to you:
     and your right hand upholds me.

10   Those that seek my life are marked for destruction:
     they shall go down to the deep places of the earth.

11   They shall be delivered to the sword:
     they shall be a portion for jackals.

12   The king will rejoice in God,
     and all who take oaths on his name shall glory:
     but the mouths of liars shall be stopped.

Psalm 64

1   Hear my voice, O God, in my complaining:
preserve my life from fear of the enemy.

2   Hide me from the conspiracy of the wicked:
from the throng of evildoers,

3   Who sharpen their tongues like swords:
who string the bow, who take arrows of bitter words,

4   To shoot from hiding at the blameless man:
to strike at him suddenly and unseen.

5   They are confirmed in an evil purpose:
they confide it to one another while they lay the snares,
saying 'Who will see them?'

6   They hatch mischief, they hide a well-considered plan:
for the mind and heart of man is very deep.

7   But God will shoot at them with his swift arrows:
they shall be suddenly struck through.

8   The Lord will bring them down
for what their tongues have spoken:
and all that see it shall toss their heads in scorn.

9   Then all men shall fear:
and tell what the Lord has done, and ponder his works.

10   The righteous man shall rejoice in the Lord,
and find in him his refuge:
and all the upright in heart shall exult.

Psalm 65

1 You are to be praised, O God, in Zion:
  to you shall vows be paid, you that answer prayer.

2 To you shall all flesh come to confess their sins:
  when our misdeeds prevail against us,
  you will purge them away.

3 Blessed is the man whom you choose and take to yourself
  to dwell within your courts:
  we shall be filled with the good things of your house,
  of your holy temple.

4 You will answer us in your righteousness
  with terrible deeds, O God our saviour:
  you that are the hope of all the ends of the earth
  and of the distant seas;

5 Who by your strength made fast the mountains:
  you that are girded with power;

6 Who stilled the raging of the seas,
  the roaring of the waves:
  and the tumult of the peoples.

7 Those who dwell at the ends of the earth
  are afraid at your wonders:
  the dawn and the evening sing your praises.

8 You tend the earth and water it:
  you make it rich and fertile.

9 The river of God is full of water:
  and so providing for the earth, you provide grain for men.

10 You drench its furrows, you level the ridges between:
  you soften it with showers and bless its early growth.

11   You crown the year with your goodness:
and the tracks where you have passed drip with fatness.

12   The pastures of the wilderness run over:
and the hills are girded with joy.

13   The meadows are clothed with sheep:
and the valleys stand so thick with corn,
they shout for joy and sing.

Psalm 66

1   O shout with joy to God, all the earth:
sing to the honour of his name,
and give him glory as his praise.

2   Say to God 'How fearful are your works:
because of your great might
your enemies shall cower before you'.

3   All the earth shall worship you:
and sing to you, and sing praises to your name.

4   Come then and see what God has done:
how terrible are his dealings with the children of men.

5   He turned the sea into dry land,
they crossed the river on foot:
then were we joyful because of him.

6   By his power he rules for ever,
his eyes keep watch on the nations:
and rebels shall never rise against him.

7   O bless our God, you peoples:
      and cause his praises to resound,

8   Who has held our souls in life:
      who has not suffered our feet to slip.

9   For you have proved us, O God:
      you have tried us as silver is tried.

10   You brought us into the net:
      you laid sharp torment on our loins.

11   You let men ride over our heads,
      we went through fire and water:
      but you brought us out into a place of liberty.

12   I will come into your house with burnt-offerings:
      and I will pay you my vows,

13   The vows that opened my lips:
      that my mouth uttered when I was in trouble.

14   I will offer you burnt-offerings of fattened beasts,
      with the sweet smoke of rams:
      I will sacrifice a bull and the flesh of goats.

15   Come then and hear, all you that fear God:
      and I will tell what he has done for me.

16   I called to him with my mouth:
      and his praise was on my tongue.

17   If I had cherished wickedness in my heart:
      the Lord would not have heard me.

18   But God has heard me:
      he has heeded the voice of my prayer.

19   Praise be to God:
        who has not turned back my prayer,
        or his steadfast love from me.

Psalm 67

1   Let God be gracious to us and bless us:
        and make his face shine upon us,

2   That your ways may be known on earth:
        your liberating power among all nations.

3   Let the peoples praise you, O God:
        let all the peoples praise you.

4   Let the nations be glad and sing:
        for you judge the peoples with integrity,
        and govern the nations upon earth.

5   Let the peoples praise you, O God:
        let all the peoples praise you.

6   Then the earth will yield its fruitfulness:
        and God, our God, will bless us.

7   God shall bless us:
        and all the ends of the earth will fear him.

Psalm 68

1   God shall arise, and his enemies shall be scattered:
those that hate him shall flee before his face.

2   As smoke is dispersed, so shall they be dispersed:
as wax melts before a fire,
so shall the wicked perish at the presence of God.

3   But the righteous shall be glad and exult before God:
they shall rejoice with gladness.

4   O sing to God, sing praises to his name:
glorify him that rode through the deserts,
him whose name is the Lord, and exult before him.

5   He is the father of the fatherless,
he upholds the cause of the widow:
God in his holy dwelling place.

6   He gives the desolate a home to dwell in,
and brings the prisoners out into prosperity:
but rebels must dwell in a barren land.

7   O God, when you went out before your people:
when you marched through the wilderness,

8   The earth shook, the heavens poured down water:
before the God of Sinai, before God, the God of Israel.

9   You showered down a generous rain, O God:
you prepared the land of your possession when it was weary.

10   And there your people settled:
in the place that your goodness, O God,
had made ready for the poor.

11   The Lord spoke the word,
      and great was the company of those that carried the tidings:
      'Kings with their armies are fleeing, are fleeing away.

12   'Even the women at home may share in the spoil:
      and will you sit idly among the sheepfolds?

13   'There are images of doves
      whose wings are covered with silver:
      and their pinions with shining gold.'

14   When the Almighty scattered kings:
      they were like snow falling upon Mount Zalmon.

15   The mountain of Bashan is a mighty mountain:
      the mountain of Bashan is a mountain of many peaks.

16   O mountains of many peaks, why look so enviously:
      at the mountain where God is pleased to dwell,
      where the Lord will remain for ever?

17   The chariots of God are twice ten thousand,
      and thousands upon thousands:
      the Lord came from Sinai into his holy place.

18   When you ascended the heights,
      you led the enemy captive,
      you received tribute from men:
      but rebels shall not dwell in the presence of God.

19   Blessed be the Lord day by day,
      who bears us as his burden:
      he is the God of our deliverance.

20   God is to us a God who saves:
      by God the Lord do we escape death.

[21   But God shall smite the heads of his enemies:
            the hairy scalp of those that walk in their sins.

22   The Lord said 'I will bring them back from Bashan:
            I will bring them again from the deep sea';

23   That you may dip your feet in blood:
            and the tongues of your dogs in the blood of your enemies.]

24   Your procession is seen, O God:
            the procession of my God and King in the sanctuary.

25   The singers go before, the musicians come after:
            and around them the maidens beating on the timbrels.

26   In their choirs they bless God:
            those that are sprung from the fount of Israel bless the Lord.

27   There is the little tribe of Benjamin leading them:
            the throng of the princes of Judah, the princes of Zebulun
            and the princes of Naphtali.

28   Give the command, my God,
            in accordance with your power:
            that godlike power whereby you act for us.

29   Give the command from your temple at Jerusalem:
            and kings shall bring you tribute.

30   Rebuke the beast of the reeds,
            the herd of bulls amidst the brutish peoples:
            tread down those that are greedy for silver,
            scatter the peoples that relish war.

31   Let them bring bronze from Egypt:
            let the hands of the Nubians carry it swiftly to God.

32   Sing to God, you kingdoms of the earth:
      O sing praises to the Lord,

33   To him that rides upon the highest heavens,
      that were from the beginning:
      who utters his voice, which is a mighty voice.

34   Ascribe power to God, whose majesty is over Israel:
      and his might is in the clouds.

35   Terrible is God who comes from his holy place:
      the God of Israel who gives power and strength to his people.
      Blessed be God.

Psalm 69

1   Save me, O God:
      for the waters have come up even to my throat.

2   I sink in the deep mire where no footing is:
      I have come into deep waters
      and the flood sweeps over me.

3   I am weary with crying out, my throat is parched:
      my eyes fail with watching so long for my God.

4   Those that hate me without cause
      are more in number than the hairs of my head:
      those that would destroy me are many,
      they oppose me wrongfully
      – for I must restore things that I never took.

5   O God, you know my foolishness:
      and my sins are not hidden from you.

6 Let not those who wait for you
  be shamed because of me, O Lord God of hosts:
  let not those who seek you
  be disgraced on my account, O God of Israel.

7 For your sake have I suffered reproach:
  and shame has covered my face.

8 I have become a stranger to my brothers:
  an alien to my own mother's sons.

9 Zeal for your house has eaten me up:
  and the taunts of those who taunt you
  have fallen on me.

10 I afflicted myself with fasting:
  and that was turned to my reproach.

11 I made sackcloth my clothing:
  and I became a byword to them.

12 Those who sit in the gate talk of me:
  and the drunkards make songs about me.

13 But to you, Lord, I make my prayer:
  at an acceptable time.

14 Answer me, O God, in your abundant goodness:
  and with your sure deliverance.

15 Bring me out of the mire, so that I may not sink:
  let me be delivered from my enemies,
  and from the deep waters.

16 Let not the flood overwhelm me
  or the depths swallow me up:
  let not the Pit shut its mouth upon me.

17 Hear me, O Lord, as your loving-kindness is good:
    turn to me, as your compassion is great.

18 Do not hide your face from your servant:
    for I am in trouble – O be swift to answer me!

19 Draw near to me and redeem me:
    O ransom me because of my enemies!

20 You know all their taunts:
    my adversaries are all in your sight.

21 Insults have broken my heart:
    my shame and disgrace are past healing.

22 I looked for someone to have pity on me,
    but there was no man:
    for some to comfort me, but found none.

23 They gave me poison for food:
    and when I was thirsty, they gave me vinegar to drink.

[24 Let their table become a snare:
    and their sacrificial feasts a trap.

25 Let their eyes be darkened, so that they cannot see:
    and make their loins shake continually.

26 Pour out your wrath upon them:
    and let your fierce anger overtake them.

27 Let their camp be desolate:
    and let no man dwell in their tents.

28 For they persecute him whom you have stricken:
    and multiply the pain of him whom you have wounded.

29   Let them have punishment upon punishment:
      let them not receive your forgiveness.

30   Let them be blotted out of the book of the living:
      let them not be written down among the righteous.]

31   As for me, I am poor and in misery:
      O God, let your deliverance lift me up.

32   And I will praise the name of God in a song:
      and glorify him with thanksgiving.

33   And that will please the Lord more than an ox:
      more than a bull with horns and cloven hoof.

34   Consider this, you that are meek, and rejoice:
      seek God, and let your heart be glad.

35   For the Lord listens to the poor:
      he does not despise his servants in captivity.

36   Let the heavens and the earth praise him:
      the seas and all that moves in them.

37   For God will save Zion:
      he will rebuild the cities of Judah.

38   His people shall live there and possess it,
      the seed of his servants shall inherit it:
      and those who love his name shall dwell in it.

Psalm 70

1   O God, be pleased to deliver me:
    O Lord, make haste to help me.

2   Let them be put to shame and confounded
    who seek my life:
    let them be turned back and disgraced
    who wish me evil.

3   Let them turn away for shame:
    who say to me 'Aha, aha!'

4   Let all who seek you be joyful and glad because of you:
    let those who love your salvation say always 'God is great'.

5   As for me, I am poor and needy:
    O God, be swift to save me.

6   You are my helper and my deliverer:
    O Lord, make no delay.

Psalm 71

1   To you, Lord, have I come for shelter:
    let me never be put to shame.

2   In your righteousness rescue and deliver me:
    incline your ear to me and save me.

3   Be for me a rock of refuge, a fortress to defend me:
    for you are my high rock, and my stronghold.

4   Rescue me, O my God, from the hand of the wicked:
    from the grasp of the pitiless and unjust.

5   For you, Lord, are my hope:
        you are my confidence, O God, from my youth upward.

6   On you have I leaned since my birth:
        you are he that brought me out of my mother's womb,
        and my praise is of you continually.

7   I have become as a fearful warning to many:
        but you are my strength and my refuge.

8   My mouth shall be filled with your praises:
        I shall sing of your glory all the day long.

9   Cast me not away in the time of old age:
        nor forsake me when my strength fails.

10   For my enemies speak against me:
        and those that watch for my life conspire together, saying,

11   'God has forsaken him:
        pursue him, take him, for there is none to save him.'

12   Be not far from me, O God:
        my God, make haste to help me.

13   Let my adversaries be confounded and put to shame:
        let those who seek my hurt
        be covered with scorn and disgrace.

14   As for me, I will wait in hope continually:
        and I will praise you more and more.

15   My mouth shall speak of your righteousness all the day:
        and tell of your salvation, though it exceeds my telling.

16   I will begin with the mighty acts of the Lord my God:
        and declare your righteous dealing – yours alone.

17   O God, you have taught me from my youth upward:
and to this day, I proclaim your marvellous works.

18   Forsake me not, O God, in my old age,
when I am grey-headed:
till I have shown the strength of your arm
to future generations,
and your might to those that come after.

19   Your righteousness, O God, reaches to the heavens:
great are the things that you have done;
O God, who is like you?

20   You have burdened me with many and bitter troubles,
O turn and renew me:
and raise me up again from the depths of the earth.

21   Bless me beyond my former greatness:
O turn to me again, and comfort me.

22   Then will I praise you upon the lute
for your faithfulness, O my God:
and sing your praises to the harp,
O Holy One of Israel.

23   My lips shall rejoice in my singing:
and my soul also, for you have ransomed me.

24   My tongue shall speak of your righteous dealing
all the day long:
for they shall be put to shame and disgraced
that seek to do me evil.

Psalm 72

1   Give the king your judgement, O God:
    and your righteousness to the son of a king,

2   That he may judge your people rightly:
    and the poor of the land with equity.

3   Let the mountains be laden with peace
    because of his righteousness:
    and the hills also with prosperity for his people.

4   May he give justice to the poor among the people:
    and rescue the children of the needy,
    and crush the oppressor.

5   May he live while the sun endures:
    and while the moon gives light,
    throughout all generations.

6   May he come down like rain upon the new-mown fields:
    and as showers that water the earth.

7   In his time shall righteousness flourish:
    and abundance of peace, till the moon shall be no more.

8   His dominion shall stretch from sea to sea:
    from the Great River to the ends of the earth.

9   His adversaries shall bow down before him:
    and his enemies shall lick the dust.

10   The kings of Tarshish and of the isles shall bring tribute:
    the kings of Sheba and Seba shall offer gifts.

11   All kings shall fall down before him:
    and all nations do him service.

12   He will deliver the needy when they cry:
         and the poor man that has no helper.

13   He will pity the helpless and the needy:
         and save the lives of the poor.

14   He will redeem them from oppression and violence:
         and their blood shall be precious in his sight.

15   Long may he live,
         and be given of the gold of Sheba:
         may prayer be made for him continually,
         and men bless him every day.

16   Let there be abundance of wheat in the land:
         let it flourish on the tops of the mountains;

17   Let its ears grow fat like the grain of Lebanon:
         and its sheaves thicken like the grass of the field.

18   Let his name live for ever:
         and endure as long as the sun.

19   Let all peoples use his name in blessing:
         and all nations call him blessed.

20   Blessed be the Lord God, the God of Israel:
         who alone does great wonders.

21   Blessed be his glorious name for ever:
         and let the whole earth be filled with his glory.
         Amen, Amen.

Psalm 73

1   God is indeed good to Israel:
to those whose hearts are pure.

2   Nevertheless, my feet were almost gone:
my steps had well-nigh slipped.

3   For I was filled with envy at the boastful:
when I saw the ungodly had such tranquillity.

4   For they suffer no pain:
and their bodies are hale and fat.

5   They come to no misfortune like other folk:
nor are they plagued like other men.

6   Therefore they put on pride as a necklace:
and clothe themselves in violence as in a garment.

7   Their eyes shine from folds of fatness:
and they have all that heart could wish.

8   Their talk is malice and mockery:
and they hand down slanders from on high.

9   Their mouths blaspheme against heaven:
and their tongues go to and fro on earth.

10   Therefore my people turn to them:
and find in them no fault.

11   They say 'How can God know:
is there understanding in the Most High?'

12   Behold, these are the ungodly:
yet they prosper and increase in riches.

13 Was it for nothing then that I cleansed my heart:
  and washed my hands in innocence?

14 Have I been stricken all day long in vain:
  and rebuked every morning?

15 If I had said 'I will speak thus':
  I should have betrayed the family of your children.

16 Then I thought to understand this:
  but it was too hard for me,

17 Till I went into the sanctuary of God:
  and then I understood what their end will be.

18 For you set them in slippery places:
  and cause them to fall from their treacherous footholds.

19 How suddenly they are laid waste:
  they come to an end, they perish in terror.

20 As with a dream when one awakes:
  so when you rouse yourself, O Lord,
  you will despise their image.

21 When my heart was soured:
  and I was wounded to the core,

22 I was but brutish and ignorant:
  no better than a beast before you.

23 Nevertheless, I am always with you:
  for you hold me by my right hand.

24 You will guide me with your counsel:
  and afterwards you will lead me to glory.

25   Whom have I in heaven but you?:
       and there is no one upon earth that I desire
       in comparison with you.

26   Though my flesh and my heart fail me:
       you, O God, are my portion for ever.

27   Behold, those who forsake you shall perish:
       and all who whore after other gods you will destroy.

28   But it is good for me to draw near to God:
       I have made the Lord God my refuge,
       and I will tell of all that you have done.

Psalm 74

1   O Lord our God, why cast us off so utterly:
      why does your anger burn
      against the sheep of your pasture?

2   Remember your congregation,
      whom you took to yourself of old:
      the people that you redeemed to be your own possession,
      and Mount Zion where you have dwelt.

3   Rouse yourself and go to the utter ruins:
      to all the harm that the enemy has done in the sanctuary.

4   Your adversaries have made uproar
      in the place appointed for your praise:
      they have set up their standards in triumph.

5   They have destroyed on every side:
      like those who take axes up to a thicket of trees.

6   All the carved woodwork they have broken down:
      and smashed it with hammers and hatchets.

7   They have set fire to your sanctuary:
           and defiled to the ground the dwelling-place of your name.

8   They have said in their hearts
           'Let us make havoc of them':
           they have burned down
           all the holy places of God in the land.

9   We see no signs, there is not one prophet left:
           there is none who knows how long these things shall be.

10   How long shall the adversary taunt you, O God:
           shall the enemy blaspheme your name for ever?

11   Why do you hold back your hand:
           why do you keep your right hand in your bosom?

12   Yet God is my king from of old:
           who wrought deliverance upon the earth.

13   You divided the sea by your might:
           you shattered the heads of the dragons in the waters.

14   You crushed the heads of Leviathan:
           and gave him as food to the creatures of the desert waste.

15   You cleft open spring and fountain:
           you dried up the everflowing waters.

16   The day is yours, and so also is the night:
           you have established the moon and the sun.

17   You set all the boundaries of the earth:
           you created winter and summer.

18   Remember, O Lord, the taunts of the enemy:
           how a mindless people have blasphemed your name.

19   Do not give to the wild beasts the soul that praises you:
     do not forget for ever the life of your afflicted.

20   Look on all that you have made:
     for it is full of darkness, and violence inhabits the earth.

21   Let not the oppressed and reviled turn away rejected:
     but let the poor and needy praise your name.

22   Arise, O God, plead your own cause:
     remember how a mindless people taunt you all day long.

23   Do not forget the clamour of your adversaries:
     or how the shouting of your enemies ascends continually.

Psalm 75

1   We give you thanks, O God, we give you thanks:
     we call upon your name
     and tell of all the wonders you have done.

2   'I will surely appoint a time:
     when I, the Lord, will judge with equity.

3   'Though the earth shake, and all who dwell in it:
     it is I that have founded its pillars.

4   'I will say to the boasters "Boast no more":
     and to the wicked "Do not flaunt your horns;

5   '"Do not flaunt your horns so high:
     or speak so proud and stiff-necked."'

6   For there is none from the east or from the west:
     or from the wilderness who can raise up;

7   But it is God who is the judge:
     who puts down one and exalts another.

8   For there is a cup in the Lord's hand:
         and the wine foams and is richly mixed;

9   He gives it in turn to each of the wicked of the earth:
         they drink it and drain it to the dregs.

10   But I will sing praises to the God of Jacob:
         I will glorify his name for ever.

11   All the horns of the wicked I will break:
         but the horns of the righteous shall be lifted high.

Psalm 76

1   In Judah God is known:
         his name is great in Israel.

2   At Salem is his tabernacle:
         and his dwelling is in Zion.

3   There he broke in pieces the flashing arrows of the bow:
         the shield, the sword and the weapons of battle.

4   Radiant in light are you:
         greater in majesty than the eternal hills.

5   The valiant were dumbfounded, they sleep their sleep:
         and all the men of war have lost their strength.

6   At the blast of your voice, O God of Jacob:
         both horse and chariot were cast asleep.

7   Terrible are you, Lord God:
         and who may stand before you when you are angry?

8   You caused your sentence to be heard from heaven:
         the earth feared and was still,

9 When God arose to judgement:
  to save all the meek of the earth.

10 For you crushed the wrath of man:
  you bridled the remnant of the wrathful.

11 O make vows to the Lord your God, and keep them:
  let all around him bring gifts
  to him that is worthy to be feared.

12 For he cuts down the fury of princes:
  and he is terrible to the kings of the earth.

Psalm 77

1 I call to my God, I cry out toward him:
  I call to my God, and surely he will answer.

2 In the day of my distress I seek the Lord,
  I stretch out my hands to him by night:
  my soul is poured out without ceasing,
  it refuses all comfort.

3 I think upon God and groan aloud:
  I muse, and my spirit faints.

4 You hold my eyelids open:
  I am so dazed that I cannot flee.

5 I consider the times that are past:
  I remember the years of long ago.

6 At night I am grieved to the heart:
  I ponder, and my spirit makes search;

| 7 | 'Will the Lord cast us off for ever: |
| | will he show us his favour no more? |

| 8 | 'Is his mercy clean gone for ever: |
| | and his promise come to an end for all generations? |

| 9 | 'Has God forgotten to be gracious: |
| | has he shut up his pity in displeasure?' |

10	And I say
	'Has the right hand of the Most High lost its strength:
	has the arm of the Lord changed?'

| 11 | I will declare the mighty acts of the Lord: |
| | I will call to mind your wonders of old. |

| 12 | I will think on all that you have done: |
| | and meditate upon your works. |

| 13 | Your way, O God, is holy: |
| | who is so great a god as our God? |

| 14 | You are the God that works wonders: |
| | you made known your power among the nations; |

| 15 | By your mighty arm you redeemed your people: |
| | the children of Jacob and Joseph. |

16	The waters saw you, O God,
	the waters saw you and were afraid:
	the depths also were troubled.

| 17 | The clouds poured out water, the heavens spoke: |
| | and your arrows darted forth. |

18	The voice of your thunder was heard in the whirlwind:
	your lightnings lit the world,
	the earth shuddered and quaked.

19   Your way was in the sea, your path in the great waters:
         and your footsteps were not seen.

20   You led your people like sheep:
         by the hand of Moses and Aaron.

Psalm 78

1   Give heed to my teaching, O my people:
         incline your ears to the words of my mouth;

2   For I will open my mouth in a parable:
         and expound the mysteries of former times.

3   What we have heard and known:
         what our forefathers have told us,

4   We will not hide from their children,
         but declare to a generation yet to come:
         the praiseworthy acts of the Lord,
         his mighty and wonderful works.

5   He established a law in Jacob and made a decree in Israel:
         which he commanded our forefathers to teach their children,

6   That future generations might know,
         and the children yet unborn:
         that they in turn might teach it to their sons;

7   So that they might put their confidence in God:
         and not forget his works, but keep his commandments,

8   And not be as their forefathers,
         a stubborn and rebellious generation:
         a generation that did not set their heart aright,
         whose spirit was not faithful to God.

9   The children of Ephraim, armed with the bow:
turned back in the day of battle.

10   They did not keep God's covenant,
they refused to walk in his law:
they forgot what he had done,
and the wonders he had shown them.

11   For he did marvellous things in the sight of their fathers:
in the land of Egypt, in the country of Zoan.

12   He divided the sea and let them pass through:
he made the waters stand up in a heap.

13   In the daytime he led them with a cloud:
and all night long with the light of fire.

14   He cleft rocks in the wilderness:
and gave them drink in abundance as from springs of water.

15   He brought streams out of the rock:
and caused the waters to flow down like rivers.

16   But for all this they sinned yet more against him:
and rebelled against the Most High in the desert.

17   They wilfully put God to the test:
and demanded food for their appetite.

18   They spoke against God, and said:
'Can God prepare a table in the wilderness?

19   'He indeed struck the rock,
so that the waters gushed and the streams overflowed:
but can he also give bread,
or provide meat for his people?'

20   When the Lord heard it he was angry,
        and a fire was kindled against Jacob:
        his wrath blazed against Israel.

21   For they put no trust in God:
        nor would they believe his power to save.

22   Then he commanded the clouds above:
        and opened the doors of heaven.

23   He rained down manna for them to eat:
        and gave them the grain of heaven.

24   So men ate the bread of angels:
        and he sent them food in abundance.

25   He stirred up the south east wind in the heavens:
        and guided it by his power.

26   He rained down meat upon them thick as dust:
        and winged birds like the sands of the sea.

27   He made them fall into the midst of their camp:
        and all about their tents.

28   So they ate and were well-filled:
        for he had given them what they desired.

29   But before they had satisfied their craving:
        while the food was still in their mouths,

30   The anger of God blazed up against them:
        and he slew their strongest men,
        and laid low the youth of Israel.

31   But for all this they sinned yet more:
        and put no faith in his wonders.

32 So he ended their days like a breath:
and their years with sudden terror.

33 When he struck them down, then they sought him:
they turned, and sought eagerly for God.

34 They remembered that God was their rock:
that God Most High was their redeemer.

35 But they lied to him with their mouths:
and dissembled with their tongues;

36 For their hearts were not fixed upon him:
nor were they true to his covenant.

37 Yet he, being merciful,
forgave their iniquity and did not destroy them:
many times he turned his anger aside,
and would not wholly arouse his fury.

38 He remembered that they were but flesh:
like a wind that passes, and does not return.

39 How often they rebelled against him in the wilderness:
and grieved him in the desert!

40 Again and again they put God to the test:
and provoked the Holy One of Israel.

41 They did not remember his power:
or the day when he redeemed them from the enemy;

42 How he wrought his signs in Egypt:
his wonders in the country of Zoan.

43   For he turned their rivers into blood:
       so that they could not drink from the streams.

44   He sent swarms of flies that devoured them:
       and frogs that laid them waste.

45   He gave their crops to the locust:
       and the fruits of their labour to the grasshopper.

46   He struck down their vines with hailstones:
       and their sycomore trees with frost.

47   He gave up their cattle to the hail:
       and their flocks to the flash of the lightning.

48   He loosed on them the fierceness of his anger,
       his fury, his indignation and distress:
       and these were his messengers of destruction.

49   He opened a path for his fury:
       he would not spare them from death,
       but gave up their lives to the pestilence.

50   He struck down the firstborn of Egypt:
       the first-fruits of their manhood
       in the dwellings of Ham.

51   As for his own people, he led them out like sheep:
       and guided them in the wilderness like a flock.

52   He led them in safety, and they were not afraid:
       but the sea covered their enemies.

53   He brought them to his holy land:
       to the mountains that his own right hand had won.

54   He drove out the nations before them,
and apportioned their lands as a possession:
and settled the tribes of Israel in their tents.

55   But they rebelled against God Most High
and put him to the test:
they would not obey his commandments.

56   They turned back and dealt treacherously like their fathers:
they turned aside, slack as an unstrung bow.

57   They provoked him to anger with their heathen shrines:
and moved him to jealousy with their carved images.

58   God heard and was angry, he utterly rejected Israel:
he forsook the tabernacle at Shiloh,
the tent where he dwelt among men.

59   He gave the ark of his might into captivity:
and his glory into the hands of the enemy.

60   He delivered his people to the sword:
and was enraged against his own possession.

61   Fire devoured the young men:
there was no one to bewail the maidens;

62   Their priests fell by the sword:
and there was none to mourn for the widows.

63   Then the Lord awoke like a man out of sleep:
like a warrior that had been overcome with wine.

64   He struck the backs of his enemies as they fled:
and put them to perpetual shame.

65   He rejected the family of Joseph:
he refused the tribe of Ephraim.

66   But he chose the tribe of Judah:
and the hill of Zion which he loved.

67   He built his sanctuary like the heights of heaven:
like the earth which he had founded for ever.

68   He chose David his servant:
and took him from the sheepfolds;

69   He brought him from following the ewes:
to be the shepherd of his people Jacob,
and of Israel his own possession.

70   So he tended them with upright heart:
and guided them with skilful hand.

Psalm 79

1   O God, the heathen have come into your land:
they have defiled your holy temple,
they have made Jerusalem a heap of stones.

2   They have given the dead bodies of your servants
as food to the birds of the air:
and the flesh of your faithful ones
to the wild beasts of the earth.

3   Their blood they have spilt like water
on every side of Jerusalem:
and there is none to bury them.

4   We have become a mockery to our neighbours:
the scorn and laughing-stock of those about us.

5   How long, O Lord, shall your anger be so extreme:
       will your jealous fury burn like fire?

6   Pour out your wrath on the nations that do not know you:
       on the kingdoms that have not called upon your name.

7   For they have devoured Jacob:
       and made his dwelling-place a desolation.

8   Do not remember against us the sin of former times:
       but let your compassion hasten to meet us,
       for we are brought very low.

9   Help us, O God our saviour, for the honour of your name:
       O deliver us and expiate our sins, for your name's sake.

[10   Why should the heathen say 'Where is their God?':
       O let vengeance for the blood of your servants that is shed
       be shown upon the nations in our sight.]

11   Let the sorrowful sighing of the prisoners come before you:
       and as your power is great, reprieve those condemned to die.

[12   For the taunts
       with which our neighbours have taunted you, O Lord:
       repay them seven times over into their bosoms.]

13   So we that are your people and the sheep of your pasture
       shall give you thanks for ever:
       we will declare your praise in every generation.

Psalm 80

1   Hear, O Shepherd of Israel,
       you that led Joseph like a flock:
       you that are enthroned upon the cherubim,
       shine out in glory;

2 Before Ephraim, Benjamin and Manasseh:
  stir up your power, and come to save us.

3 *Restore us again, O Lord of hosts:*
  show us the light of your countenance,
  and we shall be saved.

4 O Lord God of hosts:
  how long will you be angry at your people's prayer?

5 You have fed them with the bread of tears:
  and given them tears to drink in good measure.

6 You have made us the victim of our neighbours:
  and our enemies laugh us to scorn.

7 *Restore us again, O Lord of hosts:*
  show us the light of your countenance,
  and we shall be saved.

8 You brought a vine out of Egypt:
  you drove out the nations, and planted it in.

9 You cleared the ground before it:
  and it struck root and filled the land.

10 The hills were covered with its shadow:
  and its boughs were like the boughs of the great cedars.

11 It stretched out its branches to the sea:
  and its tender shoots to the Great River.

12 Why then have you broken down its walls:
  so that every passer-by can pluck its fruit?

13 The wild boar out of the woods roots it up:
  and the locusts from the wild places devour it.

14   Turn to us again, O Lord of hosts:
       look down from heaven, and see.

15   Bestow your care upon this vine:
       the stock which your own right hand has planted.

16   As for those that burn it with fire and cut it down:
       let them perish at the rebuke of your countenance.

17   Let your power rest on the man at your right hand:
       on that son of man whom you made so strong for yourself.

18   And so we shall not turn back from you:
       give us life, and we will call upon your name.

19   Restore us again, O Lord of hosts:
       show us the light of your countenance,
       and we shall be saved.

Psalm 81

1   O sing joyfully to God our strength:
       shout in triumph to the God of Jacob.

2   Make music and beat upon the drum:
       sound the lute and the melodious harp.

3   Blow the ram's horn at the new moon:
       and at the full moon of our day of festival.

4   For this was a statute for Israel:
       a commandment of the God of Jacob,

5   Which he laid on Joseph as a solemn charge:
       when he came out of the land of Egypt.

6   I heard a voice that I had not known, saying:
'I eased your shoulders of the burden,
and your hands were freed from the load.

7   'You called to me in trouble, and I rescued you:
I answered you from the secret place of my thunder,
I put you to the test at the waters of Meribah.

8   'Listen, my people, and I will admonish you:
O Israel, if only you would hear me.

9   'There shall be no strange god among you:
nor shall you bow down to an alien god.

10   'I am the Lord your God,
who brought you up from the land of Egypt:
open wide your mouth, and I will fill it.

11   'But my people would not listen to my voice:
and Israel would have none of me.

12   'So I left them to the stubbornness of their hearts:
to walk according to their own designs.

13   'If only my people would listen:
if Israel would but walk in my ways,

14   'I would soon put down their enemies:
and turn my hand against their adversaries.

15   'Those that hate the Lord would cringe before him:
and their punishment would last for ever.

16   'But Israel I would feed with the finest wheat:
and satisfy you with honey from the rocks.'

Psalm 82

1   God has stood up in the council of heaven:
    in the midst of the gods he gives judgement.

2   'How long will you judge unjustly:
    and favour the cause of the wicked?

3   'Judge for the poor and fatherless:
    vindicate the afflicted and oppressed.

4   `Rescue the poor and needy:
    and save them from the hands of the wicked.

5   'They do not know, they do not understand,
    they walk about in darkness:
    all the foundations of the earth are shaken.

6   'Therefore I say, "Though you are gods:
    and all of you sons of the Most High,

7   '"Nevertheless you shall die like man:
    and fall like one of the princes."'

8   Arise, O God, and judge the earth:
    for you shall take all nations as your possession.

Psalm 83

1   Hold not your peace, O God:
    O God, be not silent or unmoved.

2   See how your enemies make uproar:
    how those that hate you have lifted up their heads.

3   For they lay shrewd plots against your people:
        they scheme against those whom you have cherished.

4   'Come', they say, 'let us destroy them,
        that they may no longer be a nation:
        that the very name of Israel may be remembered no more.'

5   With one mind they conspire together:
        they make alliance against you,

6   The tribes of Edom and the Ishmaelites:
        the people of Moab and the Hagarites,

7   Gebal and Ammon and Amalek:
        Philistia, and the inhabitants of Tyre;

8   Asshur also is joined with them:
        and lends a friendly arm to the children of Lot.

9   Do to them as you did to Midian:
        as to Sisera and Jabin at the river of Kishon,

10   Who were destroyed at Endor:
        and became like dung for the earth.

11   Make their leaders as Oreb and Zeeb:
        and all their princes like Zebah and Zalmunna,

12   Who said 'Let us take possession:
        let us seize the pastures of God'.

13   Make them like thistledown, my God:
        or like chaff blown before the wind.

14   As fire consuming a thicket:
        or as flame that sets the hillsides ablaze,

15   Pursue them with your tempest:
        and terrify them with your storm-wind.

16   Cover their faces with shame, O Lord:
       that they may seek your name.

[17   Let them be disgraced and dismayed for ever:
       let them be confounded and perish,]

18   That they may know that you, whose name is the Lord:
       are alone the Most High over all the earth.

Psalm 84

1   How lovely is your dwelling-place:
       O Lord God of hosts!

2   My soul has a desire and longing
       to enter the courts of the Lord:
       my heart and my flesh rejoice in the living God.

3   The sparrow has found her a home,
       and the swallow a nest where she may lay her young:
       even your altar, O Lord of hosts, my King and my God.

4   Blessed are those who dwell in your house:
       they will always be praising you.

5   Blessed is the man whose strength is in you:
       in whose heart are the highways to Zion;

6   Who, going through the valley of dryness,
       finds there a spring from which to drink:
       till the autumn rain shall clothe it with blessings.

7   They go from strength to strength:
       they appear, every one of them,
       before the God of gods in Zion.

8   O Lord God of hosts, hear my prayer:
        give ear, O God of Jacob.

9   Behold, O God, him who reigns over us:
        and look upon the face of your anointed.

10   One day in your courts is better than a thousand:
        I would rather stand at the threshold
        of the house of my God
        than dwell in the tents of ungodliness.

11   For the Lord God is a rampart and a shield,
        the Lord gives favour and honour:
        and no good thing will he withhold
        from those who walk in innocence.

12   O Lord God of hosts:
        blessed is the man who puts his trust in you.

Psalm 85

1   O Lord, you were gracious to your land:
        you restored the fortunes of Jacob.

2   You forgave the iniquity of your people:
        and covered all their sin.

3   You put aside all your wrath:
        and turned away from your fierce indignation.

4   Return to us again, O God our saviour:
        and let your anger cease from us.

5   Will you be displeased with us for ever:
will you stretch out your wrath
from one generation to another?

6   Will you not give us life again:
that your people may rejoice in you?

7   Show us your mercy, O Lord:
and grant us your salvation.

8   I will hear what the Lord God will speak:
for he will speak peace to his people,
to his faithful ones, whose hearts are turned to him.

9   Truly his salvation is near to those that fear him:
and his glory shall dwell in our land.

10   Mercy and truth are met together:
righteousness and peace have kissed each other;

11   Truth shall flourish out of the earth:
and righteousness shall look down from heaven.

12   The Lord will also give us all that is good:
and our land shall yield its plenty.

13   For righteousness shall go before him:
and tread the path before his feet.

Psalm 86

1   Incline your ear to me, O God, and answer me:
for I am poor and in misery.

2   Preserve my life, for I am faithful:
My God, save your servant who puts his trust in you.

3   Be merciful to me, O Lord:
    for I call to you all the day long.

4   O make glad the soul of your servant:
    for I put my hope in you, O Lord.

5   For you, Lord, are good and forgiving:
    of great and continuing kindness
    to all who call upon you.

6   Hear my prayer, O Lord:
    and give heed to the voice of my supplication.

7   In the day of my trouble I call upon you:
    for you will surely answer.

8   Among the gods there is none like you, O Lord:
    nor are there any deeds like yours.

9   All the nations you have made
    shall come and worship before you:
    O Lord, they shall glorify your name.

10 For you are great and do marvellous things:
    and you alone are God.

11 Show me your way, O Lord, and I will walk in your truth:
    let my heart delight to fear your name.

12 I will praise you, O Lord my God, with all my heart:
    and I will glorify your name for ever.

13 For great is your abiding love toward me:
    and you have delivered my life
    from the lowest depths of the grave.

14   Insolent men, O God, have risen against me:
      a band of ruthless men seek my life,
      they have not set God before their eyes.

15   But you, Lord, are a God gracious and compassionate:
      slow to anger, full of goodness and truth.

16   Turn to me and be merciful,
      give your strength to your servant:
      and save the son of your handmaid.

17   Show me some token of your goodness:
      that those who hate me may see it and be ashamed,
      because you, Lord, are my helper and my comforter.

Psalm 87

1   He has founded it upon a holy hill:
      and the Lord loves the gates of Zion
      more than all the dwellings of Jacob.

2   Glorious things shall be spoken of you:
      O Zion, city of our God.

3   I might speak of my kinsmen in Egypt or in Babylon:
      in Philistia, Tyre or Nubia, where each was born.

4   But of Zion it shall be said:
      many were born in her,
      he that is Most High has established her.

5   When the Lord draws up the record of the nations:
      he shall take note where every man was born.

6   And the singers and the dancers together:
      shall make their song to your name.

Psalm 88

1   O Lord my God, I call for help by day:
     and by night also I cry out before you.

2   Let my prayer come into your presence:
     and turn your ear to my loud crying.

3   For my soul is filled with trouble:
     and my life has come even to the brink of the grave.

4   I am reckoned among those that go down to the Pit:
     I am a man that has no help.

5   I lie among the dead, like the slain that sleep in the grave:
     whom you remember no more,
     who are cut off from your power.

6   You have laid me in the lowest Pit:
     in darkness and in the watery depths.

7   Your wrath lies heavy upon me:
     and all your waves are brought against me.

8   You have put my friends far from me:
     and made me to be abhorred by them.

9   I am so fast in prison I cannot get free:
     my eyes fail because of my affliction.

10   Lord, I call to you every day:
     I stretch out my hands toward you.

11   Will you work wonders for the dead:
     or will the shades rise up again to praise you?

12   Shall your love be declared in the grave:
     or your faithfulness in the place of destruction?

13   Will your wonders be made known in the dark:
    or your righteousness
    in the land where all things are forgotten?

14   But to you, Lord, will I cry:
    early in the morning my prayer shall come before you.

15   O Lord, why have you rejected me:
    why do you hide your face from me?

16   I have been afflicted and wearied from my youth upward:
    I am tossed high and low, I cease to be.

17   Your fierce anger has overwhelmed me:
    and your terrors have put me to silence

18   They surround me like a flood all the day long:
    they close upon me from every side.

19   Friend and acquaintance you have put far from me:
    and kept my companions from my sight.

Psalm 89

1   Lord, I will sing for ever of your loving-kindnesses:
    my mouth shall proclaim your faithfulness
    throughout all generations.

2   I have said of your loving-kindness that it is built for ever:
    you have established your faithfulness in the heavens.

3   The Lord said 'I have made a covenant with my chosen:
    I have sworn an oath to my servant David.

4   'I will establish your line for ever:
    and build up your throne for all generations.'

5   Let the heavens praise your wonders, O Lord:
     and let your faithfulness be sung
     in the assembly of the holy ones.

6   For who amidst the clouds can be compared to the Lord:
     or who is like the Lord among the sons of heaven?

7   – A God to be feared in the council of the holy ones:
     great and terrible above all that are around him.

8   O Lord God of hosts, who is like you?:
     your power and your faithfulness are all about you.

9   You rule the raging of the sea:
     when its waves surge, you still them.

10   You crushed Rahab like a carcase:
     you scattered your enemies by your mighty arm.

11   The heavens are yours, so also is the earth:
     you founded the world and all that is in it.

12   You created the north and the south:
     Tabor and Mount Hermon shall sing of your name.

13   Mighty is your arm:
     strong is your hand, and your right hand is lifted high.

14   Righteousness and justice are the foundation of your throne:
     loving-kindness and faithfulness attend your presence.

15   Happy the people who know the triumphal shout:
     who walk, O Lord, in the light of your countenance.

16   They rejoice all the day long because of your name:
     because of your righteousness they are exalted.

17   For you are their glory and their strength:
     and our heads are uplifted by your favour.

18   Our king belongs to the Lord:
       he that rules over us to the Holy One of Israel.

19   You spoke once in a vision:
       and said to your faithful one,

20   'I have set a youth above a warrior:
       I have exalted a young man out of the people.

21   'I have found my servant David:
       and anointed him with my holy oil.

22   'My hand shall uphold him:
       and my arm shall strengthen him.

23   'No enemy shall deceive him:
       no evil man shall hurt him.

24   'I will crush his adversaries before him:
       and strike down those that hate him.

25   'My faithfulness and loving-kindness shall be with him:
       and through my name his head shall be lifted high.

26   'I will set the hand of his dominion upon the Western Sea:
       and his right hand shall stretch
       to the streams of Mesopotamia.

27   'He will call to me "You are my Father:
       my God, and the Rock of my salvation".

28   'I will make him my first-born son:
       and highest among the kings of the earth.

29   'I will ever maintain my loving-kindness toward him:
       and my covenant with him shall stand firm.

30 'I will establish his line for ever:
    and his throne like the days of heaven.

31 'If his children forsake my law:
    and will not walk in my judgements;

32 'If they profane my statutes:
    and do not keep my commandments,

33 'Then I will punish their rebellion with the rod:
    and their iniquity with blows.

34 'But I will not cause my loving-kindness to cease from him:
    nor will I betray my faithfulness.

35 'I will not profane my covenant:
    or alter what has passed from my lips.

36 'Once and for all I have sworn by my holiness:
    I will not prove false to David.

37 'His posterity shall endure for ever:
    and his throne be as the sun before me;

38 'Like the moon that is established for ever:
    and stands in the heavens for evermore.'

39 Yet you have been enraged against your anointed:
    you have abhorred him and rejected him.

40 You have spurned the covenant with your servant:
    and defiled his crown to the dust.

41 You have broken down all his walls:
    and made his strongholds desolate.

42 All that pass by plunder him:
    he has become the scorn of his neighbours.

43   You have exalted the right hand of his adversaries:
and gladdened all his enemies.

44   His bright sword you have turned backward:
you have not enabled him to stand in the battle.

45   You have brought his lustre to an end:
you have cast his throne to the ground.

46   You have cut short the days of his youth:
and clothed him with dishonour.

47   How long, O Lord, will you hide yourself so utterly:
how long shall your fury burn like fire?

48   Remember how I draw to my eternal end:
have you created all mankind for nothing?

49   Where is the man who can live and not see death:
who can deliver his life from the power of the grave?

50   Where, O Lord, are your loving-kindnesses of old:
which you have vowed to David in your faithfulness?

51   Remember, O Lord, how your servant is reviled:
how I bear in my bosom the onslaught of the peoples;

52   Remember how your enemies taunt:
how they mock the footsteps of your anointed.

53   Blessed be the Lord for ever:
Amen and amen.

Psalm 90

1   Lord, you have been our refuge:
from one generation to another.

2   Before the mountains were born
or the earth and the world were brought to be:
from eternity to eternity you are God.

3   You turn man back into dust:
saying 'Return to dust, you sons of Adam'.

4   For a thousand years in your sight
are like yesterday passing:
or like one watch of the night.

5   You cut them short like a dream:
like the fresh grass of the morning;

6   In the morning it is green and flourishes:
at evening it is withered and dried up.

7   And we are consumed by your anger:
because of your indignation we cease to be.

8   You have brought our iniquities before you:
and our secret sins to the light of your countenance.

9   Our days decline beneath your wrath:
and our years pass away like a sigh.

10   The days of our life are three score years and ten,
or if we have strength, four score:
the pride of our labours is but toil and sorrow,
for it passes quickly away and we are gone.

11   Who can know the power of your wrath:
who can know your indignation like those that fear you?

12   Teach us so to number our days:
        that we may apply our hearts to wisdom.

13   Relent, O Lord; how long will you be angry?:
        take pity on your servants.

14   O satisfy us early with your mercy:
        that all our days we may rejoice and sing.

15   Give us joy for all the days you have afflicted us:
        for the years we have suffered adversity.

16   Show your servants your work:
        and let their children see your glory.

17   May the gracious favour of the Lord our God be upon us:
        prosper the work of our hands,
        O prosper the work of our hands!

Psalm 91

1   He who dwells in the shelter of the Most High:
        who abides under the shadow of the Almighty,

2   He will say to the Lord
        'You are my refuge and my stronghold:
        my God in whom I trust'.

3   For he will deliver you from the snare of the hunter:
        and from the destroying curse.

4   He will cover you with his wings,
        and you will be safe under his feathers:
        his faithfulness will be your shield and defence.

5   You shall not be afraid of any terror by night:
    or of the arrow that flies by day,

6   Of the pestilence that walks about in darkness:
    or the plague that destroys at noonday.

7   A thousand may fall beside you,
    and ten thousand at your right hand:
    but you it shall not touch;

8   Your own eyes shall see:
    and look on the reward of the ungodly.

9   The Lord himself is your refuge:
    you have made the Most High your stronghold.

10 Therefore no harm will befall you:
    nor will any scourge come near your tent.

11 For he will command his angels:
    to keep you in all your ways.

12 They will bear you up in their hands:
    lest you dash your foot against a stone.

13 You will tread on the lion and the adder:
    the young lion and the serpent you will trample under foot.

14 'He has set his love upon me,
    and therefore I will deliver him:
    I will lift him out of danger, because he has known my name.

15 'When he calls upon me I will answer him:
    I will be with him in trouble,
    I will rescue him and bring him to honour.

16 'With long life I will satisfy him:
    and fill him with my salvation.'

Psalm 92

1   How good to give thanks to the Lord:
     to sing praises to your name, O Most High,

2   To declare your love in the morning:
     and at night to sing of your faithfulness,

3   Upon the lute, upon the lute of ten strings:
     and to the melody of the Iyre.

4   For in all you have done, O Lord,
     you have made me glad:
     I will sing for joy because of the works of your hands.

5   Lord, how glorious are your works:
     your thoughts are very deep.

6   The brutish do not consider:
     and the fool cannot understand

7   That though the wicked sprout like grass:
     and all wrongdoers flourish,

8   They flourish to be destroyed for ever:
     but you, Lord, are exalted for evermore.

9   For behold, your enemies, O Lord,
     your enemies shall perish:
     and all the workers of wickedness shall be scattered.

10   You have lifted up my head
     like the horns of the wild oxen:
     I am anointed with fresh oil;

11   My eyes have looked down on my enemies:
     and my ears have heard the ruin
     of those who rose up against me.

12   The righteous shall flourish like the palm tree:
        they shall spread abroad like a cedar in Lebanon;

13   For they are planted in the house of the Lord:
        and flourish in the courts of our God.

14   In old age they shall be full of sap:
        they shall be sturdy and laden with branches;

15   And they will say that the Lord is just:
        the Lord my Rock, in whom is no unrighteousness.

Psalm 93

1   The Lord is king, and has put on robes of glory:
        the Lord has put on his glory,
        he has girded himself with strength.

2   He has made the world so firm:
        that it cannot be moved.

3   Your throne is established from of old:
        you are from everlasting.

4   The floods have lifted up, O Lord,
        the floods have lifted up their voice:
        the floods lift up their pounding.

5   But mightier than the sound of many waters,
        than the mighty waters or the breakers of the sea:
        the Lord on high is mighty.

6   Your decrees are very sure:
        and holiness, O Lord, adorns your house for ever.

Psalm 94

1   O Lord God to whom vengeance belongs:
      O God to whom vengeance belongs, shine out in glory.

2   Arise, judge of the earth:
      and requite the proud as they deserve.

3   Lord, how long shall the wicked:
      how long shall the wicked triumph?

4   How long shall all evildoers pour out words:
      how long shall they boast and flaunt themselves?

5   They crush your people, O Lord:
      they oppress your own possession.

6   They murder the widow and the alien:
      they put the fatherless to death.

7   And they say 'The Lord does not see:
      nor does the God of Jacob consider it'.

8   Consider this, you senseless among the people:
      fools, when will you understand?

9   He who planted the ear, does he not hear:
      he who formed the eye, does he not see?

10   He who disciplines the nations, will he not punish:
      has the teacher of mankind no knowledge?

11   The Lord knows the thoughts of man:
      he knows that they are mere breath.

12   Blessed is the man whom you discipline, O Lord:
      and teach from your law,

13   Giving him rest from days of misery:
      till a pit is dug for the wicked.

14   The Lord will not cast off his people:
      nor will he forsake his own.

15   For justice shall return to the righteous man:
      and, with him, to all the true of heart.

16   Who will stand up for me against the wicked:
      who will take my part against the evildoers?

17   If the Lord had not been my helper:
      I would soon have dwelt in the land of silence.

18   But when I said 'My foot has slipped':
      your mercy, O Lord, was holding me.

19   In all the doubts of my heart:
      your consolations delighted my soul.

20   Will you be any friend to the court of wickedness:
      that contrives evil by means of law?

21   They band together against the life of the righteous:
      and condemn innocent blood.

22   But the Lord is my stronghold:
      my God is my rock and my refuge.

23   Let him requite them for their wickedness,
      and silence them for their evil:
      the Lord our God shall silence them.

Psalm 95

1   O come, let us sing out to the Lord:
    let us shout in triumph to the rock of our salvation.

2   Let us come before his face with thanksgiving:
    and cry out to him joyfully in psalms.

3   For the Lord is a great God:
    and a great king above all gods.

4   In his hand are the depths of the earth:
    and the peaks of the mountains are his also.

5   The sea is his and he made it:
    his hands moulded dry land.

6   Come, let us worship and bow down:
    and kneel before the Lord our maker.

7   For he is the Lord our God:
    we are his people and the sheep of his pasture.

8   Today if only you would hear his voice
    'Do not harden your hearts as at Meribah:
    as on that day at Massah in the wilderness;

9   'When your fathers tested me:
    put me to proof, though they had seen my works.

10   'Forty years long I loathed that generation and said:
    "It is a people who err in their hearts,
    for they do not know my ways";

11   'Of whom I swore in my wrath:
    "They shall not enter my rest."'

Psalm 96

1   O sing to the Lord a new song:
     sing to the Lord, all the earth.

2   Sing to the Lord and bless his holy name:
     proclaim the good news of his salvation
     from day to day.

3   Declare his glory among the nations:
     and his wonders among all peoples.

4   For great is the Lord, and greatly to be praised:
     he is more to be feared than all gods.

5   As for all the gods of the nations,
     they are mere idols:
     it is the Lord who made the heavens.

6   Majesty and glory are before him:
     beauty and power are in his sanctuary.

7   Render to the Lord, you families of the nations:
     render to the Lord glory and might.

8   Render to the Lord the honour due to his name:
     bring offerings and come into his courts.

9   O worship the Lord in the beauty of his holiness:
     let the whole earth stand in awe of him.

10   Say among the nations that the Lord is king:
     he has made the world so firm
     that it can never be moved;
     and he shall judge the peoples with equity.

11   Let the heavens rejoice and let the earth be glad:
     let the sea roar, and all that fills it;

12   Let the fields rejoice, and everything in them:
         then shall all the trees of the wood
         shout with joy before the Lord;

13   For he comes, he comes to judge the earth:
         he shall judge the world with righteousness,
         and the peoples with his truth.

Psalm 97

1   The Lord is king; let the earth rejoice:
         let the multitude of islands be glad.

2   Clouds and darkness are round about him:
         righteousness and justice
         are the foundation of his throne.

3   Fire goes before him:
         and burns up his enemies on every side.

4   His lightnings light the world:
         the earth sees it and quakes.

5   The mountains melt like wax before his face:
         from before the face of the Lord of all the earth.

6   The heavens have proclaimed his righteousness:
         and all peoples have seen his glory.

7   They are ashamed, all those who serve idols
         and glory in mere nothings:
         all gods bow down before him.

8   Zion heard and was glad,
         and the daughters of Judah rejoiced:
         because of your judgements, O God.

9 For you, Lord, are most high over all the earth:
 you are exalted far above all gods.

10 The Lord loves those that hate evil:
 the Lord guards the life of the faithful,
 and delivers them from the hand of the ungodly.

11 Light dawns for the righteous:
 and joy for the true of heart.

12 Rejoice in the Lord, you righteous:
 and give thanks to his holy name.

Psalm 98

1 O sing to the Lord a new song:
 for he has done marvellous things;

2 His right hand and his holy arm:
 they have got him the victory.

3 The Lord has made known his salvation:
 he has revealed his just deliverance
 in the sight of the nations.

4 He has remembered his mercy and faithfulness
 towards the house of Israel:
 and all the ends of the earth
 have seen the salvation of our God.

5 Shout with joy to the Lord, all the earth:
 break into singing and make melody.

6 Make melody to the Lord upon the harp:
 upon the harp and with the sounds of praise.

7   With trumpets and with horns:
      cry out in triumph before the Lord, the king.

8   Let the sea roar, and all that fills it:
      the good earth and those who live upon it.

9   Let the rivers clap their hands:
      and let the mountains ring out together before the Lord;

10   For he comes to judge the earth:
      he shall judge the world with righteousness,
      and the peoples with equity.

Psalm 99

1   The Lord is king, let the nations tremble:
      he is enthroned upon the cherubim; let the earth quake.

2   The Lord is great in Zion:
      he is high above all nations.

3   Let them praise your great and terrible name:
      for holy is the Lord.

4   The Mighty One is king and loves justice:
      you have established equity,
      you have dealt righteousness and justice in Jacob.

5   *O exalt the Lord our God:*
      and bow down before his footstool, for he is holy.

6   Moses and Aaron among his priests,
      and Samuel among those who call upon his name:
      they called to the Lord and he answered.

7   He spoke to them from the pillar of cloud:
      they kept to his teachings
      and the law that he gave them.

8   You answered them, O Lord our God:
      you were a forgiving God to them,
      and pardoned their wrongdoing.

9   *O exalt the Lord our God:*
      and bow down towards his holy hill,
      for the Lord our God is holy.

Psalm 100

1   O shout to the Lord in triumph, all the earth:
      serve the Lord with gladness,
      and come before his face with songs of joy.

2   Know that the Lord he is God:
      it is he who has made us and we are his;
      we are his people and the sheep of his pasture.

3   Come into his gates with thanksgiving,
      and into his courts with praise:
      give thanks to him, and bless his holy name.

4   For the Lord is good,
      his loving mercy is for ever:
      his faithfulness throughout all generations.

Psalm 101

1   My song shall be of steadfastness and justice:
       to you, Lord, will I sing.

2   I will be wise in the way of innocence:
       O when will you come to me?

3   I will walk within my house:
       in purity of heart.

4   I will set nothing evil before my eyes:
       I hate the sin of backsliders, it shall get no hold on me.

5   Crookedness of heart shall depart from me:
       I will know nothing of wickedness.

[6   The man who secretly slanders his neighbour I will destroy:
       the proud look and the arrogant heart I will not endure.]

7   My eyes shall look to the faithful in the land,
       and they shall make their home with me:
       one who walks in the way of innocence,
       he shall minister to me.

8   No man who practises deceit shall live in my house:
       no one who utters lies shall stand in my sight.

[9   Morning by morning
       I will destroy all the wicked of the land:
       and cut off all evildoers from the city of the Lord.]

Psalm 102

1   O Lord, hear my prayer:
       and let my cry come to you.

2   Do not hide your face from me in the day of my trouble:
      turn your ear to me; and when I call, be swift to answer.

3   For my days pass away like smoke:
      and my bones burn as in a furnace.

4   My heart is scorched and withered like grass:
      and I forget to eat my bread.

5   I am weary with the sound of my groaning:
      my bones stick fast to my skin.

6   I have become like an owl in the wilderness:
      like a speech-owl among the ruins.

7   I keep watch and flit to and fro:
      like a sparrow upon a housetop.

8   My enemies taunt me all day long:
      and those who rave at me make oaths against me.

9   Surely I have eaten ashes for bread:
      and mingled my drink with tears,

10   Because of your wrath and indignation:
      for you have taken me up and tossed me aside.

11   My days decline like a shadow:
      and I wither away like grass.

12   But you, Lord, are enthroned for ever:
      and your name shall be known
      throughout all generations.

13   You will arise and have mercy upon Zion:
      for it is time to pity her, the appointed time has come.

14   Your servants love even her stones:
        and her dust moves them to pity.

15   Then shall the nations fear your name, O Lord:
        and all the kings of the earth your glory,

16   When the Lord has built up Zion:
        when he shows himself in his glory,

17   When he turns to the prayer of the destitute:
        and does not despise their supplication.

18   Let this be written down for those who come after:
        and a people yet unborn will praise the Lord.

19   For the Lord has looked down
        from the height of his holiness:
        from heaven he has looked upon the earth,

20   To hear the groaning of the prisoner:
        to deliver those condemned to die;

21   That they may proclaim the name of the Lord in Zion:
        and his praises in Jerusalem,

22   When the nations are gathered together:
        and the kingdoms, to serve the Lord.

23   He has broken my strength before my time:
        he has cut short my days.

24   Do not take me away, O God, in the midst of my life:
        you, whose years extend through all generations.

25   In the beginning you laid the foundations of the earth:
        and the heavens are the work of your hands.

26   They shall perish, but you will endure:
        they shall all grow old like a garment;
        like clothes you will change them,
        and they shall pass away.

27   But you are the same for ever:
        and your years will never fail.

28   The children of your servants shall rest secure:
        and their seed shall be established in your sight.

Psalm 103

1   Praise the Lord, O my soul:
        and all that is within me, praise his holy name.

2   Praise the Lord, O my soul:
        and forget not all his benefits,

3   Who forgives all your sin:
        and heals all your infirmities,

4   Who redeems your life from the Pit:
        and crowns you with mercy and compassion;

5   Who satisfies your being with good things:
        so that your youth is renewed like an eagle's.

6   The Lord works righteousness:
        and justice for all who are oppressed.

7   He made known his ways to Moses:
        and his works to the children of Israel.

8   The Lord is full of compassion and mercy:
     slow to anger and of great goodness.

9   He will not always be chiding:
     nor will he keep his anger for ever.

10   He has not dealt with us according to our sins:
     nor rewarded us according to our wickedness.

11   For as the heavens are high above the earth:
     so great is his mercy over those that fear him;

12   As far as the east is from the west:
     so far has he set our sins from us.

13   As a father is tender towards his children:
     so is the Lord tender to those that fear him.

14   For he knows of what we are made:
     he remembers that we are but dust.

15   The days of man are but as grass:
     he flourishes like a flower of the field;

16   When the wind goes over it, it is gone:
     and its place will know it no more.

17   But the merciful goodness of the Lord
     endures for ever and ever
     toward those that fear him:
     and his righteousness upon their children's children;

18   Upon those who keep his covenant:
     and remember his commandments to do them.

19   The Lord has established his throne in heaven:
     and his kingdom rules over all.

20   Praise the Lord, all you his angels,
      you that excel in strength:
      you that fulfil his word,
      and obey the voice of his commandment.

21   Praise the Lord, all you his hosts:
      his servants who do his will.

22   Praise the Lord, all his works,
      in all places of his dominion:
      praise the Lord, O my soul!

Psalm 104

1   Bless the Lord, O my soul:
      O Lord my God, how great you are!

2   Clothed with majesty and honour:
      wrapped in light as in a garment.

3   You have stretched out the heavens like a tent-cloth:
      and laid the beams of your dwelling upon their waters;

4   You make the clouds your chariot:
      and ride upon the wings of the wind;

5   You make the winds your messengers:
      and flames of fire your ministers;

6   You have set the earth on its foundations:
      so that it shall never be moved.

7   The deep covered it as with a mantle:
      the waters stood above the hills.

8   At your rebuke they fled:
      at the voice of your thunder they hurried away;

9   They went up to the mountains,
         they went down by the valleys:
         to the place which you had appointed for them.

10   You fixed a limit which they may not pass:
         they shall not return again to cover the earth.

11   You send springs into the gullies:
         which run between the hills;

12   They give drink to every beast of the field:
         and the wild asses quench their thirst.

13   Beside them the birds of the air build their nests:
         and sing among the branches.

14   You water the mountains from your dwelling on high:
         and the earth is filled by the fruits of your work.

15   You cause the grass to grow for the cattle:
         and all green things for the servants of mankind.

16   You bring food out of the earth:
         and wine that makes glad the heart of man,

17   Oil to give him a shining countenance:
         and bread to strengthen his heart.

18   The trees of the Lord are well-watered:
         the cedars of Lebanon that he has planted,

19   Where the birds build their nests:
         and the stork makes her home in the pine-tops.

20   The high hills are a refuge for the wild goats:
         and the crags a cover for the conies.

21   You created the moon to mark the seasons:
and the sun knows the hour of its setting.

22   You make darkness, and it is night:
in which all the beasts of the forest move by stealth.

23   The lions roar for their prey:
seeking their food from God.

24   When the sun rises, they retire:
and lay themselves down in their dens.

25   Man goes out to his work:
and to his labour until the evening.

26   Lord, how various are your works:
in wisdom you have made them all,
and the earth is full of your creatures.

27   There is the wide, immeasurable sea:
there move living things without number,
great and small;

28   There go the ships, to and fro:
and there is that Leviathan
whom you formed to sport in the deep.

29   These all look to you:
to give them their food in due season.

30   When you give it to them, they gather it:
when you open your hand
they are satisfied with good things.

31   When you hide your face, they are troubled:
when you take away their breath,
they die and return to their dust.

32   When you send forth your spirit they are created:
and you renew the face of the earth.

33   May the glory of the Lord endure for ever:
may the Lord rejoice in his works.

34   If he look upon the earth, it shall tremble:
if he but touch the mountains, they shall smoke.

35   I will sing to the Lord as long as I live:
I will praise my God while I have any being.

36   May my meditation be pleasing to him:
for my joy shall be in the Lord.

37   May sinners perish from the earth,
let the wicked be no more:
bless the Lord, O my soul; O praise the Lord.

Psalm 105

1   O give thanks to the Lord and call upon his name:
tell among the peoples what things he has done.

2   Sing to him, O sing praises:
and be telling of all his marvellous works.

3   Exult in his holy name:
and let those that seek the Lord be joyful in heart.

4   Seek the Lord and his strength:
O seek his face continually.

5   Call to mind what wonders he has done:
his marvellous acts, and the judgements of his mouth,

6   O seed of Abraham his servant:
       O children of Jacob his chosen one.

7   For he is the Lord our God:
       and his judgements are in all the earth.

8   He has remembered his covenant for ever:
       the word that he ordained for a thousand generations,

9   The covenant that he made with Abraham:
       the oath that he swore to Isaac,

10   And confirmed it to Jacob as a statute:
       to Israel as an everlasting covenant,

11   Saying 'I will give you the land of Canaan:
       to be the portion of your inheritance',

12   And that when they were but few:
       little in number and aliens in the land.

13   They wandered from nation to nation:
       from one people and kingdom to another.

14   He suffered no man to do them wrong:
       but reproved even kings for their sake,

15   Saying 'Touch not my anointed:
       and do my prophets no harm'.

16   Then he called down a famine on the land:
       and destroyed the bread that was their stay.

17   But he had sent a man ahead of them:
       Joseph who was sold into slavery,

18   Whose feet they fastened with fetters:
      and thrust his neck into a hoop of iron.

19   Till the time that his words proved true:
      he was tested by the Lord's command.

20   Then the king sent and loosed him:
      the ruler of nations set him free;

21   He made him master of his household:
      and ruler over all his possessions,

22   To rebuke his officers at will:
      and to teach his counsellors wisdom.

23   Then Israel came into Egypt:
      and Jacob dwelt in the land of Ham.

24   There the Lord made his people fruitful:
      too numerous for their enemies,

25   Whose hearts he turned to hate his people:
      and to deal deceitfully with his servants.

26   Then he sent Moses his servant:
      And Aaron whom he had chosen.

27   Through them he manifested his signs:
      and his wonders in the land of Ham.

28   He sent darkness, and it was dark:
      yet they would not obey his commands.

29   He turned their waters into blood:
      and slew the fish therein.

30   Their country swarmed with frogs:
      even the inner chambers of their kings.

31   He spoke the word, and there carne great swarms of flies:
      and gnats within all their borders.

32   He sent them storms of hail:
      and darts of fire into their land.

33   He struck their vines and their fig-trees:
      and shattered the trees within their borders.

34   He commanded, and there came grasshoppers:
      and young locusts without number.

35   They ate up every green thing in the land:
      and devoured the fruit of the soil.

36   He smote all the first-born in their land:
      the first-fruits of all their manhood.

37   He brought Israel out with silver and with gold:
      and not one among their tribes was seen to stumble.

38   Egypt was glad at their going:
      for dread of Israel had fallen upon them.

39   He spread out a cloud for a covering:
      and fire to lighten the night.

40   The people asked, and he brought them quails:
      and satisfied them with the bread from heaven.

41   He opened a rock, so that the waters gushed:
      and ran in the parched land like a river.

42   For he had remembered his holy word:
      that he gave to Abraham his servant.

43   So he led out his people with rejoicing:
      his chosen ones with shouts of joy;

44   He gave them the land of the nations:
and they took possession of the fruit of other men's toil,

45   So that they might keep his statutes:
and faithfully obey his laws.
O praise the Lord.

Psalm 106

1   Praise the Lord;
O give thanks to the Lord, for he is good:
and his mercy endures for ever.

2   Who can express the mighty acts of the Lord:
or fully voice his praise?

3   Blessed are those who act according to justice:
who at all times do the right.

4   Remember me, O Lord,
when you visit your people with your favour:
and come to me also with your salvation,

5   That I may see the prosperity of your chosen:
that I may rejoice with the rejoicing on your people,
and exult with those who are your own.

6   We have sinned like our fathers:
we have acted perversely and done wrong.

7   Our fathers when they were in Egypt:
took no heed of your wonders;

8   They did not remember
the multitude of your loving-kindnesses:
but they rebelled at the Red Sea.

9   Nevertheless, he saved them for his name's sake:
         that he might make known his power.

10   He commanded the Red Sea, and it dried up:
         and he led them through the deep as through a desert.

11   He delivered them from the hand of their adversary:
         and redeemed them from the power of the enemy.

12   The waters closed over their oppressors:
         so that not one was left alive.

13   Then they believed his words:
         and sang him songs of praise.

14   But in a little while they forgot what he had done:
         and would wait for his counsel no more.

15   Greed took hold of them in the desert:
         and they put God to the test in the wilderness.

16   So he gave them that which they desired:
         but sent a wasting sickness among them.

17   Then they grew envious of Moses in the camp:
         and of Aaron, the holy one of the Lord;

18   Whereupon the earth opened and swallowed up Dathan:
         it closed over the company of Abiram;

19   Fire flared out against their number:
         and flame devoured the ungodly.

20   At Horeb they made themselves a calf:
         and bowed down in worship to an image.

21   And so they exchanged the glory of God:
         for the likeness of an ox that eats hay.

| 22 | They forgot God who was their saviour: |
| | that had done such great things in Egypt, |

| 23 | Who had worked his wonders in the land of Ham: |
| | and his terrible deeds at the Red Sea. |

24	Therefore he thought to destroy them:
	had not Moses his servant stood before him in the breach,
	to turn away his wrath from destroying them.

| 25 | Then they despised the pleasant land: |
| | and put no faith in his promise, |

| 26 | But murmured in their tents: |
| | and would not obey the voice of the Lord. |

| 27 | So he lifted his hand to swear an oath against them: |
| | that he would strike them down in the wilderness, |

| 28 | And cast out their children among the nations: |
| | and scatter them through all the lands. |

| 29 | Then they joined themselves to the Baal of Peor: |
| | and ate things sacrificed to gods that have no life. |

| 30 | They provoked him to anger with their wanton deeds: |
| | and plague broke out among them. |

| 31 | Then stood up Phinehas and interposed: |
| | and so the plague was ended; |

| 32 | And that was counted to him for righteousness: |
| | throughout all generations for evermore. |

| 33 | They angered God also at the waters of Meribah: |
| | so that Moses suffered for their misdeeds; |

167

34   For they had embittered his spirit:
    and he spoke rashly with his lips.

35   They did not destroy the peoples:
    as the Lord had commanded them to do,

36   But they mingled themselves with the heathen:
    and learned to follow their ways.

37   They worshipped foreign idols:
    and these became their snare,

38   So that they sacrificed their sons:
    and their own daughters to demons.

39   They shed innocent blood:
    even the blood of their own sons and daughters,

40   Whom they offered to the idols of Canaan:
    and the land was defiled with blood.

41   They made themselves foul by their acts:
    and with wanton deeds whored after strange gods.

42   Then was the wrath of the Lord kindled against his people:
    and he loathed his own possession;

43   He gave them into the hands of the nations:
    and their adversaries ruled over them.

44   Their enemies became their oppressors:
    and they were brought into subjection beneath their power.

45   Many a time he saved them:
    but they rebelled against him to follow their own designs
    and were brought down by their wickedness.

46 Nevertheless, he looked on their distress:
    when he heard their loud crying.

47 He remembered his covenant with them:
    and relented,
    according to the abundance of his loving-kindness.

48 And he caused them to be pitied:
    even by those that held them captive.

49 Save us, O Lord our God,
    and gather us from among the nations:
    that we may give thanks to your holy name,
    and make our boast in your praises.

50 Blessed be the Lord, the God of Israel,
    from everlasting to everlasting:
    and let all the people say, Amen.
    Praise the Lord.

Psalm 107

1   O give thanks to the Lord, for he is good:
    for his loving mercy is for ever.

2   Let the Lord's redeemed say so:
    whom he has redeemed from the hand of the enemy,

3   And gathered in from every land,
    from the east and from the west:
    from the north and from the south.

4   Some went astray in the wilderness and in the desert:
    and found no path to an inhabited city;

5   They were hungry and thirsty:
    and their heart fainted within them.

6   Then they cried to the Lord in their distress:
and he took them out of their trouble.

7   He led them by the right path:
till they came to an inhabited city.

8   *Let them thank the Lord for his goodness:
and for the wonders that he does for the children of men;*

9   *For he satisfies the thirsty:
and fills the hungry with good things.*

10   Some sat in darkness and in deadly shadow:
bound fast in affliction and iron,

11   Because they had rebelled against the words of God:
and scorned the purposes of the Most High.

12   So he bowed down their hearts with affliction:
they tripped headlong, with none to help them.

13   Then they cried to the Lord in their distress:
and he took them out of their trouble.

14   He brought them out from darkness and deadly shadow:
and broke their chains in two.

15   *Let them thank the Lord for his goodness:
and for the wonders that he does for the children of men;*

16   *For he shatters the doors of bronze:
and cleaves the bars of iron.*

17   Fools were far gone in transgression:
and because of their sins were afflicted.

18   They sickened at any food:
      and had come to the gates of death.

19   Then they cried to the Lord in their distress:
      and he took them out of their trouble.

20   He sent his word and healed them:
      and saved their life from the Pit.

21   *Let them thank the Lord for his goodness:*
      and for the wonders that he does for the children of men;

22   *Let them offer sacrifices of thanksgiving:*
      and tell what he has done with shouts of joy.

23   Those who go down to the sea in ships:
      and follow their trade on great waters,

24   These men have seen the works of God:
      and his wonders in the deep.

25   For he spoke, and raised the storm-wind:
      and it lifted high the waves of the sea.

26   They go up to the sky, and down again to the depths:
      their courage melts away in the face of disaster.

27   They reel and stagger like drunken men:
      and are at their wits' end.

28   Then they cried to the Lord in their distress:
      and he took them out of their trouble.

29   He calmed the storm to a silence:
      and the waves of the sea were stilled.

30   Then they were glad because they were quiet:
      and he brought them to the haven they longed for.

31   *Let them thank the Lord for his goodness:*
       and for the wonders that he does for the children of men;

32   *Let them exalt him in the assembly of the people:*
       and praise him in the council of elders.

33   He turns the rivers into desert:
       and springs of water into thirsty ground.

34   He makes of a fruitful land a salty waste:
       because its inhabitants are evil.

35   He turns the wilderness into a pool of water:
       and parched ground into flowing springs.

36   And there he settles the hungry:
       and they build a city to live in.

37   They sow fields and plant vineyards:
       which give them fruitful harvest.

38   He blesses them, and they multiply greatly:
       he does not let their cattle diminish.

39   But he pours contempt upon princes:
       and makes them stray in the pathless desert;

40   They are weakened and brought low:
       through stress of adversity and sorrow.

41   But he lifts the poor out of misery:
       and increases their families like flocks of sheep.

42   The upright shall see it and rejoice:
       and all wickedness shall shut its mouth.

43   Whoever is wise, let him observe these things:
       and consider the loving-kindness of the Lord.

Psalm 108

1   My heart is fixed, O God, my heart is fixed:
       I will sing and make melody.

2   Awake my soul, awake lute and harp:
       for I will awaken the morning.

3   I will give you thanks, O Lord, among the peoples:
       I will sing your praise among the nations.

4   For the greatness of your mercy reaches to the heavens:
       and your faithfulness to the clouds.

5   Be exalted, O God, above the heavens:
       and let your glory be over all the earth;

6   That those whom you love may be delivered:
       O save us by your right hand, and answer me.

7   God has said in his holy place:
       'I will exult and divide Shechem,
       I will parcel out the valley of Succoth.

8   'Gilead is mine, and Manasseh is mine:
       Ephraim is my helmet, and Judah my rod of command.

9   'Moab is my wash-bowl, over Edom will I cast my shoe:
       against Philistia will I shout in triumph.'

10   Who will lead me into the fortified city:
       who will bring me into Edom?

11   Have you not cast us off, O God?:
       you go not out with our armies.

12   Give us your help against the enemy:
       for vain is the help of man.

13   By the power of our God we shall do valiantly:
       for it is he that will tread down our enemies.

Psalm 109

1   O God of my praise, do not be silent:
       for evil and deceitful mouths are opened against me.

2   They speak of me with lying tongues:
       they surround me with words of hatred,
       they fight against me without cause.

3   In return for my friendship they oppose me:
       and that for no fault of mine.

4   They repay me evil for good:
       and hatred for my affection.

[5   Appoint an evil man to stand against him:
       and let an adversary be at his right hand.

6   When he is judged, let him be found guilty:
       let his prayer for help be counted as sin.

7   Let his days be few:
       and let another take what he has hoarded.

8   Let his children be made fatherless:
       and his wife become a widow.

9   Let his children be vagabonds and beggars:
       let them seek alms far from their own homes.

10   Let the usurer exact all that he has:
and let strangers plunder the fruit of his toil.

11   Let no man be loyal to him:
and let no one have pity on his fatherless children.

12   Let his line become extinct:
in one generation let their name be blotted out.

13   Let the sins of his fathers be remembered by the Lord:
and his mother's iniquity not be wiped away.

14   Let their sins be constantly before the Lord:
may he root out their memory from the earth.

15   For he was a man that did not remember to show loyalty:
but he persecuted the humble,
the poor and the crushed in spirit,
and sought to put them to death.

16   He loved to curse – let curses fall on him:
he took no pleasure in blessing, so let it be far from him.

17   He clothed himself in cursing like a garment:
so let it seep like water into his body
and like oil into his bones.

18   Let it be as the clothes he wraps about him:
or like the girdle that he wears each day.

19   This is the Lord's recompense to those that oppose him:
to those that speak evil against me.]

20   Act for me, O Lord my God, for your name's sake:
and deliver me, as your steadfast love is good.

21   For I am poor and needy:
and my heart writhes within me.

22   I fade like a lengthening shadow:
        I am shaken off like a locust.

23   My knees are weak from fasting:
        my flesh grows lean and shrunken.

24   I have become the scorn of my enemies:
        and when they see me, they toss their heads in derision.

25   Help me, O Lord my God:
        and save me for your mercy's sake,

26   That men may know it was your hand:
        that you, O Lord, have done it.

27   Though they curse, yet give me your blessing:
        and those that come against me will be put to shame,
        and your servant shall rejoice.

28   Let those that oppose me be covered with disgrace:
        let them wear their shame as a garment.

29   And I will give the Lord great thanks with my mouth:
        and praise him in the midst of a multitude.

30   For the Lord will stand at the right hand of the poor:
        to save him from those that would condemn him.

Psalm 110

1   The Lord said to my lord:
        'Sit at my right hand,
        until I make your enemies your footstool.'

2   The Lord commits to you the sceptre of your power:
        reign from Zion in the midst of your enemies.

3   Noble are you,
from the day of your birth upon the holy hill:
radiant are you, even from the womb,
in the morning dew of your youth.

4   The Lord has sworn and will not turn back:
'You are a priest for ever after the order of Melchizedek.'

5   The king shall stand at your right hand, O Lord:
and shatter kings in the day of his wrath.

6   Glorious in majesty, he shall judge among the nations:
and shatter heads over a wide land.

7   He shall slake his thirst from the brook beside the way:
therefore shall he lift up his head.

Psalm 111

1   O praise the Lord.
I will praise the Lord with my whole heart:
in the company of the upright and among the congregation.

2   The works of the Lord are great:
and studied by all who take delight in them.

3   His deeds are majestic and glorious:
and his righteousness stands for ever.

4   His marvellous acts
have won him a name to be remembered:
the Lord is gracious and merciful.

5   He gives food to those that fear him:
he remembers his covenant for ever.

6   He showed his people the power of his acts:
in giving them the heritage of the heathen.

7   The works of his hands are faithful and just:
and all his commandments are sure;

8   They stand firm for ever and ever:
they are done in faithfulness and in truth.

9   He sent redemption to his people,
he ordained his covenant for ever:
holy is his name and worthy to be feared.

10   The fear of the Lord is the beginning of wisdom,
and of good understanding
are those that keep his commandments:
his praise shall endure for ever.

Psalm 112

1   O praise the Lord.
Blessed is the man who fears the Lord:
and greatly delights in his commandments.

2   His children shall be mighty in the land:
a race of upright men who will be blessed.

3   Riches and plenty shall be in his house:
and his righteousness stands for ever.

4   Light arises in darkness for the upright:
gracious and merciful is the righteous man.

5   It goes well with the man who acts generously and lends:
who guides his affairs with justice.

6   Surely he shall never be moved:
        the righteous shall be held in everlasting remembrance.

7   He will not fear bad tidings:
        his heart is steadfast, trusting in the Lord.

8   His heart is confident and will not fear:
        he will see the downfall of his enemies.

9   He gives freely to the poor:
        his righteousness stands for ever,
        his head is uplifted in glory.

10   The wicked man shall see it and be angry:
        he shall gnash his teeth and consume away;
        and the hope of the wicked shall fail:

Psalm 113

1   Praise the Lord, O sing praises, you that are his servants:
        O praise the name of the Lord.

2   Let the name of the Lord be blessed:
        from this time forward and for ever.

3   From the rising of the sun to its going down:
        let the name of the Lord be praised.

4   The Lord is exalted over all the nations:
        and his glory is above the heavens.

5   Who can be likened to the Lord our God:
        in heaven or upon the earth,

6   Who has his dwelling so high:
        yet condescends to look on things beneath?

7   He raises the lowly from the dust:
     and lifts the poor from out of the dungheap;

8   He gives them a place among the princes:
     even among the princes of his people.

9   He causes the barren woman to keep house:
     and makes her a joyful mother of children.
     Praise the Lord.

Psalm 114

1   When Israel came out of Egypt:
     and the house of Jacob
     from among a people of an alien tongue,

2   Judah became his sanctuary:
     and Israel his dominion.

3   The sea saw that, and fled:
     Jordan was driven back.

4   The mountains skipped like rams:
     and the little hills like young sheep.

5   What ailed you, O sea, that you fled:
     O Jordan, that you were driven back?

6   You mountains, that you skipped like rams:
     and you little hills like young sheep?

7   Tremble, O earth, at the presence of the Lord:
     at the presence of the God of Jacob,

8   Who turned the rock into a pool of water:
     and the flint-stone into a welling spring.

Psalm 115

1   Not to us, O Lord, not to us
     but to your name give the glory:
     for the sake of your faithfulness
     and your loving-kindness.

2   Why should the heathen say 'Where is their God?':
     our God is in heaven, he does whatever he wills.

3   As for their idols, they are silver and gold:
     the work of a man's hand.

4   They have mouths, but speak not:
     they have eyes, but they cannot see.

5   They have ears, yet hear nothing:
     they have noses, but cannot smell.

6   Hands they have, but handle nothing,
     feet, but they do not walk:
     they make no sound with their throats.

7   Those who make them shall be like them:
     so shall everyone that trusts in them.

8   O Israel, trust in the Lord:
     he is your help and your shield.

9   O house of Aaron, trust in the Lord:
     he is your help and your shield.

10   You that fear the Lord, trust in the Lord:
     he is your help and your shield.

11   The Lord has remembered us and he will bless us:
     he will bless the house of Israel,
     he will bless the house of Aaron.

12   He will bless all those that fear the Lord:
      both high and low together.

13   May the Lord increase you greatly:
      you and your children after you.

14   The blessing of the Lord be upon you:
      he that made heaven and earth.

15   As for the heavens, they are the Lord's:
      but the earth he has given to the children of men.

16   The dead do not praise the Lord:
      nor do any that go down to silence.

17   But we will bless the Lord:
      both now and for evermore.
      O praise the Lord.

Psalm 116

1   I love the Lord, because he heard my voice:
      the voice of my supplication;

2   Because he inclined his ear to me:
      in the day that I called to him.

3   The cords of death encompassed me,
      the snares of the grave took hold on me:
      I was in anguish and sorrow.

4   Then I called upon the name of the Lord:
      'O Lord, I beseech you, deliver me !'

5   Gracious and righteous is the Lord:
      full of compassion is our God.

6   The Lord preserves the simple:
     when I was brought low, he saved me.

7   Return, O my soul, to your rest:
     for the Lord has rewarded you.

8   For you, O Lord, have delivered my soul from death:
     my eyes from tears and my feet from falling.

9   I will walk before the Lord:
     in the land of the living.

10   I believed that I would perish, I was brought very low:
     I said in my haste 'All men are liars'.

11   How shall I repay the Lord:
     for all his benefits to me?

12   I will take up the cup of salvation:
     and call upon the name of the Lord.

13   I will pay my vows to the Lord:
     in the presence of all his people.

14   Grievous in the sight of the Lord:
     is the death of his faithful ones.

15   O Lord, I am your servant,
     your servant and the son of your handmaid:
     you have unloosed my bonds.

16   I will offer you a sacrifice of thanksgiving:
     and call upon the name of the Lord.

17   I will pay my vows to the Lord:
     in the presence of all his people,

18   In the courts of the house of the Lord:
      even in your midst, O Jerusalem.
      Praise the Lord.

Psalm 117

1   O praise the Lord, all you nations:
      O praise him, all you peoples.

2   For great is his loving-kindness toward us:
      and the faithfulness of the Lord endures for ever.
      Praise the Lord.

Psalm 118

1   O give thanks to the Lord, for he is good:
      his mercy endures for ever.

2   Let Israel now proclaim:
      that his mercy endures for ever.

3   Let the house of Aaron proclaim:
      that his mercy endures for ever.

4   Let those who fear the Lord proclaim:
      that his mercy endures for ever.

5   In my danger I called to the Lord:
      he answered and set me free.

6   The Lord is on my side, I shall not fear:
      what can man do to me?

7   The Lord is at my side as my helper:
      I shall see the downfall of my enemies.

8   It is better to take refuge in the Lord:
          than to put your trust in man:

9   It is better to take refuge in the Lord:
          than to put your trust in princes.

10   All the nations surrounded me:
          but in the name of the Lord I drove them back.

11   They surrounded, they surrounded me on every side:
          but in the name of the Lord I drove them back.

12   They swarmed about me like bees,
          they blazed like fire among the thorns:
          in the name of the Lord I drove them back.

13   I was pressed so hard that I almost fell:
          but the Lord was my helper.

14   The Lord is my strength and my song:
          and has become my salvation.

15   The sounds of joy and deliverance:
          are in the tents of the righteous.

16   The right hand of the Lord does mighty things:
          the right hand of the Lord raises up.

17   I shall not die but live:
          and proclaim the works of the Lord.

18   The Lord has disciplined me hard:
          but he has not given me over to death.

19   Open me the gates of righteousness:
          and I will enter and give thanks to the Lord.

20   This is the gate of the Lord:
      the righteous shall enter it.

21   I will praise you, for you answered me:
      and have become my salvation.

22   The stone that the builders rejected:
      has become the head of the corner.

23   This is the Lord's doing:
      and it is marvellous in our eyes.

24   This is the day that the Lord has made:
      let us rejoice and be glad in it.

25   O Lord, save us, we pray:
      O Lord, send us prosperity.

26   Blessed is he who comes, in the name of the Lord:
      from the house of the Lord we bless you.

27   The Lord is God, and he has given us light:
      guide the festal throng up to the horns of the altar.

28   You are my God and I will praise you:
      you are my God, I will exalt you.

29   O give thanks to the Lord, for he is good:
      and his mercy endures for ever.

Psalm 119

1

1   Blessed are those whose way is blameless:
      who walk in the law of the Lord.

2   Blessed are those who keep his commands:
      and seek him with their whole heart;

3   Those who do no wrong:
        but walk in the ways of our God.

4   For you, Lord, have commanded us:
        to persevere in all your precepts.

5   If only my ways were unerring:
        towards the keeping of your statutes!

6   Then I should not be ashamed:
        when I looked on all your commandments.

7   I will praise you with sincerity of heart:
        as I learn your righteous judgements.

8   I will keep your statutes:
        O forsake me not utterly.

2

9   How shall a young man's path be pure:
        unless he keep to your word?

10   I have sought you with my whole heart:
        let me not stray from your commandments.

11   I have treasured your words in my heart:
        that I might not sin against you.

12   Blessed are you, Lord God:
        O teach me your statutes.

13   With my lips I have been telling:
        all the judgements of your mouth;

14   And I find more joy in the way of your commands:
        than in all manner of riches.

15 I will meditate on your precepts:
  and give heed to your ways;

16 For my delight is wholly in your statutes:
  and I will not forget your word.

3

17 O be bountiful to your servant that I may live:
  in obedience to your word.

18 Take away the veil from my eyes:
  that I may see the wonders of your law.

19 I am but a stranger on the earth:
  do not hide your commandments from me.

20 My soul is consumed with longing:
  for your judgements day and night.

21 You have rebuked the proud:
  and cursed are those who stray from your commandments;

22 Turn away from me their reproach and scorn:
  for I have kept your commands.

23 Though princes sit and plot together against me:
  your servant shall meditate on your statutes;

24 For your commands are my delight:
  and they are counsellors in my defence.

4

25 I am humbled to the dust:
  O give me life according to your word.

26 If I examine my ways:
   surely you will answer me – O teach me your statutes!

27 Make me to understand the way of your precepts:
   and I shall meditate on your marvellous works.

28 My soul pines away for sorrow:
   O raise me up according to your word.

29 Keep me far from the way of deception:
   and grant me the grace of your law.

30 I have chosen the way of truth:
   and have set your judgements before me.

31 I hold fast to your commands:
   O Lord, let me never be confounded.

32 Let me run the way of your commandments:
   for you will liberate my heart.

5

33 Teach me, O Lord, the way of your statutes:
   and I will honour it to the end.

34 Give me understanding, that I may keep your law:
   that I may keep it with my whole heart.

35 Guide me in the path of your commandments:
   for therein is my delight.

36 Incline my heart to your commands:
   and not to selfish gain.

37 Turn away my eyes from looking on vanities:
   as I walk in your way give me life.

38   Make good your promise to your servant:
       the promise that endures for all who fear you.

39   Turn aside the taunts that I dread:
       for your judgements are very good.

40   Lord, I long for your precepts:
       in your righteousness give me life.

6

41   Let your loving mercy come to me, O Lord:
       and your salvation, according to your word.

42   Then I shall have an answer for those who reproach me:
       for I trust in your word.

43   Do not take the word of truth utterly out of my mouth:
       for in your judgements is my hope.

44   Let me keep your law continually:
       O let me keep it for ever.

45   And so I shall walk at liberty:
       because I have sought your precepts.

46   I shall speak of your commands before kings:
       and shall not be put to shame.

47   My delight shall be in your commandments:
       which I have greatly loved;

48   I shall worship you with outstretched hands:
       and I shall meditate on your statutes.

7

49   Remember your word to your servant:
on which you have built my hope.

50   This has been my comfort in my affliction:
for your word has brought me life.

51   Though the proud have laughed me to scorn:
I have not turned aside from your law;

52   But I called to mind, O Lord, your judgements of old:
and in them I have found consolation.

53   I am seized with indignation at the wicked:
for they have forsaken your law.

54   But your statutes have become my songs:
in the house of my pilgrimage.

55   I think on your name, O Lord, in the night:
and I observe your law;

56   This has been my reward:
because I have kept your precepts.

8

57   The Lord is my portion:
I have promised to keep your words.

58   I have sought your favour with my whole heart:
O be gracious to me according to your word.

59   I have taken stock of my ways:
and have turned back my feet to your commands.

60 I made haste and did not delay:
  to keep your commandments.

61 The snares of the wicked encompassed me:
  but I did not forget your law;

62 At midnight I rise to give you thanks:
  for the righteousness of your judgements.

63 I am a friend to all who fear you:
  to those who keep your precepts.

64 The earth, O Lord, is full of your loving mercy:
  O teach me your statutes.

9

65 Lord, you have done good to your servant:
  in accordance with your word.

66 O teach me right judgement and knowledge:
  for I trust in your commandments.

67 Before I was afflicted I went astray:
  but now I keep your word.

68 You are good, and you do good:
  O teach me your statutes.

69 The proud have smeared me with lies:
  but I will keep your precepts with my whole heart.

70 Their hearts are gross like fat:
  but my delight is in your law.

71 It is good for me that I was afflicted:
  so I might learn your statutes.

72   The law of your mouth is dearer to me:
      than a wealth of gold and silver.

10

73   Your hands have made me and fashioned me:
      O give me understanding,
      that I may learn your commandments.

74   Those who fear you shall see me and rejoice:
      for my hope is in your word.

75   I know, Lord, that your judgements are right:
      and that in faithfulness you have afflicted me.

76   Let your merciful kindness be my comfort:
      according to your promise to your servant.

77   O let your mercy come to me that I may live:
      for your law is my delight.

78   Let the proud be shamed
      who steal my rights through their lies:
      but I will meditate on your precepts.

79   Let those who fear you turn to me:
      and they shall know your commands.

80   O let my heart be sound in your statutes:
      that I may never be put to shame.

11

81   My soul languishes for your salvation:
      but my hope is in your word;

82 My eyes fail with watching for your promise:
    saying 'O when will you comfort me?'

83 I am parched as a wineskin in the smoke:
    yet I do not forget your statutes.

84 How many are the days of your servant:
    and when will you judge my persecutors?

85 The proud have dug pitfalls for me:
    in defiance of your law.

86 All your commandments are true:
    but they persecute me with lies – O come to my help!

87 They have almost made an end of me on the earth:
    but I have not forsaken your precepts.

88 In your merciful goodness give me life:
    that I may keep the commands of your mouth.

12

89 Lord, your word is for ever:
    it stands firm in the heavens.

90 Your faithfulness abides from one generation to another:
    firm as the earth which you have made.

91 As for your judgements, they stand fast this day:
    for all things are your servants.

92 If your law had not been my delight:
    I would have perished in my affliction.

93 I will never forget your precepts:
    for by them you have given me life.

94   I am yours, O save me:
        for I have sought your precepts.

95   The wicked have lain in wait for me to destroy me:
        but I think on your commands.

96   I have seen that all perfection comes to an end:
        only your commandment has no bounds.

13

97   Lord, how I love your law:
        it is my meditation all the day long.

98   Your commandments have made me wiser than my enemies:
        for they remain with me for ever.

99   I have more understanding than all my teachers:
        for I study your commands.

100   I am wiser than the aged:
        because I have kept your precepts.

101   I have held back my feet from every evil path:
        that I might keep your word;

102   I have not turned aside from your judgements:
        for you yourself are my teacher.

103   How sweet are your words to my tongue:
        sweeter than honey to my mouth.

104   Through your precepts I get understanding:
        therefore I hate all lying ways.

14

105   Your word is a lantern to my feet:
and a light to my path.

106   I have vowed and sworn an oath:
to keep your righteous judgements.

107   I have been afflicted beyond measure:
Lord, give me life according to your word.

108   Accept, O Lord, the freewill offerings of my mouth:
and teach me your judgements.

109   I take my life in my hands continually:
yet I do not forget your law.

110   The wicked have laid a snare for me:
but I have not strayed from your precepts.

111   Your commands are my inheritance for ever:
they are the joy of my heart.

112   I have set my heart to fulfil your statutes:
always, even to the end.

15

113   I loathe those who are double-minded:
but your law do I love.

114   You are my shelter and my shield:
and in your word is my hope.

115   Away from me, all you that do evil:
I will keep the commandments of my God.

116   Be my stay, according to your word, that I may live:
       and do not disappoint me in my hope.

117   Hold me up, and I shall be safe:
       and I will ever delight in your statutes.

118   You scorn all those who swerve from your statutes:
       for their calumnies against me are lies;

119   All the ungodly of the earth you count as dross:
       therefore I love your commands.

120   My flesh shrinks for fear of you:
       and I am afraid of your judgements.

16

121   I have done what is just and right:
       O do not give me over to my oppressors.

122   Stand surety for your servant's good:
       let not the proud oppress me.

123   My eyes fail with watching for your salvation:
       for the fulfilment of your righteous word.

124   O deal with your servant according to your loving mercy:
       and teach me your statutes.

125   I am your servant, O give me understanding:
       that I may know your commands.

126   It is time for the Lord to act:
       for they violate your law.

127   Therefore I love your commandments:
       more than gold, more than the finest gold;

128   Therefore I straighten my paths by all your precepts:
and I hate all lying ways.

17

129   Wonderful are your commands:
and therefore my soul keeps them.

130   The unfolding of your word gives light:
it gives understanding to the simple.

131   I open my mouth and draw in my breath:
for I yearn for your commandments.

132   O turn to me and be merciful to me:
as is your way with those who love your name.

133   Order my steps according to your word:
that no evil may get mastery over me.

134   Deliver me from man's oppression:
that I may keep your precepts.

135   Make your face shine upon your servant:
and teach me your statutes.

136   My eyes gush out with streams of water:
because they pay no heed to your law.

18

137   Righteous are you, Lord God:
and just are your judgements;

138   The commands that you have commanded:
are exceedingly righteous and true.

139   Zeal and indignation have choked my mouth:
        because my enemies have forgotten your words.

140   Your word has been tried in the fire:
        and therefore your servant loves it.

141   I am small and of no account:
        but I have not forgotten your precepts.

142   Your righteousness is an everlasting righteousness:
        and your law is the truth.

143   Trouble and anguish have taken hold on me:
        but your commandments are my delight.

144   The righteousness of your commands is everlasting:
        O give me understanding, and I shall live.

19

145   I call with my whole heart:
        hear me, O Lord, I will keep your statutes.

146   I cry out to you; O save me:
        and I will heed your commands.

147   Before the morning light I rise and I call:
        for in your word is my hope.

148   Before the night watch my eyes wake:
        that I may meditate upon your words.

149   Hear my voice, O Lord, in your loving mercy:
        and according to your judgements, give me life.

150   They draw near to me who maliciously persecute me:
        but they are far from your law.

151 You, Lord, are close at hand:
and all your commandments are true.

152 I have known long since from your commands:
that you have founded them for ever.

20

153 Consider my affliction and deliver me:
for I do not forget your law.

154 Plead my cause and set me free:
O give me life, according to your word.

155 Salvation is far from the wicked:
for they do not seek your statutes.

156 Numberless, O Lord, are your tender mercies:
according to your judgements, give me life.

157 Many there are that persecute me and trouble me:
but I have not swerved from your commands.

158 I am cut to the heart when I see the faithless:
for they do not keep your word.

159 Consider, O Lord, how I love your precepts:
and in your mercy, give me life.

160 The sum of your word is truth:
and all your righteous judgements stand for ever.

21

161   Princes have persecuted me without a cause:
but my heart stands in awe of your word.

162   I am as glad of your word:
as one who finds rich spoil.

163   Lies I hate and abhor:
but your law do I love.

164   Seven times a day I praise you:
because of your righteous judgements.

165   Great is the peace of those who love your law:
and nothing shall make them stumble.

166   Lord, I have waited for your salvation:
and I have done your commandments.

167   My soul has heeded your commands:
and I love them beyond measure.

168   I have kept your precepts and commands:
for all my ways are open before you.

22

169   Let my cry come to you, O Lord:
O give me understanding, according to your word.

170   Let my supplication come before you:
and deliver me according to your promise.

171   My lips shall pour forth your praise:
because you teach me your statutes;

172   My tongue shall sing of your word:
for all your commandments are righteousness.

173   Let your hand be swift to help me:
for I have chosen your precepts.

174   Lord, I have longed for your salvation:
and your law is my delight.

175   O let my soul live, that I may praise you:
and let your judgements be my help.

176   I have gone astray like a sheep that is lost:
O seek your servant,
for I do not forget your commandments.

Psalm 120

1   I call to the Lord in my trouble:
that he may answer me.

2   O Lord, deliver me from lying lips:
and from the treacherous tongue.

3   What will he do to you, and what more will he do to you,
O treacherous tongue?:
you are sharp as the arrows of a warrior,
that are tempered in coals of juniper.

4   Alas for me, I am like a stranger in Meshech:
like one who dwells amidst the tents of Kedar.

5   My soul has been too long:
among those who are enemies to peace.

6   I am for peace, but when I speak of it:
they make themselves ready for war.

Psalm 121

1 I lift up my eyes to the hills:
 but where shall I find help?

2 My help comes from the Lord:
 who has made heaven and earth.

3 He will not suffer your foot to stumble:
 and he who watches over you will not sleep.

4 Be sure he who has charge of Israel:
 will neither slumber nor sleep.

5 The Lord himself is your keeper:
 the Lord is your defence upon your right hand;

6 The sun shall not strike you by day:
 nor shall the moon by night.

7 The Lord will defend you from all evil:
 it is he who will guard your life.

8 The Lord will defend your going out and your coming in:
 from this time forward for evermore.

Psalm 122

1 I was glad when they said to me:
 'Let us go to the house of the Lord.'

2 And now our feet are standing:
 within your gates, O Jerusalem;

3 Jerusalem which is built as a city:
 where the pilgrims gather in unity.

4   There the tribes go up, the tribes of the Lord:
        as he commanded Israel,
        to give thanks to the name of the Lord.

5   There are set thrones of judgement:
        the thrones of the house of David.

6   O pray for the peace of Jerusalem:
        may those who love you prosper.

7   Peace be within your walls:
        and prosperity in your palaces.

8   For the sake of my brothers and companions:
        I will pray that peace be with you.

9   For the sake of the house of the Lord our God:
        I will seek for your good.

Psalm 123

1   To you I lift up my eyes:
        you who are enthroned in the heavens.

2   As the eyes of servants look to the hand of their master:
        or as the eyes of a maid toward the hand of her mistress,

3   So our eyes look to the Lord our God:
        until he show us his mercy.

4   Have mercy upon us, O Lord, have mercy upon us:
        for we have had our fill of derision.

5   Our souls overflow with the mockery of those at ease:
        and with the contempt of the proud.

Psalm 124

1   If the Lord had not been on our side,
now may Israel say:
if the Lord had not been on our side,
when men rose up against us,

2   Then they would have swallowed us alive:
when their anger was kindled against us.

3   Then the waters would have overwhelmed us,
and the torrent gone over us:
the raging waters would have gone clean over us.

4   But praised be the Lord:
who has not given us as a prey to their teeth.

5   We have escaped like a bird from the snare of the fowler:
the snare is broken, and we have gone free.

6   Our help is in the name of the Lord:
who has made heaven and earth.

Psalm 125

1   Those who put their trust in the Lord
shall be as Mount Zion:
which cannot be shaken, but endures for ever.

2   As the mountains stand about Jerusalem,
so stands the Lord about his people:
from this time forward for evermore.

3   For the sceptre of wickedness shall have no sway
over the land apportioned to the righteous:
lest the righteous set their hands to do evil.

4   Do good, O Lord, to those who are good:
       to those that are upright in heart.

5   As for those who turn aside to crooked ways,
       let the Lord lead them away with the evildoers:
       and in Israel let there be peace.

Psalm 126

1   When the Lord turned again the fortunes of Zion:
       then were we like men restored to life.

2   Then was our mouth filled with laughter:
       and our tongue with singing.

3   Then said they among the heathen:
       'The Lord has done great things for them.'

4   Truly the Lord has done great things for us:
       and therefore we rejoiced.

5   Turn again our fortunes, O Lord:
       as the streams return to the dry south.

6   Those that sow in tears:
       shall reap with songs of joy.

7   He who goes out weeping, bearing the seed:
       shall come again in gladness, bringing his sheaves with him.

Psalm 127

1   Unless the Lord builds the house:
       their labour is but lost that build it.

2   Unless the Lord keeps the city:
      the watchmen watch in vain.

3   It is in vain that you rise up early and go so late to rest,
      eating the bread of toil:
      for the Lord bestows honour
      – and on those whom he loves.

4   Behold, children are a heritage from the Lord:
      and the fruit of the womb is his gift.

5   Like arrows in the hand of a warrior:
      are the sons of a man's youth.

6   Happy the man who has his quiver full of them:
      he will not be put to shame
      when he confronts his enemies at the gate.

Psalm 128

1   Blessed is everyone who fears the Lord:
      and walks in the confine of his ways.

2   You will eat the fruit of your labours:
      happy shall you be, and all shall go well with you.

3   Your wife within your house:
      shall be as a fruitful vine;

4   Your children around your table:
      like the fresh shoots of the olive.

5   Behold, thus shall the man be blessed:
      who lives in the fear of the Lord.

6   May the Lord so bless you from Zion:
     that you see Jerusalem in prosperity
     all the days of your life.

7   May you see your children's children:
     and in Israel let there be peace.

Psalm 129

1   Many a time from my youth upward
     have they fought against me:
     now may Israel say,

2   Many a time from my youth upward
     have they fought against me:
     but they have not prevailed.

3   They have scored my back as with a ploughshare:
     they have opened long furrows.

4   But the Lord is righteous:
     and he has cut me free from the thongs of the wicked.

5   They shall be confounded and turned backward:
     all those who hate Zion.

6   They shall be as the grass that grows upon the housetops:
     which withers before it comes to any good,

7   With which no reaper may fill his hand:
     nor the binder of sheaves his bosom.

8   And none who pass by shall say to them
     'The blessing of the Lord be upon you:
     we bless you in the name of the Lord'.

Psalm 130

1   Out of the depths have I called to you, O Lord:
Lord, hear my voice;

2   O let your ears consider well:
the voice of my supplication.

3   If you, Lord, should note what we do wrong:
who then, O Lord, could stand?

4   But there is forgiveness with you:
so that you shall be feared.

5   I wait for the Lord, my soul waits for him:
and in his word is my hope.

6   My soul looks for the Lord:
more than watchmen for the morning,
more, I say, than watchmen for the morning.

7   O Israel, trust in the Lord,
for with the Lord there is mercy:
and with him is ample redemption.

8   He will redeem Israel:
from the multitude of his sins.

Psalm 131

1   O Lord, my heart is not proud:
nor are my eyes haughty.

2   I do not busy myself in great matters:
or in things too wonderful for me.

3   But I have calmed and quieted my soul
    like a weaned child upon its mother's breast:
    like a child on its mother's breast is my soul within me.

4   O Israel, trust in the Lord:
    from this time forward and for ever.

Psalm 132

1   Lord, remember David and all his trouble:
    how he swore an oath to the Lord,
    and vowed to the Mighty One of Jacob;

2   'I will not enter the shelter of my house:
    nor climb into the comfort of my bed;

3   'I will not give sleep to my eyes:
    or slumber to my eyelids,

4   'Till I find out a place for the ark of the Lord:
    a dwelling for the Mighty One of Jacob.'

5   Lo, we heard of it at Ephrathah:
    we found it in the fields of Ja-ar.

6   Let us go to the place of his dwelling:
    let us fall upon our knees before his footstool.

7   Arise, O Lord, into your resting-place:
    you, and the ark of your might.

8   Let your priests be clothed with righteousness:
    and let your faithful ones shout for joy.

9   For the sake of David your servant:
    do not turn away the face of your anointed.

10   The Lord has sworn to David:
      an oath which he will not break;

11   'One who is the fruit of your body:
      I will set upon your throne.

12   'If your children will keep my covenant
      and the commands which I teach them:
      their children also shall sit upon your throne for ever.'

13   For the Lord has chosen Zion for himself:
      he has desired it for his habitation.

14   'This shall be my resting-place for ever:
      here will I dwell, for my delight is in her.

15   'I will bless her provisions with abundance:
      I will satisfy her poor with bread.

16   'I will clothe her priests with salvation:
      and her faithful ones shall shout for joy.

17   'There will I make a horn to sprout for the family of David:
      I have prepared a lamp for my anointed.

18   'As for his enemies, I will cover them with shame:
      but upon his head shall his crown be bright.'

Psalm 133

1   Behold how good and how lovely it is:
      when brothers live together in unity.

2   It is fragrant as oil upon the head,
      that runs down over the beard:
      fragrant as oil upon the beard of Aaron,
      that ran down over the collar of his robe.

3   It is like a dew of Hermon:
     like the dew that falls upon the hill of Zion.

4   For there the Lord has commanded his blessing:
     which is life for evermore.

Psalm 134

1   Come bless the Lord, all you servants of the Lord:
     you that by night stand in the house of our God.

2   Lift up your hands toward the holy place
     and bless the Lord:
     may the Lord bless you from Zion,
     the Lord who made heaven and earth.

Psalm 135

1   Praise the Lord, praise the name of the Lord:
     praise him, you servants of the Lord,

2   Who stand in the house of the Lord:
     in the courts of the house of our God.

3   Praise the Lord, for the Lord is gracious:
     sing praises to his name, for it is good.

4   For the Lord has chosen Jacob for himself:
     and Israel as his own possession.

5   I know that the Lord is great:
     and that our Lord is above all gods.

6   He does whatever he wills,
     in heaven and upon the earth:
     in the seas and in the great depths.

7   He brings up clouds from the ends of the earth:
    he makes lightning for the rain
    and brings the wind out of his storehouses.

8   He struck down the firstborn of Egypt:
    both man and beast alike.

9   He sent signs and wonders into your midst, O Egypt:
    against Pharaoh and against all his servants.

10 He struck down great nations:
    and slew mighty kings,

11 Sihon, king of the Amorites, and Og, the king of Bashan:
    and all the princes of Canaan.

12 He made over their land as a heritage:
    a heritage for Israel his people.

13 O Lord, your name shall endure for ever:
    so shall your renown, throughout all generations.

14 For the Lord will vindicate his people:
    he will take pity on his servants.

15 As for the idols of the nations,
    they are but silver and gold:
    the work of a man's hand.

16 They have mouths, but speak not:
    they have eyes, but they cannot see.

17 They have ears, yet hear nothing:
    there is no breath in their nostrils.

18 Those who make them shall be like them:
    so shall everyone that trusts in them.

19   Bless the Lord, O house of Israel:
        bless the Lord, O house of Aaron.

20   Bless the Lord, O house of Levi:
        you that fear the Lord, bless the Lord.

21   Blessed be the Lord from Zion:
        he that dwells in Jerusalem.
        Praise the Lord.

Psalm 136

1   O give thanks to the Lord, for he is good:
        for his mercy endures for ever.

2   O give thanks to the God of gods:
        for his mercy endures for ever.

3   O give thanks to the Lord of lords:
        for his mercy endures for ever;

4   To him who alone does great wonders:
        for his mercy endures for ever;

5   Who by wisdom made the heavens:
        for his mercy endures for ever;

6   Who stretched out the earth upon the waters:
        for his mercy endures for ever;

7   Who made the great lights:
        for his mercy endures for ever,

8   The sun to rule the day:
        for his mercy endures for ever,

9   The moon and the stars to govern the night:
for his mercy endures for ever;

10   Who struck down Egypt and its firstborn:
for his mercy endures for ever;

11   Who brought out Israel from among them:
for his mercy endures for ever,

12   With a strong hand and with outstretched arm:
for his mercy endures for ever;

13   Who divided the Red Sea into two parts:
for his mercy endures for ever,

14   And made Israel pass through the midst of it:
for his mercy endures for ever;

15   Who cast off Pharaoh and his host into the Red Sea:
for his mercy endures for ever;

16   Who led his people through the wilderness:
for his mercy endures for ever;

17   Who struck down great kings:
for his mercy endures for ever;

18   Who slew mighty kings:
for his mercy endures for ever,

19   Sihon, king of the Amorites:
for his mercy endures for ever,

20   And Og, the king of Bashan:
for his mercy endures for ever;

21   Who made over their land as a heritage:
for his mercy endures for ever,

| 22 | As a heritage for Israel, his servant: |
| | for his mercy endures for ever; |

| 23 | Who remembered us in our humiliation: |
| | for his mercy endures for ever, |

| 24 | And delivered us from our enemies: |
| | for his mercy endures for ever; |

| 25 | Who gives food to all that lives: |
| | for his mercy endures for ever. |

| 26 | O give thanks to the God of heaven: |
| | for his mercy endures for ever. |

Psalm 137

| 1 | By the waters of Babylon we sat down and wept: |
| | when we remembered Zion. |

| 2 | As for our harps we hung them up: |
| | upon the trees that are in that land. |

3	For there those who led us away captive
	required of us a song:
	and those who had despoiled us demanded mirth,
	saying 'Sing us one of the songs of Zion'.

| 4 | How can we sing the Lord's song in a strange land? |

| 5 | If I forget you, O Jerusalem: |
| | let my right hand forget its mastery. |

6	Let my tongue cling to the roof of my mouth:
	if I do not remember you,
	if I do not prefer Jerusalem above my chief joy.

[7   Remember, O Lord, against the Edomites
the day of Jerusalem:
how they said 'Down with it, down with it,
raze it to its foundations'.

8   O daughter of Babylon, you that lay waste:
happy shall he be who serves you as you have served us;

9   Happy shall he be who takes your little ones:
and dashes them against the stones.]

Psalm 138

1   I will give you thanks, O Lord, with my whole heart:
even before the gods will I sing your praises.

2   I will bow down toward your holy temple
and give thanks to your name:
because of your faithfulness and your loving-kindness,
for you have made your name
and your word supreme over all things.

3   At a time when I called to you, you gave me answer:
and put new strength within my soul.

4   All the kings of the earth shall praise you, O Lord:
for they have heard the words of your mouth;

5   And they shall sing of the ways of the Lord:
that the glory of the Lord is great.

6   For though the Lord is exalted, he looks upon the lowly:
but he humbles the proud from afar.

7   Though I walk in the midst of danger,
yet will you preserve my life:
you will stretch out your hand
against the fury of my enemies,
and your right hand shall save me.

8   The Lord will complete his purpose for me:
your loving-kindness, O Lord, endures for ever;
do not forsake the work of your own hands.

Psalm 139

1   O Lord, you have searched me out and known me:
you know when I sit or when I stand,
you comprehend my thoughts long before.

2   You discern my path and the places where I rest:
you are acquainted with all my ways.

3   For there is not a word on my tongue:
but you, Lord, know it altogether.

4   You have encompassed me behind and before:
and have laid your hand upon me.

5   Such knowledge is too wonderful for me:
so high that I cannot endure it.

6   Where shall I go from your spirit:
or where shall I flee from your presence?

7   If I ascend into heaven you are there:
if I make my bed in the grave you are there also.

8   If I spread out my wings towards the morning:
or dwell in the uttermost parts of the sea,

9   Even there your hand shall lead me:
     and your right hand shall hold me.

10   If I say 'Surely the darkness will cover me:
     and the night will enclose me',

11   The darkness is no darkness with you,
     but the night is as clear as the day:
     the darkness and the light are both alike.

12   For you have created my inward parts:
     you knit me together in my mother's womb.

13   I will praise you, for you are to be feared:
     fearful are your acts, and wonderful your works.

14   You knew my soul,
     and my bones were not hidden from you:
     when I was formed in secret,
     and woven in the depths of the earth.

15   Your eyes saw my limbs when they were yet imperfect:
     and in your book were all my members written;

16   Day by day they were fashioned:
     and not one was late in growing.

17   How deep are your thoughts to me, O God:
     and how great is the sum of them!

18   Were I to count them,
     they are more in number than the sand:
     were I to come to the end, I would still be with you.

[19 If only you would slay the wicked, O God:
     if only the men of blood would depart from me!

20   For they affront you by their evil:
         and your enemies exalt themselves against you.

21   Do I not hate them, O Lord, that hate you:
         do I not loathe those who rebel against you?

22   I hate them with a perfect hatred:
         they have become my enemies.]

23   Search me out, O God, and know my heart:
         put me to the proof and know my thoughts.

24   Look well lest there be any way of wickedness in me:
         and lead me in the way that is everlasting.

Psalm 140

1   Deliver me, O Lord, from evil men:
         and preserve me from violent men.

2   Who devise mischief in their hearts:
         who stir up enmity day by day.

3   They have sharpened their tongues like a serpent's:
         and the venom of asps is under their lips.

4   Keep me, O Lord, from the power of the wicked:
         preserve me from violent men,
         who think to thrust me from my course.

5   The arrogant have laid a snare for me,
         and rogues have stretched the net:
         they have set traps along my way.

6   But I have said to the Lord 'You are my God':
         hear, O Lord, the voice of my pleading.

7   O Lord my God and my sure stronghold:
      you have covered my head in the day of battle.

8   Do not fulfil, O Lord, the desire of the wicked:
      nor further the evil that he has devised.

[9   Let not those that beset me lift their heads:
      but let the mischief that is on their lips bury them.

10   Let hot burning coals be poured upon them:
      let them be plunged into that miry pit
      from which they shall never arise.

11   Let no man of evil tongue find footing in the land:
      the evil, the violent man – let him be hunted to the end.]

12   I know that the Lord will work justice for the oppressed:
      and right judgements for the poor.

13   Surely the righteous shall have cause to praise your name:
      and the just shall dwell in your sight.

Psalm 141

1   O Lord, I call to you, make haste to help me:
      and hear my voice when I cry.

2   Let my prayer be as incense before you:
      and the lifting up of my hands as the evening sacrifice.

3   Set a guard, O Lord, on my mouth:
      and keep the door of my lips.

4   Let not my heart incline to evil speech,
      to join in wickedness with wrongdoers:
      let me not taste the pleasures of their table.

5   But let the righteous man chastise me:
         and the faithful man rebuke me.

6   Let not the oil of the wicked anoint my head:
         for I pray to you still against their wickedness.

7   They shall be cast down
         by that Mighty One who is their judge:
         and how pleasing shall my words be to them then!

8   As when a farmer breaks the ground:
         so shall their bones lie scattered at the mouth of Sheol.

9   But my eyes look to you, O Lord my God:
         to you I come for refuge, do not pour out my life.

10   Keep me from the snare that they have laid for me:
         and from the traps of the evildoers.

11   Let the wicked fall together into their own nets:
         whilst I pass safely by.

Psalm 142

1   I call to the Lord with a loud voice:
         with loud voice I entreat his favour.

2   I pour out my complaint before him:
         and tell him all my trouble.

3   When my spirit is faint within me, you know my path:
         in the way where I walk they have hidden a snare for me.

4   I look to my right hand and see:
         but no man will know me;

5   All escape is gone:
         and there is no one who cares for me.

6   I call to you, O Lord, I say 'You are my refuge:
        you are my portion in the land of the living'.

7   Heed my loud crying, for I am brought very low:
        O save me from my persecutors,
        for they are too strong for me.

8   Bring me out of the prison-house:
        that I may praise your name.

9   When you have given me my reward:
        then will the righteous gather about me.

Psalm 143

1   Hear my prayer, O Lord:
        in your faithfulness consider my petition,
        and in your righteousness give me answer.

2   Bring not your servant into judgement:
        for in your sight can no man living be justified.

3   For the enemy has pursued me,
        he has crushed my life to the ground:
        he has made me dwell in darkness,
        like those for ever dead.

4   Therefore my spirit grows faint:
        and my heart is appalled within me.

5   I remember the days of old,
        I think on all that you have done:
        I consider the works of your hands.

6   I stretch out my hands toward you:
        my soul yearns for you like a thirsty land.

7   Be swift to hear me, O Lord, for my spirit fails:
hide not your face from me,
lest I be like those who go down to the Pit.

8   O let me hear of your merciful kindness in the morning,
for my trust is in you:
show me the way that I should go, for you are my hope.

9   Deliver me from my enemies, O Lord:
for I run to you for shelter.

10   Teach me to do your will, for you are my God:
let your kindly spirit lead me in an even path.

11   For your name's sake, O Lord, preserve my life:
and for the sake of your righteousness,
bring me out of trouble.

[12   In your merciful goodness slay my enemies,
and destroy all those that come against me:
for truly I am your servant.]

Psalm 144

1   Blessed be the Lord my Rock:
who teaches my hands to war
and my fingers to fight;

2   My strength and my stronghold,
my fortress and my deliverer:
my shield, to whom I come for refuge,
who subdues the peoples under me.

3   Lord, what is man,
that you should be mindful of him:
or the son of man,
that you should consider him?

224

4   Man is but a breath of wind:
       his days are like a shadow that passes away.

5   Part the heavens, O Lord, and come down:
       touch the mountains, and they shall smoke.

6   Dart forth your lightnings, and scatter them on every side:
       let loose your arrows, with the roar of the thunderbolt.

7   Reach down your hand from on high, rescue me,
       and pluck me out of the great waters:
       out of the hands of the aliens,

8   Whose mouths speak perjury:
       and their right hand is a right hand of falsehood.

9   I will sing you a new song, O God:
       on the ten-stringed lute will I sing your praises.

10   You have given victory to kings:
       and deliverance to David your servant.

11   O save me from the peril of the sword:
       pluck me out of the hands of the aliens,

12   Whose mouths speak perjury:
       and their right hand is a right hand of falsehood.

13   Our sons in their youth shall be like sturdy plants:
       and our daughters as the carved corners of palaces.

14   Our barns shall be full and give food of every kind:
       the sheep shall lamb in our fields in thousands
       and tens of thousands.

15   Our cattle shall be heavy with calf,
       there shall be no miscarriage or untimely birth:
       and no loud crying in our streets.

16   Happy the people whose lot is such as this:
      happy that people who have the Lord for their God!

Psalm 145

1   I will exalt you, O God my king:
      I will bless your name for ever and ever.

2   Every day will I bless you:
      and praise your name for ever and ever.

3   Great is the Lord, and wonderfully worthy to be praised:
      his greatness is past searching out.

4   One generation shall praise your works to another:
      and declare your mighty acts.

5   As for me,
      I will be talking of the glorious splendour of your majesty:
      I will tell the story of your marvellous works.

6   Men shall recount the power of your terrible deeds:
      and I will proclaim your greatness.

7   Their lips shall flow with the remembrance
      of your abundant goodness:
      they shall shout for joy at your righteousness.

8   The Lord is gracious and compassionate:
      slow to anger and of great goodness.

9   The Lord is loving to every man:
      and his mercy is over all his works.

10   All creation praises you, O Lord:
      and your faithful servants bless your name.

11 They speak of the glory of your kingdom:
and tell of your great might,

12 That all mankind may know your mighty acts:
and the glorious splendour of your kingdom.

13 Your kingdom is an everlasting kingdom:
and your dominion endures through all generations.

14 The Lord upholds all those who stumble:
and raises up those that are bowed down.

15 The eyes of all look to you in hope:
and you give them their food in due season;

16 You open wide your hand:
and fill all things living with your bounteous gift.

17 The Lord is just in all his ways:
and faithful in all his dealings.

18 The Lord is near to all who call upon him:
to all who call upon him in truth.

19 He will fulfil the desire of those that fear him:
he will hear their cry, and save them.

20 The Lord preserves all those that love him:
but the wicked he will utterly destroy.

21 My mouth shall speak the praises of the Lord:
and let all flesh bless his holy name, for ever and ever.

Psalm 146

1 Praise the Lord, praise the Lord, O my soul:
while I live I will praise the Lord;

2   While I have any being:
I will sing praises to my God.

3   Put not your trust in princes:
nor in the sons of men, who cannot save.

4   For when their breath goes from them,
they return again to the earth:
and on that day all their thoughts perish.

5   Blessed is the man whose help is the God of Jacob:
whose hope is in the Lord his God,

6   The God who made heaven and earth:
the sea, and all that is in them,

7   Who keeps faith for ever:
who deals justice to those that are oppressed.

8   The Lord gives food to the hungry:
and sets the captives free.

9   The Lord gives sight to the blind:
the Lord lifts up those that are bowed down.

10   The Lord loves the righteous:
the Lord cares for the stranger in the land.

11   He upholds the widow and the fatherless:
as for the way of the wicked, he turns it upside down.

12   The Lord shall be king for ever:
your God, O Zion, shall reign through all generations.
Praise the Lord.

Psalm 147

1   O praise the Lord,
        for it is good to sing praises to our God:
        and to praise him is joyful and right.

2   The Lord is rebuilding Jerusalem:
        he is gathering together the scattered outcasts of Israel.

3   He heals the broken in spirit:
        and binds up their wounds.

4   He counts the number of the stars:
        and calls them all by name.

5   Great is our Lord, and great is his power:
        there is no measuring his understanding.

6   The Lord restores the humble:
        but he brings down the wicked to the dust.

7   O sing to the Lord a song of thanksgiving:
        sing praises to our God upon the harp.

8   He covers the heavens with cloud,
        and prepares rain for the earth:
        and makes the grass to sprout upon the mountains.

9   He gives the cattle their food:
        and feeds the young ravens that call to him.

10   He takes no pleasure in the strength of a horse:
        nor does he delight in any man's legs,

11   But the Lord's delight is in those that fear him:
        who wait in hope for his mercy.

12   Praise the Lord, O Jerusalem:
      sing praises to your God, O Zion.

13   For he has strengthened the bars of your gates:
      and blessed your children within you.

14   He makes peace within your borders:
      and satisfies you with the finest wheat.

15   He sends his command to the earth:
      and his word runs very swiftly.

16   He gives snow like wool:
      and scatters the hoar-frost like ashes.

17   He sprinkles his ice like morsels of bread:
      and the waters harden at his frost.

18   He sends out his word and melts them:
      he blows with his wind and the waters flow.

19   He made his word known to Jacob:
      his statutes and judgements to Israel.

20   He has not dealt so with any other nation:
      nor have they knowledge of his laws.
      Praise the Lord.

Psalm 148

1   Praise the Lord,
      praise the Lord from heaven:
      O praise him in the heights.

2   Praise him, all his angels:
      O praise him, all his host.

3   Praise him, sun and moon:
       praise him, all you stars of light.

4   Praise him, you highest heaven:
       and you waters that are above the heavens.

5   Let them praise the name of the Lord:
       for he commanded and they were made.

6   He established them for ever and ever:
       he made an ordinance which shall not pass away.

7   O praise the Lord from the earth:
       praise him, you sea-monsters and all deeps;

8   Fire and hail, mist and snow:
       and storm-wind fulfilling his command;

9   Mountains and all hills:
       fruiting trees and all cedars;

10   Beasts of the wild, and all cattle:
       creeping things and winged birds;

11   Kings of the earth, and all peoples:
       princes, and all rulers of the world;

12   Young men and maidens:
       old men and children together.

13   Let them praise the name of the Lord:
       for his name alone is exalted.

14   His glory is above earth and heaven:
       and he has lifted high the horn of his people.

15   Therefore he is the praise of all his servants:
       of the children of Israel, a people that is near him.
       Praise the Lord.

Psalm 149

1   O praise the Lord,
and sing to the Lord a new song:
O praise him in the assembly of the faithful.

2   Let Israel rejoice in him that made him:
let the children of Zion be joyful in their king.

3   Let them praise him in the dance:
let them sing his praise with timbrel and with harp.

4   For the Lord takes delight in his people:
he adorns the meek with his salvation.

5   Let his faithful ones exult in his glory:
let them sing for joy upon their beds.

6   Let the high praises of God be in their mouths:
and a two-edged sword in their hands,

7   To execute vengeance on the nations:
and chastisement upon the peoples,

8   To bind their kings in chains:
and their nobles with fetters of iron,

9   To visit upon them the judgement that is decreed:
such honour belongs to all his faithful servants.
Praise the Lord.

Psalm 150

1   Praise the Lord. O praise God in his sanctuary:
    praise him in the firmament of his power.

2   Praise him for his mighty acts:
    praise him according to his abundant goodness.

3   Praise him in the blast of the ram's horn:
    praise him upon the lute and harp.

4   Praise him with the timbrel and dances:
    praise him upon the strings and pipe.

5   Praise him on the high-sounding cymbals:
    praise him upon the loud cymbals.

6   Let everything that has breath praise the Lord:
    O praise the Lord!

NOTES ON THE TEXT

by

A. A. Macintosh

(This information was originally made available in a booklet from

COLLINS LITURGICAL PUBLICATIONS

and

CHURCH INFORMATION OFFICE

ABBREVIATIONS

C.	Miles Coverdale's version of the Psalms in the *Book of Common Prayer.*
H.	Denotes 'Hebrew' or 'Hebrew text'. For the latter, see *Biblia Hebraica* ed. R. Kittel, 3rd ed., *or Biblia Hebraica Stuttgartensia* ed. H. Bardtke.
LXX	The Septuagint (Greek) version of the O.T.
Aq.	Aquila)
Symm.	Symmachus) The Minor Greek versions of the O.T.
Theod.	Theodotion)
Targum	The Aramaic translation of the O.T.
Pesh. *or* **Peshitta**	The Syriac translation of the O.T.
Jer. *or* **Jerome**	The Latin translation of the Psalms made by Jerome from the Hebrew O.T. (called I.H., *Iuxta Hebraeos*).
Vulg. *or* **Vulgate**	The Latin translation of the Greek (LXX) version of the Psalms.
Ms(s)	Manuscript(s)
R.P.	*The Revised Psalter*
R.V.	*The Revised Version*
R.S.V.	*The Revised Standard Version*
N.E.B.	*The New English Bible*
>	denotes 'whence' or 'becoming'
<	denotes 'deriving from'

INTRODUCTION

These notes were compiled by the Secretary of the translation panel at the request of the Chairman of the Liturgical Commission of the Church of England. They are designed to give some account of the differences between the new translation and that of Miles Coverdale in the Book of Common Prayer. Where it is thought useful, some comparison has been made with other translations of the Psalms and especially those of the *Revised Psalter* and the *New English Bible.* The notes are written in order to meet the requirements of those who are not Hebraists and should not be regarded as a full and comprehensive commentary on the textual and philological decisions of the translation panel.

August 1977   A. A. Macintosh

1. GENERAL NOTE ON *nephesh*

The word *nephesh* has a wide range of meanings, though in C. it is consistently translated 'soul'. In places it has a physical sense and denotes 'the throat' or 'neck' (see e.g. Pss. 69: 1, 105: 18). Elsewhere it denotes the inner personality or the self and is often rendered in this translation simply by 'I' or 'me' < 'my soul') or 'they', 'them' < 'their soul'). When it is said e.g. that the wicked 'band together against the *nephesh* of the righteous' (Ps. 94: 24), 'life' seems to be an appropriate translation of the term and it has been adopted in such passages. The panel chose to avoid rendering *nephesh* consistently by 'soul' on the grounds that it is in some places wrong, and also because it might suggest the later theological ideas of the soul (as opposed to the body). There are a few places, however, where 'soul' has been retained; here it was judged to express the meaning best in English and without the danger of its being misunderstood (e.g. Ps. 55: 20).

2. GENERAL NOTE ON *emeth*

The H. noun is derived from a root meaning 'reliable, faithful, sure'. Used in connexion with persons, it denotes reliability and trustworthiness. C.'s translation 'truth' was judged misleading, for it suggests philosophical ideas which are not part of the H. word.

PSALM 1

Verse 7 *cares for:* The H. word sometimes has the meaning 'care for' as well as the more usual 'know'. The former meaning fits this context better than the latter (so R.P. and N.E.B.; C. has 'knoweth').

PSALM 2

Verse 10 *govern yourselves in fear and trembling:* C.'s 'Rejoice unto him with reverence' (lit. 'rejoice with trembling') is unlikely to be correct. Similarly C.'s 'Kiss the Son'. Rabbinic commentators of the 10th and 11th centuries suggest a tradition that the H. word usually translated 'rejoice' could also carry the meaning 'display fear' and that the H. word usually translated 'kiss' could also mean 'be properly governed, ordered'. (Cf. R.V. note at Gen. 41: 40). The evidence of comparative philology now substantiates these meanings which fit the context admirably. The translations 'kiss his feet with trembling' (so e.g. R.P., R.S.V.), 'Kiss the

King' (N.E.B.) are based upon conjectural emendations. The consonants interpreted 'son' (implausible in itself because that word is Aramaic rather than Hebrew) are likely to be a corrupt dittograph.

PSALM 4

Verse 3 *his wonderful kindness:* The translation is based upon a small correction to H. by comparison with Ps. 31: 23, cf. N.E.B. The traditional text appears to mean 'The Lord has separated for himself a pious one' (cf. C. and R.P.) which does not fit the context as well.

Verse 6 *has gone from us:* A small change of the pointing (not of the consonantal text) gives this meaning appropriate on the lips of the 'many' who are speaking, cf. N.E.B. The way in which the H. word is spelt tells against the meaning 'Lift up' (so C. and R.P.).

PSALM 6

Verse 3 *how long will you delay . . . . :* H.'s 'how long?' is thus expanded to give the sense. (cf. R.P.).

Verse 7 *eyes:* This is what the text means (cf. R.V., R.P. and N.E.B.); not 'beauty' (C.).

PSALM 7

Verse 1 *come for shelter:* The word has this meaning rather than 'trust' (C.), cf. N.E.B.

Verse 2 *throat:* See general note on *nephesh.*
carry me *off:* The H. word means 'to tear, snatch away'. It is here taken to mean 'to take off (as prey)' (cf. N.E.B.), rather than 'to rip into pieces' (so C. and R.P.).

Verse 4 *plundered:* The H. word is attested with this meaning as well as 'to set free, deliver'. The panel took the view that the former sense was correct here (cf. R.P.). C.'s translation does not fit the conditional sentence of H. and N.E.B. supposes that it was a sin to free an enemy, which is unlikely here.

Verse 8 *take your seat:* A small correction to H. (cf. N.E.B.) which otherwise appears to mean 'on high, return'. (> C. 'lift thyself again' cf. R.P.)

sit in judgement: A small correction to H. which otherwise seems to mean 'The Lord will judge...' R.P. emends the text in a different (and less satisfactory) way. N.E.B. treats the H. phrase as a relative clause, but the panel thought an imperative was more natural in the context. The meaning 'sit' is partly derived from 'sit in judgement' immediately before.

Verse 11 *over me:* A small correction to H. which otherwise seems to mean 'my shield upon God'. (> C. 'My help cometh of God'.) R.P. is dubious.

PSALM 8

Verse 2 *is yet recounted:* The H. word is clearly attested with this meaning (cf. Judges 5: 11). The traditional pointing appears to understand the consonants as an imperative, which gives no sense. C.'s 'thou hast set' is highly dubious. A change of pointing (but not of consonants) gives the passive meaning, cf. N.E.B.; R.P. emends the consonantal text.

babes and sucklings: this is taken with the 'majesty recounted above the heavens' rather than with the following phrase, which contributes to a separate stanza or verse. (Contrast C., R.P. and N.E.B.)

Verse 6 *god:* The H. word means 'gods', 'god' or 'God'. Early Jewish tradition interpreted the word as 'angels' (so C. and R.P.). The meaning of the Psalm is that man is the chief creature of God's creation, only a little less than divine.

PSALM 9

Verse 6 *strongholds:* The H. word usually means 'desolations' (C. 'destructions'). However, there is evidence in other Semitic languages to suggest that here the word means 'strongholds', cf. N.E.B. and Job 3: 14. R.P.'s translation is dubious and there is no evidence in its favour.

Verse 7 *confounds them:* Two slight corrections have been made to H. First, one letter of a word has been altered (the word as written seems to mean 'they' – which is strange (> C. 'with them'; which is highly dubious). Secondly, the word is read with this verse rather than with the previous one. N.E.B.'s solution is similar but gives the meaning 'The Lord thunders', which is less likely in the context.

Verse 17 *death:* Lit. 'Sheol', i.e. the abode of the dead. Cf. Greek 'Hades' – not hell in the sense of the place of torment.

PSALM 10

Verse 3 *He spurns:* So, probably (in accordance with Jewish tradition), H.'s 'He blesses' (> C. 'speaketh good of') is understood, cf. R.P. 'He blesses' in the H. is itself likely to be a euphemism which avoids putting in writing the unseemly words 'curse God' (even when such action is predicated of the wicked), cf. Job 1: 5 and 2: 5, 9. C.'s 'speaketh good of the covetous whom God abhorreth' is an ingenious interpretation of H., but it fails to understand the word 'He blesses'. (N.E.B.'s translation depends upon an emendation of H.).

Verse 4 *God will not avenge:* Lit. 'He will not seek *(sc.* vengeance)'. C., R.P. and N.E.B. take God as the object and understand the phrase to mean 'he careth not for God'. It is more likely, however, that two sentiments of the ungodly are here quoted.

Verse 5 *He is settled in all his ways:* Lit. 'at all times his ways are firm.' Cf. R.P. and contrast C. (so N.E.B.) 'his ways are alway grievous'.

Verse 6 *I shall walk secure ... :* There has been some rearrangement of the H. verse division. The resulting reading is taken to mean lit. 'I will walk not with the hurt of a curse'. N.E.B.'s solution is very similar. C.'s (so R.P.) 'there shall no harm happen unto me' is dubious.

Verse 11 *The upright are crushed:* The H. word 'upright' is supplied on the grounds that the (acrostic) structure of the poem requires it, cf. R.P. and N.E.B. The change also helps to restore the metre.

Verse 20 *be terrified:* Such is the meaning of the H. word rather than 'exalt' (so C.), cf. R.P. and N.E.B.

PSALM 11

Verse 1 *refuge:* Cf. Ps. 7: 1.

Verse 6 *coals of fire:* H. has 'snares'. A slight change (made on the authority of Symmachus) gives the much more suitable meaning 'coals', cf. R.P. and N.E.B.

PSALM 12

Verse 6 *crucible . . . gold:* 'crucible' is the likely meaning of the word in question (left untranslated in C.). The change of one letter in another word gives the meaning 'gold' rather than 'to the earth', which is obscure if not corrupt, cf. R.P. and N.E.B.

PSALM 14

Verses 5-7 of C.'s version are not in H. They derive ultimately from other parts of the O.T. *via* Romans 3: 13-18 where they are collected and whence they found their way into the Ms tradition of the LXX (Greek) version of Psalm 14. It is because this version lay behind the Latin (Vulgate) Psalms known to C. that the verses are present in C.

Verse 7 *turns again the fortunes:* The H. phrase is now understood in this way, cf. R.P. and N.E.B. The translation 'turn the captivity' (so C.) is a later Jewish interpretation of the H. phrase which is quite unsuitable in some contexts. (The ancient versions in a number of places in the O.T. support the meaning given here.)

PSALM 15

Verse 5 *to his neighbour:* A slight change is made to H. on the authority of one of the ancient versions (LXX). As it stands, H. appears to mean 'to do evil' which does not make sense. C. has given a double translation of the word. 'To his own hindrance' (so also R.P. and N.E.B.) is a doubtful interpretation of 'to do evil'.

PSALM 16

Verse 2 *all my good depends on you:* Cf. R.P. Lit. 'my good, does it not depend on you?' This is preferable to C.'s 'my goods are nothing unto thee'.

Verse 3 *As for those who are held holy:* The text probably refers to holy (gods), i.e. idols (cf. N.E.B.), rather than to holy (people), whence C.'s 'saints'. R.P. emends the text.

PSALM 17

Verse 4 *My mouth . . . of others:* Lit. 'My mouth does not transgress according to the deeds of men'. There has been a rearrangement of H.'s verse division.

Verse 7 *refuge:* Cf. on Ps. 7: 1.

Verse 14 *Slay them by your hand, O Lord:* A change of pointing (but not of the consonantal text) gives this appropriate sense (A literal 'slaying them' >, in English, 'Slay them'). The traditional pointing may have suggested 'From the men of your hand' (so C. and R.P.), but this gives poor sense and is highly dubious as a translation of H. N.E.B. emends the verb to give a sense achieved here without (consonantal) emendation.

Verse 14 *destroy them:* The pointing of the H. word (but not the consonants) is emended on the authority of one of the ancient versions (LXX), and the verb is given this meaning on philological grounds, cf. N.E.B. H. as pointed means 'their portion' (so C. and R.P.) which is obscure in the context. R.P.'s attempt to make sense of the traditional pointing is inconsistent with O.T. views of life and death.

Verse 15 *cherished ones:* H. 'thy hidden, cherished (ones)' refers to people rather than to treasure (C., cf. R.P.).
let their sons be satisfied: continues the sense of the verse more satisfactorily than 'they are satisfied with sons' (so C.'s 'they have children at their desire', cf. R.P. and N.E.B.).

PSALM 18

The tenses of the Psalm have been understood to have a past reference, i.e. to a past deliverance of God for which the psalmist gives thanks.

Verse 2 *refuge:* Cf. Ps. 7: 1.

Verse 3 *with loud lamentation:* A small correction. The word so translated is very similar to that translated 'worthy to be praised' (C., cf. R.P. and N.E.B.). In this context the former is more likely to be correct.

Verse 9 *from his nostrils:* The literal meaning of the H. word, cf. R.P. and N.E.B. Contrast C.'s 'out in his presence'.

Verse 10 *He parted:* Lit. 'He pushed aside'.

Verse 14 H. adds 'hailstones and coals of fire' at the end of the verse: a mistaken repetition from the previous verse. Cf. II Sam. 22: 14. The phrase is omitted by some H. Mss.

Verse 15 *with the roar of the thunderbolt:* Lit. 'and sent them (i.e. his lightnings) roaring'. C.'s 'and destroyed them' mistakenly assumes that the object of the verb is (God's) enemies. But all the verbs of the verse have as their objects God's arrows and lightnings. Cf. N.E.B.

Verse 27 *faithful:* Cf. N.E.B. ('loyal'). This is the meaning rather than 'holy' (C.).

Verse 36 *arrow of bronze:* The metal denoted is 'bronze' not 'steel' (C.). The verb means 'to aim' not 'to break' (C.). The word translated 'arrow' can mean 'bow' (so C. and R.P. - but bows were not made of bronze) or *arrow,* cf. N.E.B.

Verse 46 *aliens humbled themselves before me:* Lit. 'the sons of the foreigner (> C. 'strange children') shall be obsequious before me'. The H. verb can mean 'to lie' (C. 'dissemble') and 'to be obsequious'. The latter meaning is more likely here, cf. R.P. and N.E.B.

Verse 47 *The strength of the aliens withered away:* Lit. 'The sons of the alien (i.e. 'aliens') wither away'. The word 'strength' is supplied in English *ad sensum,* cf. R.P.

PSALM 19

Verse 5 *strong man:* A more accurate translation than C.'s 'giant', cf. R.P. and N.E.B.

PSALM 20

Verse 5 *victory:* The word usually translated 'salvation' (so C.) has often, as here, the force 'triumph, victory', cf. R.P. and N.E.B.

Verse 9 *king:* The word is the object of the verb (so R.P. and N.E.B.) rather than a vocative (so C. who adds 'of heaven' as a gloss).

PSALM 22

Verse 9 *brought* me *to lie at peace:* The H. word is, on philological grounds, likely to retain here its originally physical meaning 'to make to lie flat' (cf. Jer. 12: 5). The word generally has the connotation of security, and that is here conveyed by the words 'at peace'. C.'s 'my hope' is derived from the LXX and 'when I hanged yet' is probably supplied *ad sensum.*

Verse 15 *my mouth:* The order of two H. consonants is inverted to give this meaning which well suits the context, cf. R.P. and N.E.B. H. unaltered has 'my strength' (so C.).

Verse 16 *are withered:* A variant Ms. reading is attested which, on philological grounds, is likely to have the meaning 'be shrunken, shortened'. The reference is therefore probably to diseased rather than to tortured limbs. H., unaltered, has 'like the lion' which in the context gives no sense. C.'s 'they pierced' is probably derived from the Vulgate (if not from the LXX). There is a Hebrew verb near in form to the word 'like a lion' but it is attested with the meaning 'to dig' and not with the meaning 'to pierce'. N.E.B's 'they have hacked off' is based upon a comparison with a very dubious Akkadian verb. R.P.'s attempt to preserve the meaning 'pierce' by appeal to the same philological theory that lies behind the N.E.B. is even more dubious. For reasons of metre as well as of sense, the words my *hands and my feet are withered* are transferred to the beginning of this verse. In H. they occur after the words 'hem me in' (here verse 17).

Verse 22 *afflicted soul:* This reading is suggested by the LXX and other ancient versions and it fits the context well, cf. R.P. and N.E.B. H., unaltered, seems to mean 'thou hast answered me' (cf. C.'s 'thou hast heard me'); such a meaning, however, scarcely fits the context in which there are a number of (imperative) cries for help.

wild oxen: such is the meaning of the H. word rather than the mythical 'unicorn'.

Verse 27 *of the sacrifice:* These words, which are not in H., are supplied in English *ad sensum. their hearts:* a change to H. is made by reference to the LXX and another ancient version. Cf. N.E.B. H. unaltered: 'your heart' (cf. C. and R.P.).

Verse 30 *How can those who sleep in the earth do him homage:* A conjectural restoration of the text gives this meaning, cf. R.P. and N.E.B. H., unaltered, seems to mean 'they have eaten and have done homage, all the fat of the earth', which is nonsensical (cf. C.).

Verse 31 my *life:* One letter of H. is altered to enable this sense and it is done by reference to the LXX. H., unaltered, has 'his life'. R.P. emends H. as here but the translation there is less satisfactory. N.E.B. emends but also changes the pointing of another word.

for himself: is a variant H. reading to which a number of the ancient versions also bear witness, cf. R.P. and N.E.B. The other reading has 'not' (cf. C's 'no man hath quickened his own soul').

PSALM 23

Verse 2 *make me lie down:* Such is the meaning of the H. word, cf. R.P. and N.E.B. C.'s 'he shall feed me' is wrong.

still waters: The H. expression denotes 'waters of quietness', 'waters of rest', which may be simply descriptive, adjectival. It is not necessary to spell out the metaphorical possibilities. Cf. C.'s 'waters of comfort' and N.E.B's 'waters of peace'.

Verse 3 *refresh:* The H. word means 'to restore, refresh'. C.'s 'convert' is wrong in this context.

Verse 4 *shadow of death:* The greatly loved translation has been retained here. For this phrase, see further on Psalm 107: l0.

PSALM 24

Verse 4 *idols:* The H. word means, lit. 'emptiness, vanity' (cf. C.'s 'vanity'); but here it is likely specifically to denote 'idols'.

nor sworn his oath to a lie: < H. lit. 'has not sworn with reference to deceit', cf. C.'s 'nor sworn to deceive his neighbour' and R.P. 'nor sworn to his neighbour deceitfully' which are somewhat free.

Verse 5 *recompense:* The H. word means 'what is right' and here what is right for the true of heart, so 'recompense', cf. C.'s 'righteousness'.

Verse 6 *of such a kind as this:* The H. word is well attested with the meanings 'class of people' as well as 'generation'. It is the former meaning that is appropriate here. R.P. and N.E.B. on another theory understand the word to mean 'fortune, lot' which is less likely.

God of Jacob: The LXX has 'God of Jacob' and this is probably what is intended by the psalmist. H. has simply 'Jacob'.

PSALM 25

Verse 5 *because of your goodness, O Lord:* Cf. N.E.B. The words are transferred from verse 7 (in H.), where they are superfluous, to form a second, parallel line in this verse which otherwise is defective in this respect.

Verse 17 *O free my heart from pain and bring me out of my distress:* This translation is achieved by deleting one consonant of H. and by a small change to the word-division and consequent change to the pointing, cf.

R.P. and N.E.B. C.'s 'the sorrows of my heart are enlarged' is an unlikely expression in Hebrew.

Verse 18 *Give heed:* One word of H. is emended to give this sense and to restore the structure of the psalm. H.'s 'see' (cf. C.'s 'look upon' – so R.P. and N.E.B.) is unlikely in the context.

PSALM 26

Verse 2 *mind:* H. (lit.) 'kidneys' (cf. C.'s 'reins') i.e. the seat of emotion and affection.

Verse 9 *Do not sweep me away:* Such is the meaning of H. Cf. and contrast C.'s 'O shut not up', which is impossible.

me: See general note on *nephesh*.

Verse 11 *ransom me:* A fairly literal rendering of H. Contrast C.'s (so R.P.) 'deliver me'.

PSALM 27

Verse 1 *stronghold:* The H. word denotes this rather than the abstract 'strength' (so C.).

Verse 3 *yet will I trust:* H. denotes a trusting attitude; it does not say '(trust) in him' (so C. and R.P.).

Verse 5 *to seek his will in his temple:* Such is the likely meaning of H. C.'s 'visit his temple' is dubious. The H. verb denotes (lit.) 'to enquire'.

Verse 10 *his face:* H. has 'my face'. God is represented as talking with the psalmist and he commands him 'seek my face' to which the psalmist replies *('My heart has said of you')* in the affirmative. In translation the sense has been made clearer by rendering *his face*.

Verse 16 *But I believe:* Some H. Mss. omit the H. word 'if not' (cf. C.'s 'but that') and this reading is here adopted, cf. R.P. and N.E.B. C. inserts

'I should utterly have fainted' as an apodosis to what he understood to be a protasis. There is nothing, however, corresponding to these words in H.

PSALM 28

Verse 2 *holiest place of your sanctuary:* The H. expression denotes the 'holy of holies' (lit. 'the back part of thy sanctuary'). C.'s 'mercy seat of thy holy temple' is somewhat interpretative and expanded.

Verse 9 *his people:* A variant reading attested by some H. Mss. and by two of the ancient versions, cf. R.P. and N.E.B. The other reading has 'to them' which is less satisfactory.

PSALM 29

Verse 1 *sons of heaven:* The H. expression means lit. 'sons of God(s)'. C.'s 'ye mighty' (itself a free paraphrase) and 'rams' (dubious in the context) are a double translation of H. which goes back to the LXX. R.P. paraphrases 'O ye hosts of heaven'; N.E.B. has simply 'You Gods'.

Verse 6 *wild ox:* such is the meaning of H. rather than the mythical '(young) unicorn'.

Verse 8 *rends the terebinth trees:* The verb was thought to carry this meaning and the noun (repointed) means terebinths. A reference to God's destruction of forest and woodland is here more likely than to his bringing about the premature birth of animals. C. has 'maketh the hinds to bring forth young' and continues 'and discovereth the thick bushes' (cf. here *strips bare the forests).* R.P. and N.E.B. seek by (somewhat dubious) philological considerations to turn 'discovereth the thick bushes' into another reference to premature birth in the animal world. The resulting sense is little short of ludicrous.

PSALM 30

Verse 5 *For if in his anger is havoc, in his good favour is life:* cf. N.E.B. H. lit. 'for havoc is in his anger, life is in his good favour'. The word translated 'havoc' has this meaning (lit. 'disturbance') as well as 'twinkling of an eye' (so C.). Cf. and contrast C.'s 'his wrath endureth but the twinkling of an eye, and in his pleasure is life'.

PSALM 31

Verse 5 *you will redeem me:* The translation of the H. tenses in the Psalms is very uncertain. The panel took the view that since this psalm opens with a prayer for deliverance, a future reference for *you will redeem* was more likely than a past reference (so C. 'thou has redeemed me').

Verse 7 *known me:* see general note on *nephesh.*

Verse 8 *where I may walk at liberty:* Cf. R.P.'s 'where they may walk at liberty'. H. lit. 'in a broad place' > C. 'in a large room'.

Verse 9 *my throat:* See general note on *nephesh.*
my inward parts: H. lit. 'my belly'; cf. C.'s 'my body'.

Verse 11 *wag their heads in derision:* H. has a word translated 'especially' in C. One letter is changed to give the literal sense 'and nodding to my neighbours' which gives the appropriate sense: *they wag their heads in derision,* cf. R.P.'s (free) 'a byword among my neighbours'.

Verse 23 *a city besieged:* H. lit., a 'city of siege'. cf. C.'s 'strong city'. R.P.'s (so also N.E.B.) 'time of trouble' is achieved by emending the text, which is unnecessary.

Verse 27 *let your heart take courage:* 'heart' is taken as the subject of the verb, cf. R.P. and N.E.B. C. takes 'he' (i.e. the Lord) as the subject and 'heart' as the object, which is less likely as an interpretation of H.

PSALM 32

Verse 7 *trouble:* Cf. R.P. and N.E.B. One H. word is emended to give this sense. H., unaltered, appears to have (lit.) 'time of finding: but' which is dubious (> C. 'a time when thou mayest be found: but').

Verse 10 *forward course:* Cf. N.E.B. The H. word was understood to have here this meaning on the basis of philological evidence and on the authority of some medieval Jewish commentators. There is no philological

evidence to support the translation 'mouth' (so C. and R.P.), which is
likely to represent a guess.

PSALM 33

Verse 7 *water-skin:* The pointing of one H. word (but not the consonants)
is emended with the support of the LXX and Targum to give this meaning,
cf. R.P. and N.E.B. H., unaltered, reads 'heap' which is dubious in the
context.

Verse 10 *devices of the peoples:* C., on the authority of the Vulgate (and
so of the LXX), adds the words 'and casteth out the counsels of princes'
which are not present in H.

Verse 19 *We:* See general note on *nephesh.*

PSALM 35

Verse 4 *my life:* See general note on *nephesh.*

me: See general note on *nephesh.*

Verse 12 I am as one bereaved of his children: H. means (lit.) '(there is)
bereavement-of-children for me'. Cf. and contrast C. 'to the great
discomfort of my soul'. For 'soul' (C.) and 'I' in the present translation,
see general note on *nephesh.*

Verse 16 as though they were strangers I never knew: The addition of one
letter to one H. word gives the meaning 'strangers' rather than
(apparently) 'smitten ones, cripples' (cf. C.'s 'abjects'). The words 'as
though' are supplied *ad sensum.*

tore at me: H. lit. 'they rend in pieces', cf. C.'s 'making mouths'. *at me*
here (and in C.) is added *ad sensum* and is not represented in H.

Verse 17 *when I slipped:* The pointing (but not the consonants) of the H.
word is changed and the meaning established on philological grounds, cf.
R.P. and N.E.B. H., as pointed, seems to mean 'as profane men', cf. C.'s
(dubious) 'with the flatterers'. *they mocked me:* Two H. words are slightly
emended with some support from the LXX to give this sense. H.,
unaltered, seems to suggest the highly dubious meaning 'mockers of

cake'. The phrase is perhaps taken as an intensive by C., 'busy mockers'. R.P. and N.E.B. also emend, but more drastically.

PSALM 36

Verse 1 *The transgressor speaks from the wickedness in his own heart:* The pointing of two words (but not the consonants) is changed to give this sense. One reading of the H. text has also 'my heart' but a variant reading 'his heart' is here accepted, cf. N.E.B.

Verse 2 *he hates:* One consonant of the relevant H. word is deleted and the pointing emended to give this sense. N.E.B. emends more substantially. C.'s (so R.P.) 'abominable sin' is dubious.

to be found out: The pointing (but not the consonants) of H. is emended to give this passive sense.

PSALM 37

Verse 1 *Do not vie with:* Cf. N.E.B. Such is the meaning of the H. words rather than 'fret not thyself because of' (so C. and R.P.).

Verse 8 *let not envy move you:* Cf. on Verse 1 above. (C. and R.P. have 'fret not thyself, else shalt thou be moved').

Verse 13 *for his overthrow:* The words, which are not represented in H., are added to make the meaning clear.

Verse 14 *strung the bow:* The H. expression 'to tread the bow' means to prepare it for battle by stringing it rather than to aim it by bending it.

those that walk in innocence: H. lit. 'the upright way' (so here *those that walk in innocence),* cf. R.P. C. has 'such as are of a right conversation', where 'conversation' is used in an obsolete way.

Verse 20 *like fuel in a furnace:* One consonant of one H. word is changed (and the pointing of another) to give this sense, cf. R.P. and N.E.B. H., unaltered, seems to mean 'like the glory of pastures'. C.'s 'as the fat of lambs' is highly dubious.

Verse 27 *you shall dwell in the land:* The H. imperative is interpreted as conveying the consequence of obeying the previous commands 'Turn from evil and do good'. The construction is used a number of times in H., see e.g. Verse 30. The words 'in the land' are added in translation because they are implied in the H. word 'dwell', cf. and contrast C.'s 'dwell for evermore'.

Verse 29 *But the unjust shall be destroyed for ever:* H. (with its acrostic form) is restored by reference to verse 39 (H.38) and the LXX., cf. R.P. and N.E.B. C.'s 'they are preserved for ever' translates H. unaltered, taking the phrase with the preceding line (in C., the preceding verse).

Verse 38 *Observe the blameless man:* Such is the meaning of H. as pointed, cf. R.P. and N.E.B. The LXX and Jerome understood the same consonants to denote the abstract 'blamelessness' (> C. 'innocency').

upright: as *mutatis mutandis* on the note above.

for the man of peace: Cf. R.P. and N.E.B. H. means (lit.) 'For posterity will belong to the man of peace'. C.'s 'that shall bring a man peace at the last' is dubious.

PSALM 38

Verse 2 *have been aimed:* This meaning is probable on philological grounds for the H. word, cf. N.E.B. and see Ps.18: 36. C.'s (so R.P.) 'stick fast in' is dubious.

Verse 11 *hold aloof from my affliction:* H. means (lit.) 'stand over against my affliction', cf. C.'s 'did stand looking upon my trouble'.

Verse 12 *strike at me:* such is the meaning of the H. word. C.'s 'laid snares for me' is dubious.

Verse 17 *I am ready to fall:* Cf. R.P. and N.E.B. H. means (lit.) 'I am ready for stumbling'. C.'s 'l am set in the plague' is dubious. The word translated 'stumbling' can mean also 'limping' but not 'plague'.

Verse 19 *without a cause:* One H. word is emended to give this sense which provides a better parallel, cf. R.P. and N.E.B. The word unemended means 'life' (> C.'s 'mine enemies live and are mighty') which it is awkward to construe.

PSALM 39

Verse 2 *but found no comfort:* The H. preposition has a privative sense, 'without achieving any good' (> here *found no comfort*). C.'s (so R.P.) 'I kept silence from good (words)' is less likely. N.E.B. changes the pointing unnecessarily.

Verse 6 *though he stand secure:* (The division of verses at this point is somewhat different from H.) The H. word (lit. 'standing') is here taken as having concessive force (cf. N.E.B.) rather than as being a participial adjective defining every man (> C.'s 'every man living', where 'living' is a mistranslation).

Verse 7 *The riches . . . puff of wind:*

(a) *riches:* One H. word is emended to give this sense; unaltered, H. seems to mean 'they are in commotion' (the plural is very strange) > C. 'disquieteth himself'.

(b) *puff of wind:* The H. word means 'breath' or 'puff of wind'. The word was often previously rendered 'vanity'; so C.'s 'in vain'. The phrase in H. (unaltered) is lit. 'a puff of wind they are in commotion'.

Verse 12 *in putrefaction:* The H. word probably here denotes the abstract 'decay' (cf. N.E.B.) rather than the more concrete agent of it, 'the moth'. The words 'fretting a garment' in C.'s (so R.P.) 'like a moth fretting a garment' are not present in H.

Verse 15 *Turn your eye from me:* The H. word means (lit.) 'blind, smear (your eye) from me' (> here *turn your eye from me*). C.'s 'spare me a little' is dubious.
Smile again: such is the meaning of the H. word, cf. R.P. and N.E.B. C.'s 'I may recover my strength' is dubious.

PSALM 40

Verse 2 *pit of roaring waters:* The H. word in question means 'roaring' and is used in connexion with raging water. R.P.'s 'miry pit' (so N.E.B.) is achieved by emendation. C.'s 'horrible pit' is dubious as a translation of H. The word 'waters' is here supplied in order to make the meaning clear.

Verse 6 *there is none to be compared with you:* <H. (lit.) 'there is no ordering (i.e. comparing) to you'. C.'s '(there is no man) that ordereth them unto thee' is dubious.

Verse 8 *my ears you have marked for obedience:* H. means (lit.) 'you have bored ears for me', cf. Exodus 21: 6 for this institution which signified willingness on the part of a slave to continue in the service of his master.

Verse 19 *Aha, aha:* A close reproduction of the H. exclamation. Cf. C.'s 'Fie upon thee'.

PSALM 41

Verse 3 *if illness lays him low, you will overthrow it:* H. means (lit.) 'all his lying in his sickness thou wilt overthrow'. The H. word corresponding to 'lying' can also mean 'bed'. But C.'s 'make thou all his bed in his sickness' gives a dubious sense to the verb even if it avoids the comical 'overthrow his bed in his sickness'. N.E.B. emends and R.P. is dubious.

Verse 6 *gathers mischief:* Such is the meaning of the H. expression, cf. N.E.B. Contrast C.'s (so R.P.) 'conceiveth falsehood'.

Verse 8 a *deadly thing has got hold of him:* H. means (lit.) 'a thing of belial (i.e. destruction or the like) has got hold of him', cf. R.P. (though it should not be assumed that the same etymological view of 'belial' was here adopted). N.E.B. interprets the phrase as a 'spell'. C.'s 'let the sentence of guiltiness proceed against him' is dubious.

Verse 9 *has lifted his heel against me:* Cf. R.P. The meaning of the H. expression is (lit.) 'has made great his heel against me'. C.'s 'hath laid great wait for me' is dubious. N.E.B. renders freely 'exults over my misfortune'.

Verse 12 *Because of my innocence:* The H. word here denotes moral soundness rather than health, cf. R.P. and N.E.B. and contrast C.'s 'when I am in my health'.

PSALM 42

Verse 2 *when shall I come and see his face:* This is the likely meaning of the consonantal text. The traditional Jewish pointing attempted to impose a passive meaning upon the word corresponding to 'see' for reverential reasons. Hence C.'s 'when shall I come to appear (i.e. to be seen) before the presence of God'.

Verse 4 *the house of the Mighty One:*

a) *the house of:* the pointing (but not the consonantal text) is emended to give this sense, the word having (lit.) the meaning 'booth' or 'tabernacle'. The word is used of God's dwelling place in Psalm 76: 2.

b) *the Mighty One:* A variant reading is adopted to give this title of God. The other reading is obscure. This treatment (both the change of pointing and the variant reading) is supported by the LXX and it has the advantage that it restores parallelism to the verse. C.'s 'went with the multitude' (so R.P., cf. N.E.B.) is less likely to be correct.

Verse 7 *my deliverer:* H. lit. 'the deliverance of my face'. (> C. 'help of my countenance'.)

Verse 8 *from Mizar among the hills of Hermon:* Cf. R.P. and N.E.B. H. (lit.) 'and the Hermons (or 'Hermon') from the hill of Mizar'. C. translated the proper noun (Mizar) of the unidentified peak of Hermon, 'and the little hill of Hermon'.

Verse 9 *of your waters:* The obscure H. word probably refers to the primaeval waters which God, since creation, controls. Cf. R.P. and C.'s rather quaint 'water pipes'.

Verse 11 *like a mourner:* A literal translation of H.

PSALM 43

Verse 2 *my refuge:* such is the likely meaning of the H. word, (cf. N.E.B.) rather than 'strength' (C. and R.P.).

PSALM 44

Verse 2 *caused us to root and grow:* The H. verb usually means 'to throw' (> C. 'cast them out'). In some places (cf. on Ps. 80: 11) it is used of plants and means 'to throw out shoots', cf. N.E.B. A causative sense is here assumed with the meaning *you caused us to root and grow;* cf. the parallel above *planted us in.* The first person plural pronouns of the present version are adopted in translation for clarity. H. has 3rd person plural pronouns which refer to 'our fathers' (verse 1), cf. R.P.

Verse 5 *my God: who ordained:* The H. division of the consonants into words has been changed with the authority of the LXX and Peshitta and the pointing is consequently emended, cf. R.P. and N.E.B. The resulting sense fits the context well. H., unaltered, means 'O God: ordain the victory of Jacob' (cf. C.'s 'send help unto Jacob').

Verse 10 *you have cast us off:* This is the meaning of H. (cf. R.P. and N.E.B.) rather than C.'s 'thou art far off'.

Verse 16 *shame has covered my face: my face* is likely to be another object of the verb in apposition to 'me'. H. (lit.) 'shame has covered me (with respect to) my face'; cf. R.P. and contrast C. 's 'the shame of my face has covered me'.

Verse 20 *jackals:* Cf. R.P. This is the meaning of the H. word. C.'s 'dragons' derives from a confusion between this word and a similar one with the meaning 'serpent, sea-monster'. N.E.B. emends H. to obtain the meaning 'sea serpent'.

PSALM 45

Verse 3 *tread down your foes and triumph:* The H. words corresponding to this phrase are transferred from their place (in H.) at the beginning of the following verse. The sense *tread down* is achieved by a change of pointing and by omitting the H. conjunction 'and'. For the former of these changes there is support in the LXX. *your foes* is supplied in English *ad sensum.* H. unaltered seems to mean 'and your honour, prosper' (> C. (so R.P.) 'Good luck have thou with thine honour') for which it is difficult to find a coherent translation. N.E.B. emends the consonants of H. substantially and translates 'your limbs resplendent in royal armour'.

Verse 4 *for the sake of (justice):* H. is emended to give this sense. Unaltered H. appears to mean 'and meekness justice' which does not make sense. C.'s 'of meekness and righteousness' is dubious. R.P. emends H. differently to give 'to bear witness to righteousness'. N.E.B.'s '(to execute) just judgement' is dubious. The H. word translated 'righteousness' in C. and R.P. means here *justice.*

Verse 5 *in the hearts of the king's enemies:* a literal translation of H., cf. R.P. Contrast C.'s 'in the midst among the king's enemies'. N.E.B. emends the (consonantal) text.

Verse 6 *your throne is the throne of God:* H. may imply that the king's throne is like the throne of God (so R.P. and N.E.B.) or that the king is addressed by the title *Elohim.* This word usually means 'God' but may possibly be used here as an honorific title for the king. The present translation is designed to allow for both main possibilities.

Verse 8 *music:* perhaps (lit.) 'strings', cf. with R.P., Ps. 150: 4; cf. also N.E.B. C. mistakenly took the word to be a form of the preposition 'from' ('from which' > 'whereby').

Verse 9 *gold of Ophir:* So lit. H. C.'s 'vesture of gold wrought about with diverse colours' is dubious and indeed there is nothing to correspond with 'wrought about etc.' in H.

Verse 11 *your lord:* C. adds 'God' but this is not present in H.

Verse 14 *many colours:* the H. word means 'variegated stuff'. C.'s of 'needlework' is not strictly accurate, though it conveys the general sense.

PSALM 46

Verse 3 *at the rising of the sea:* H. lit. 'at his rising' (cf. C.'s 'at the tempest of the same'). *'sea'* is added in this translation *ad sensum;* it is mentioned in the previous verse.

Verse 6 *shall tremble:* The Arabic cognate suggests for this H. word here (as in some other places) the meaning 'tremble' (cf. N.E.B.'s 'surges') rather than 'melt'. C. (so R.P.) has 'melt away'.

PSALM 47

Verse 7 *well-wrought psalm:* The H. word represented by this English phrase denotes a particular type of psalm (the exact denotation is now lost to us), cf. R.P.'s 'song' and N.E.B.'s 'all your art'. The H. root appears to be similar if not identical to a well-known word which means 'to be prudent', 'have insight, understanding'. (> C.'s 'sing ye praises with understanding').

Verse 10 *For the mighty ones of the earth are become the servants of God:* H. (lit.) means 'For to God (belong) the mighty ones of the earth, he is highly exalted'.

mighty ones: the word is now recognised sometimes to mean 'rulers', 'mighty ones' and sometimes 'shield'; cf. R.P. and N.E.B. C.'s 'for God which is very high exalted, doth defend the earth, as it were with a shield' is, however, very dubious.

PSALM 48

Verse 2 *High and beautiful:* H. means lit. 'his holy hill is beautiful of height'. C.'s 'The hill of Zion is a fair place' is somewhat free.

Verse 3 *where godhead truly dwells:* The H. phrase means lit. 'the furthest parts of the North' (> C. cf. R.P. 'on the north-side lieth') which is a reference to the mythical home of the gods in the far north. The poet, equating mount Zion with this place, means that mount Zion is the true home of God (so here *where godhead truly dwells).*

Verse 4 *came on:* The H. word denotes 'to pass, move across, by or to'. Here it probably means that the kings advance on Jerusalem only to be rebuffed. C.'s (so R.P.) 'gone by' is misleading. N.E.B. has 'marching on'.

Verse 7 *that shatters:* Cf. N.E.B. The phrase is a suppressed relative in H., and the east wind is the subject of the verb rather than 'you' (i.e. God), cf. and contrast C.'s (so R.P.) 'thou shalt break'.

Verse 11 *victory:* The H. word, often rendered 'salvation' in English, here means 'salvation effected (for Zion)' so 'her victory' or 'God's victory for her'.

Verse 12 *pass through:* the meaning of this word is far from certainly known but 'pass through' is regarded as the most likely, cf. N.E.B. C.'s 'set up' is presumably conjectural.

Verse 13 *eternally:* Cf. R.P. and N.E.B. This reading, attested by many Mss., is preferable to the alternative which may mean 'upon (or) to death'.

PSALM 49

Verse 2 *children of men and sons of Adam:* This phrase is probably merely inclusive denoting 'everyman', cf. N.E.B.; it is unlikely that 'high and low' (so C. and R.P.), i.e. two types of men, are indicated.

Verse 5 *the wickedness of my deceivers surrounds me:* The pointing (but not the consonants) of H. is slightly changed (and on the authority of Origen) to give this sense, cf. R.P. and N.E.B. *my deceivers:* the word has this meaning as well as the more physical 'those at my heels' (so R.P. cf. C.).

Verses 8, 9 *For to ransom men's lives* etc.: (Verse 9) The words are parenthetical and consequently the words 'so that he may live for ever', etc. (verse 8) are, for ease of sense, placed after the words of verse 7 rather than after the words of verse 9 as in H. (so C.).

Verse 11 *The tomb is their home for ever:* With the authority of three of the ancient versions the order of two consonants is inverted to give this sense, cf. R.P. and N.E.B. H. unaltered means (lit.) 'In them their houses for ever' whence C.'s dubious 'they think that their houses shall continue for ever'.

Verse 12 *a rich man:* H. lit. 'a man with precious things/preciousness'. C. takes 'preciousness' as 'honour' which is less likely. R.P. and N.E.B. emend H. unnecessarily (> 'Man is like unto an ox').

without understanding: One letter of H. is emended with the authority of two of the ancient versions to give this sense, cf. verse 21. H. unaltered means 'will not lodge' (> C. 'will not abide in honour').

Verse 14 *They are driven:* The H. word means (lit.) 'they have been appointed (to Sheol)'.

death is their shepherd: Cf. R.P. and N.E.B. The H. word (translated here in accordance with the simile of the verse) 'is their shepherd' is capable of the sense 'to feed' (> C. 'death gnaweth upon them'), but this gives here a less likely sense.

they slip down easily into the tomb: Cf. R.P. The sense is achieved by restoring the text (a) by repointing the verb (> lit. 'they go down'); (b) by combining the consonants of two words in H. as received and by consequent repointing (> lit. 'with ease'); (c) by inverting the order of two consonants of a further word with consequent repointing (> 'to the tomb'). The verse is a very difficult one and there are a number of possible solutions. The restoration proposed here is effected with the minimum of textual alteration and gives a reasonable sense in the context.

Verse 19 *and praises you also when you prosper:* Such is the probable meaning of H. and it is achieved by adopting the reading of one H. Ms. The 'you' is anybody, or the person reading the psalm. R.P. and N.E.B. avoid the slightly difficult 'you' by emending the consonantal text.

PSALM 50

Verse 8 *for your burnt-offerings are always before me:* such is the meaning of H., cf. N.E.B. C. appears to assume that the force of the negative continues into this half of the verse from the former half; this is most unlikely.

Verse 10 *the cattle upon the mountains:* The H. phrase was taken to mean (lit.) 'the cattle upon the cattle-hills'. The second H. word translated 'cattle' can also mean 'thousand', hence C.'s and R.P. 's 'a thousand hills'. N.E.B. understands the word as 'thousand' but refers it to the 'cattle' rather than to the 'hills'. It is unlikely, however, that H. would use numerals in this way.

Verse 11 *grasshoppers:* Cf. N.E.B. 'teeming life'. C.'s 'wild beasts' is unsatisfactory in that it implies large animals, whereas the H. word denotes swarming insects.

Verse 14 a *sacrifice of thanksgiving:* The H. word can mean 'thanksgiving' or 'sacrifice of thanksgiving'. The latter meaning is intended here. Cf. C.'s 'to offer unto God thanksgiving'.

Verse 15 *I will bring you out:* The H. word means· 'to rescue' or 'bring out', cf. R.P. and N.E.B. C.'s 'I will hear thee' is dubious.

Verse 24 *sacrifice of thanksgiving:* See note on verse 14 above.

who keeps to my way: H. is amended to give this sense, cf. N.E.B. R.P.'s '(he) that ordereth (his) way (aright)' and C.'s '(that) ordereth his conversation right' are dubious.

PSALM 51

Verse 4 *in your judging:* The H. word means that God does the judging rather than that he is judged, cf. R.P. and N.E.B.; contrast C.'s 'when thou art judged'.

PSALM 52

Verse 1 *all day long: of mischief done to him that is faithful to God:*

a) *all day long:* In H. belongs to this clause rather than (as in C.) to a separate one.

b) *to him that is faithful to God:* On the authority of the Peshitta the preposition 'to' is restored, and on the same authority the pointing (but not the consonants) of one H. word is changed to give 'faithful', cf. R.P. and N.E.B. Unaltered the word means 'faithfulness' (> C. 'goodness').

Verse 4 *and every deceit of the tongue:* The H. phrase, lit. 'tongue of deceit', is more likely to be a second object to 'you love' than a vocative, cf. N.E.B. Contrast C. and R.P. 'O thou false (R.P. deceitful) tongue'.

Verse 7 *slander:* The H. word is a very difficult one, but it is thought sometimes, as here, to have the meaning 'spiteful abuse/slander', cf. N.E.B. 'wild lies'. Contrast C.'s 'wickedness' and R.P.'s 'wealth'; the latter is achieved by emendation.

Verse 9 *I will glorify:* The H. word is thought to be capable of bearing this meaning as well as 'hope in' (so C.), cf. N.E.B. R.P.'s 'I will declare' is less satisfactory as it requires textual emendation.

before the faithful: A literal translation of H. C.'s 'for thy saints like it well' is dubious.

to praise you: The words are added in English *ad sensum.* H. (lit.) 'for it is good'.

PSALM 53

Verse 5 *They shall be struck with terror:* H. as received adds 'there was not terror'. The words are deleted because they are absent in some H. Mss. (as well as in the corresponding place in Psalm xiv) and make no sense in the context (cf. R.P. and N.E.B.).

will scatter: So H. (lit.). C.'s 'hath broken' is dubious.

the ungodly: One letter of the H. word is emended on the authority of two of the ancient versions to give this sense, cf. R.P. and N.E.B. H. unaltered seems to mean 'of the one who encamps against thee' (> C. 'him that besieged thee').

Verse 6 *be put to confusion:* For two letters of the H. word, one is substituted on the authority of two of the ancient versions, cf. (but not identical) N.E.B. H., unaltered, seems to mean 'thou hast put them to confusion' (so C.).

Verse 7 *turn again the fortunes:* see on Ps. 14: 7.

PSALM 54

Verse 3 *insolent men:* One H. reading has 'strangers' (so C.). A number of H. Mss. however have the (very similar) word 'insolent men' which is here accepted as more probable, cf. Psalm 86: 14. R.P. and N.E.B. take the same view.

my life: see general note on *nephesh.*

Verse 5 recoil: An alternative pointing of the consonantal text (recorded by Jewish tradition) suggests this translation which is quite straight-forward, cf. N.E.B. As pointed, H. is made to mean (somewhat unnaturally) 'He *(sc.* God) will requite evil', cf. C. and R.P. This has the disadvantage that God is spoken of in the 3rd and 2nd person in the same verse.

Verse 7 *downfall:* the word is supplied in English *ad sensum,* cf. N.E.B. and C.'s similar 'his desire'.

PSALM 55

Verse 2 *I am restless in my complaining:* A fairly literal rendering of H., cf. N.E.B. C.'s 'I mourn (in my prayer)' is rather too free as a rendering of H. R.P.'s 'I am tormented' is achieved by unnecessary emendation.

Verse 3 *I am in turmoil:* In H. the word is included in the previous verse (cf. C.'s 'I am vexed'). In order to restore the line in H. the word is transferred to this verse.

Verse 4 *bring down:* The H. word is difficult and, on philological grounds, it is here given this meaning, cf. N.E.B.'s 'Heap (on me)' which reflects the same understanding of the word. Contrast C.'s (so R.P.) 'they are minded' for which there is no strong evidence.

Verse 9 *blast of slander:* Cf. N.E.B. The relevant H. word is thought to mean 'slander'. The phrase as a whole means 'from the wind of slander', cf. and contrast C.'s (and R.P.'s) 'stormy wind'.

Verse 10 *out of the tempest of their calumny:* The H. word corresponding to 'out of the tempest' is taken with this verse rather than with the previous verse as in H. (as received). Metre and sense are consequently improved.

their calumny: The H. word, pointing emended to give a noun rather than a verb (C. 'destroy'), is thought on philological grounds to have this meaning, cf. N.E.B.

Verse 10 *from their double tongues:* The pointing of one H. word is emended to give a noun rather than a verb (C. 'divide') and on philological grounds it is given the (related) meaning 'division, duplicity' (lit. 'the duplicity of their tongues' > *their double tongues).* The changes, which are made to the pointing rather than to the consonantal text, secure unity of thought for the psalmist's prayer.

Verse 14 *a man like myself:* H. (lit.) 'a man according to my valuation'.

Verse 16 *Let them pass away in confusion:* The meaning of H. (as received) is very uncertain. To the H. verb one letter is added and the pointing emended to give this well attested sense. The noun is attested in Post-Biblical H., with the meaning 'tumult', cf. N.E.B. The words correspond to 'walked as friends' of the previous verse in C. and R.P., but such a rendering is highly dubious. The words, on metrical grounds, are taken with the curse of vv.16 and 17.

carry them away to destruction: Such is thought to be the meaning of the H. verb. C.'s 'come hastily upon them' is derived ultimately from the LXX's rendering of an H. word similar in form and usually translated 'beguile' (> 'come deceitfully upon them' > 'come hastily upon them') which is dubious.

Verse 19 *and groan aloud:* A fairly literal rendering of H., cf. R.P. and N.E.B. C.'s 'and that instantly' is impossible.

Verse 20 *my soul:* i.e. me. See general note on *nephesh.*

Verse 21 *from those that bear down upon me:* H. is emended to give this meaning with the support of two of the ancient versions (LXX and Jer.). In addition one letter of the following H. word is deleted. Unaltered H. is almost entirely obscure. R.P. and N.E.B. emend in a similar way, but a further change to the pointing of one word is necessary to achieve the sense 'archers'. The present restoration has the advantage that it involves the least change to H.

Verse 22 *God will hear and bring them low:* R.P.'s (cf. N.E.B.) 'Ishmael and the tribes of the desert' represents an unnecessary change to the pointing, word division (and one consonant) of H. The panel have preferred to retain the traditional understanding of the word; cf. C.'s 'shall hear me and bring them down'. (The last three words, derived from the LXX, cf. Jerome, suggest a small change to the pointing of H.)

Verse 23 *they do not keep their word:* On philological grounds the H. phrase is thought to mean (lit.) 'they have no covenant/oath' (> *they do not keep their word),* cf. N.E.B. 'they have no respect for an oath'. The principal noun in the phrase (lit. 'oath') must be distinguished from another well-known word, very similar in form, having the meaning 'change', by which C.'s 'they will not turn' is presumably explained.

PSALM 56

Verses 1, 2 *tread* me *down:* A literal rendering of H., cf. R.P. C.'s 'to devour/ swallow me up' is dubious.

Verse 2 *arrogantly fight:* The H. noun is here taken adverbially in the attested sense 'proudly'. The noun elsewhere means 'height', hence C.'s dubious 'most Highest'. The emendations of the consonantal text adopted by R.P. and N.E.B. were regarded as unnecessary.

Verse 5 *they afflict me with their words:* It is assumed that one consonant in H. has been mistakenly written twice by a scribe. The consonant deleted, the sense is restored as above. Unaltered H. has 'my words' (cf. C.'s 'they daily mistake my words'). R.P.'s 'with their words they devise evil against me' involves further changes to H. and is therefore rejected.

Verse 6 *they stir up hatred:* C.'s 'they hold all together' is dubious and R.P.'s 'they gather themselves together' is achieved by unnecessary emendation.

Verse 7 *Let there be no escape:* The H. preposition which occurs erroneously at the beginning of this verse is transferred to its place before *life* in the previous verse. The pointing of another H. word is emended on the authority of four ancient versions to read 'no' rather than 'iniquity', cf. N.E.B. (> C. 'wickedness'). R.P. amends (another word) unnecessarily.

PSALM 57

Verse 1 *I (come).* See general note on *nephesh.*

Verse 4 trample me *down:* See note on Ps. 56, verses 1 and 2.

Verse 9 my *soul:* H. (lit.) 'my honour', or perhaps 'my liver'; what is denoted is the seat of honour in the inner man.

PSALM 58

Verse 1 *rulers:* The pointing of the H. word (but not the consonants) is emended to give this sense, cf. R.P. and N.E.B. C.'s 'congregation' is dubious, for the H. word (as pointed) seems to denote 'silence'.
children of men: are most naturally taken as the object of the verb rather than as a vocative, cf. R.P. and N.E.B. C. has 'O ye sons of men'.

Verse 2 *you look on:* Such, on philological grounds, is thought to be the meaning of the verb, cf. N.E.B. C.'s 'deal with' is dubious.

Verse 4 The order of the H. phrases has been changed in English in order to improve the flow, cf. N.E.B.

Verse 7 *let them be trodden down, let them wither like grass:* H. is emended to give this meaning. The emendation required for R.P. and N.E.B.'s translation is more far-reaching and therefore less attractive. Unaltered H. is virtually untranslatable and C.'s 'when they shoot their arrows let them be rooted out' is highly dubious.

Verse 8 *miscarriage:* Such, rather than 'snail' (so C.) is now thought to be the meaning of the H. word, cf. R.P. and N.E.B.

that has not seen: The H. word is emended by changing one letter. Unaltered it seems to imply a 3 m. pl. subject; cf. C.'s (unlikely) 'let them not see'.

Verse 9 *let them be cut down like:* By emendation one word of H. is made a verb 'let them be cut down' and the adverb 'like', cf. R.P. and N.E.B. C.'s 'or ever your pots be made hot with thorns' is highly dubious if indeed it is intelligible.

like brambles: This sense is achieved by emending one H. word. Unaltered the word seems to mean 'like a living (thing)'; (> C.'s 'as a thing that is raw').

angrily: H. lit. (after emending the initial letter) 'in anger' (unaltered 'like anger').

a man: Supplied in English *ad sensum.*

sweeps aside: The literal meaning of the H. verb, cf. R.P. and N.E.B. C.'s 'vex' is dubious. C.'s treatment of this (very difficult) verse is dubious ('let indignation vex him, as a thing that is raw').

Verse 11 *on earth:* So lit. H. (cf. R.P. and N.E.B.). C.'s 'judgeth the earth' is a mistranslation.

PSALM 59

Verses 3-5 The order of the phrases in English is not that of H. and has been adopted in the interests of clarity.

Verse 3 *my life:* See general note on *nephesh.*

stir up violence: Such is the meaning of the H. word rather than 'gathered' (so C. and R.P., the latter adopts a variant reading).

Verse 5 *Lord of hosts:* The H. word for 'God' is omitted as a dittograph (cf. C. 'Lord God of hosts').

Verse 7 *They return:* A literal rendering of the H. word. C.'s 'they go to and fro' is dubious as is R.P.'s (so presumably N.E.B.'s) understanding of the philology of the word.

Verse 8 *slaver:* The H. word means lit. 'bubble up'. It may denote reckless utterance (cf. N.E.B.), but R.P.'s 'they boast' is unlikely.

Verse 11 *My God:* The reading is found in a few H. Mss. and is supported by two of the ancient versions (LXX and Jer.), cf. R.P. and N.E.B.

came to meet me: A literal rendering of the H. word. C.'s 'sheweth me' is somewhat free.

Verse 12 *by your power:* So lit. H. C.'s 'among the people' is dubious.

stagger: A literal rendering of H.; C.'s 'scatter abroad' is dubious.

Verse 13 *Give them over to punishment for:*

a) Two words of verse 12 in H. are read with this verse for the sake of metre. (H.'s 'Lord' is reproduced in the English translation in the preceding verse).

b) The pointing of the verb is emended, and a 3rd pl. suffix is read rather than H.'s 1st pl. suffix.

c) The preposition 'for' (one H. letter) is added to *sin.* H. unaltered (with the words attached to verse 12) seems to mean 'O Lord, our defence' (so C., Verse 11). This translation adopts the same solution to the problem as does N.E.B.

Verse 20 *strong tower:* Two words 'my God' and 'my steadfastness' (> C. 'my merciful God') are added in H. (as received). They are likely to have been mistakenly copied from verse 11 and are consequently here deleted. They are absent in many H. Mss.

PSALM 60

Verse 3 *steeped:* There are two H. homonyms, the one meaning 'to (cause to) see'; the other 'to (cause to) be saturated with'. The latter verb is intended here, cf. R.P. and N.E.B. and contrast C.'s 'thou hast shewed'.

bitter draught: H. lit. 'something hard', cf. R.P. and N.E.B. and contrast C.'s 'heavy things'.

to make them stagger: A literal rendering of the H. expression. C.'s 'deadly' is wrong.

Verse 4 *to take flight:* The H. noun is derived from a verb 'to flee' rather than equated with the word denoting 'standard, ensign, sign' (> C. 'token'), cf. R.P.

so that they run from the bow: H. lit. 'to flee away from before the bow'. C.'s 'that they may triumph because of the truth' is dubious. The meaning 'bow' presupposes that the H. word is spelt in an unusual way.

PSALM 61

Verse 5 *my vows:* A literal translation of H., cf. R.P. and N.E.B. C.'s 'my desires' is wrong.

the desire: The H. word is taken to be from a root 'to desire' and not from a root 'to possess, inherit', cf. R.P. and N.E.B. and contrast C.'s 'heritage'.

Verse 7 *shall be his guard:* One H. word is omitted on the grounds that it makes no sense in the context. It is omitted by two H. Mss. (cf. Aq., Symm. and Jer.). If it is retained it would appear to be an imperative, 'appoint, ordain' (> C. 'O prepare').

PSALM 62

Verse 3 *to destroy him:* A variant reading is adopted to allow the active sense rather than the passive, 'you will be destroyed' (C. > 'ye shall be slain'). The variant is a variant of the pointing and not of the consonants.

a *buckling wall:* The word division of H. is slightly changed to give a more plausible H. text. The meaning is not affected. C.'s 'broken hedge' is perhaps misleading.

Verse 4 *from his height:* A literal rendering of H. C.'s 'whom God will exalt' is dubious.

Verse 9 *they fly upward:* A literal rendering of H., cf. N.E.B. C. has 'they are deceitful upon the weights' which is misleading.

Verse 12 *That to the Lord belongs a constant goodness:* H. lit., 'to thee, O Lord, belongs constant goodness', cf. C.'s 'that thou, Lord, art merciful'.

PSALM 63

Verse 1 *eagerly:* Such is the meaning of the H. word. Contrast C.'s 'early'.

Verse 6 *longing:* See general note on *nepesh.*

Verse 10 *marked for destruction:* H. lit., 'they are for destruction'. Contrast C. and R.P. which appear to take the phrase 'destruction' with 'my life' which is less satisfactory.

PSALM 64

Verse 1 *complaining:* Cf. N.E.B. Such is the meaning of the H. word rather than 'prayer' (So C. and R.P.).

Verse 3 *string the bow:* See on Ps. 37: 14. The word *bow* here is omitted in H. by ellipsis.

Verse 4 *and unseen:* Cf. R.P. and N.E.B. A very small emendation (with consequent change of pointing) is made on the authority of one of the ancient versions (the Peshitta) and yields this sense. H., unaltered, means 'and they fear not' (so C., which is less satisfactory).

Verse 8 *The Lord will bring them down for what their tongues have spoken:* H. is emended to give the literal meaning 'the Lord will cause them to stumble for their tongue', cf. R.P. H., unemended, seems to suggest that the tongue is the subject of the verb which is less likely. C.'s 'their own tongues make them fall' is not possible without emendation (cf. N.E.B., which does emend in this way).

Verse 9 *shall fear:* So one H. reading, R.P. and N.E.B. A number of Mss. (supported by one of the minor ancient Greek versions) have the variant reading 'shall see' (C. >'that see it').

PSALM 65

Verse 2 *To you shall all flesh come to confess their sins:* Two words from the following verse in H. are taken with this verse and the pointing (but not the consonants) of the H. verb is emended to give the literal sense 'to you all flesh shall bring words of sins', cf. R.P. and N.E.B. H., as pointed, has 'to you all flesh shall come. (next verse) words of sins'. C. has 'unto thee shall all flesh come' (verse ends).

against us: A variant reading is adopted (with the support of the LXX) to give this sense. The other reading is 'against me'.

Verse 3 *we shall be filled:* A literal rendering of H., cf. R.P. and N.E.B. C.'s 'he shall be satisfied' is dubious. .

Verse 10 *you level the ridges between:* A literal rendering of H., cf. R.P. and N.E.B. C.'s 'sendest rain into the little valleys thereof' is dubious.

Verse 11 *the tracks where you have passed drip with fatness:* A difficult H. phrase which seems to mean lit. 'thy tracks drip with fatness', cf. R.P. 'thy paths overflow with plenty'. N.E.B.'s 'the palm trees drip with sweet juice' is dubious.

Verse 12 *the pastures of the wilderness:* A literal rendering of H., cf. R.P. and N.E.B. C.'s 'dwellings of the wilderness' (though possible) is less satisfactory in the context.

run over: the 'pastures' are the subject and not the object of this verb, cf. R.P. and N.E.B. and contrast C.

Verse 13 *meadows:* So H., cf. N.E.B. C.'s 'folds' is not accurate and R.P.'s 'mountains' is achieved by emendation.

are clothed: A literal rendering of H. C. 's 'shall be full' is less striking.

PSALM 66

Verse 2 *cower:* Cf. R.P. and N.E.B. and contrast C.'s 'be found liars'. See note on Ps. 18: 46.

Verse 6 *rebels:* A literal rendering of H. C. 's 'such as will not believe' is wrong.

Verse 11 *place of liberty:* H. is emended by one letter on the authority of a number of the ancient versions to give this sense. Unaltered H. seems to mean 'to saturation'.

PSALM 68

Verse 2 *is dispersed,* so *shall they be dispersed:* The pointing (but not the consonants) of the two H. verbal forms is emended to give a passive rather than active sense, cf. R.P. and N.E.B.

Verse 4 *through the deserts:* A literal rendering of H. C.'s 'upon the heavens', (cf. also R.P.) is dubious. C.'s 'as it were upon an horse' is not to be found in H.

Verse 6 *the desolate a home to dwell in:* A fairly literal rendering of H., cf. R.P. and N.E.B. C.'s 'maketh men to be of one mind in an house' is impossible.

Verse 9 *you showered down:* The H. word is, on philological grounds, given this meaning, cf. N.E.B. C. has 'sentest' which is not accurate.

the land of your possession: H. 'your possession'. *'land'* is supplied in English because it is implied in H.

Verse 10 *there your people settled:* H. (lit.) 'your living (people) settled there'. The word may also denote 'troop, band' (> C. 'thy congregation').

Verses 11-13 The next few verses are amongst the most difficult in the Hebrew bible. An attempt has been made to make sense of H. without changing the received text; considerable progress in understanding the verses is achieved by recognising in them reported speech.

Verse 11 *are fleeing, are fleeing away:* The same H. verb is repeated, cf. C.'s 'did flee and were discomforted'.

Verse 12 *women at home:* H. has (lit.) 'she that is abiding at home', cf. C.'s 'they of the household'.

idly: The word is supplied in English ad *sensum.* H. has 'will you sit'.

among the sheepfolds: The probable meaning of the word, cf. R.P. and N.E.B. C.'s 'pots' is very dubious.

Verse 13 The words of this verse are taken to be descriptive of the spoil, cf. N.E.B. C. and R.P. introduce words which are not in H. C. has 'ye shall be as the wings of a dove'; R.P. 'Israel is like a dove'.

Verse 15 *The mountain of Bashan is a mighty mountain:* A fairly literal rendering of H., cf. R.P. The H. expression 'mountain of God' is here an intensive one and does not mean that the mountain is God's. C.'s 'as the hill of Basan, so is God's hill' is dubious.

Verses 15, 16 *of many peaks:* The most likely meaning for the H. word cf. N.E.B. C.'s 'high hill' and R.P. 's 'exceeding high mountain' are somewhat free.

Verse 16 *why look so enviously:* A literal translation of H., cf. R.P. and N.E.B. C.'s 'why hop ye so' is dubious.

Verse 17 *thousands upon thousands:* H. lit. 'a repetition of thousands'. C.'s 'thousands of angels' is dubious.

the Lord came from Sinai into his holy place: The division of consonants into words is changed (with consequent restoration of one letter and change to the pointing) and gives this meaning, cf. R.P. and N.E.B. H. unaltered is unintelligible. C. has 'the Lord is among them, as in the holy place of Sinai' which is dubious.

Verse 18 *you led the enemy captive:* H. lit., 'you led captive captivity' i.e. (abstract for concrete) 'captive enemies', cf. R.P. and N.E.B.

rebels: See on Ps. 66: 6. (C. here 'enemies'.)

shall not dwell in the presence of God: H. is emended on the authority of one of the ancient versions (the Peshitta) to give this sense, cf. N.E.B. C.'s (cf. R.P.) 'that the Lord God might dwell among them' is possible as a translation of H., apart from 'among them'.

Verse 19 *bears us as his burden:* A literal rendering of H., cf. R.P. and N.E.B. C.'s 'who helpeth us' is dubious.

God of our deliverance: A literal rendering of H., cf. R.P. and N.E.B. C.'s 'poureth his benefits upon us' is dubious.

Verse 23 *you may dip:* H. is emended by the change of one consonant on the authority of three of the ancient versions to give this meaning; unaltered it means 'you may smite', cf. R.P. C.'s translation is correct though it follows the tradition of the Vulgate and LXX rather than the H.

in the blood of your enemies: H. is emended to give this sense; it is unintelligible otherwise.

Verse 26 *in their choirs:* The H. word is etymologically connected with a more familiar word for 'assembly' (> C. 'in the congregations'), but it is thought here to denote 'choirs'.

those that are sprung from the fount of Israel: H. lit. '(they bless) the Lord (who are) from the fount of Israel.' C.'s 'from the ground of the heart' is highly dubious and R.P.'s 'even the Fountain of Israel *(sc.* God)' is achieved by emendation.

Verse 27 *leading them:* A literal rendering of H., cf. R.P. and N.E.B. C.'s 'their ruler' (though possible) is less satisfactory.

the throng: The H. word is, on philological grounds, given this meaning, cf. R.P. (> 'follow after') and N.E.B. (> 'the company of Judah's princes').

Verse 28 *Give the command:* The pointing (but not the consonants) of H. is emended on the authority of many H. Mss. and the versions to give this imperative meaning, cf. R.P. and N.E.B. *my God, in accordance with your power:* The division of consonants into words in H. is emended to give this sense (with consequent change to the pointing), cf. N.E.B.

Verse 28 *the godlike power whereby you act for us:* The division of consonants into words in H. is emended to give this sense (with consequent change to the pointing). H. as emended then means literally 'the strength of God whereby you act for us', cf. N.E.B.

Verse 29 *Give the command:* The force of the imperative is understood to carry over from the previous verse.

from your temple: A literal rendering of H.; contrast C.'s (cf. also R.P. and N.E.B.) 'for thy temple's sake at Jerusalem'.

Verse 30 *Rebuke the beast of the reeds:* A fairly literal rendering of H., cf. R.P. and N.E.B. C.'s 'when the company of the spearmen' is dubious. (The nations - God's enemies - are pictured as wild animals.)

the herd of bulls amidst the brutish people: H. lit., 'the herd of the bulls amongst the calves of peoples' (> *brutish people.),* cf. C.'s dubious 'multitude of the mighty are scattered abroad among the beasts of the people.'

tread down those that are greedy for silver: The pointing (but not the consonants) of one H. word is emended on the authority of one of the minor Greek versions (Symm.) to give a literal 'treading down those who desire silver'. H., unaltered, is virtually unintelligible. C. has 'so that they humbly bring pieces of silver', which is dubious.

scatter: The pointing of the H. verb (but not the consonants) is emended to give this imperative force. It is done with the support of two of the ancient versions (LXX and Jer.).

Verse 31 *Let them bring:* The pointing (but not the consonants) of H. is emended on the authority of two of the ancient versions (LXX and Jerome) to give this causative force. H. unaltered has 'let them come' (> C. 'then shall come ...').

bronze: The meaning of the H. word is not certainly known, but on philological grounds *bronze* is thought to be the most likely. C. has 'princes'; R.P. and N.E.B. have 'tribute'.

Verse 35 *who comes from his holy place:* H. means lit. 'terrible is God from thy holy place'. The sudden change of person, while possible in H., is difficult in English and so 'his' is adopted in translation. C.'s 'in thy holy places' is dubious, for the H. preposition does not mean 'in' and the plural form of the noun is a plural of local extension.

PSALM 69

Verse 1 *even my throat:* See general note on *nephesh.*

Verse 4 The verse division follows H. closely (cf. N.E.B.); C. and R.P. differ from H.

Verse 10 *I afflicted myself:* The variant reading of one of the Dead Sea Scroll fragments gives this meaning, cf. N.E.B. H. as received means 'I wept' (so C. and R.P. who have to add 'and chastened myself' *ad sensum*).

Verse 11 *a byword:* A fairly literal translation of H. C.'s 'they jested upon me' is dubious.

Verse 20 *all their taunts:* H. lit. 'my reproach', > *their taunts,* cf. N.E.B. 'what reproaches I bear'. Two words of H. are transferred to the following verse.

Verse 21 *my shame and disgrace are past healing:*

my shame and disgrace are moved to this verse from verse 20, and the H. conjunction 'and' is deleted from *my shame,* cf. N.E.B.

are past healing: The pointing of H. (but not the consonants) is emended to give this meaning, cf. N.E.B. H. unaltered is obscure. (C. 'I am full of heaviness').

Verse 24 *sacrificial feasts:* One letter of the H. word is deleted (and the pointing consequently emended) to give this sense, and this on the authority of one of the ancient versions (Targum), cf. R.P. and N.E.B. H. unaltered seems to mean 'and for security' (> C. 'the things that should have been for their wealth').

Verse 25 *and make their loins shake continually:* A fairly literal rendering of H., cf. R.P. and N.E.B. C.'s 'and ever bow down their backs' is dubious.

Verse 28 *and multiply:* The H. word is emended to give this sense on the authority of two of the ancient versions (LXX and Peshitta), cf. R.P. and N.E.B. H. unaltered has 'they recount' (> C. 'they talk').

of him whom you have wounded: A variant H. reading is adopted here to give the singular meaning *of him* etc., cf. N.E.B. (footnote). The other reading is plural.

Verse 29 *let them not receive your forgiveness:* H. lit. 'let them not come into thy righteousness' (cf. C.).

Verse 34 *consider this:* The pointing (but not the consonants) of H. is emended to permit this imperative sense. H. unaltered has (lit.) 'they see' (> C. 'shall consider this'), cf. R.P. and N.E.B.

Verse 34 *and rejoice:* The H. word is emended to allow this imperative meaning. H. unaltered seems to mean 'let them rejoice', cf. R.P. and N.E.B.

seek God: One letter of the H. verb is emended (and the pointing consequently changed) on the authority of the LXX to give this imperative sense.

let your heart be glad: H. lit. 'let your heart live'; C. 'and your soul shall live'; R.P. 'let your heart revive'; N.E.B. 'take heart'.

PSALM 70

Verse 2 *who seek my life:* See general note on *nephesh.*

Verse 3 *turn away for shame:* A fairly literal rendering of H. C.'s 'let them for their reward be soon brought to shame' is dubious.

PSALM 71

Verse 3 *of refuge:* A variant H. reading is adopted to give this sense and it is supported by some of the ancient versions, cf. Psalm 31: 3. The other reading means 'rock of dwelling' which is less satisfactory, cf. R.P.

a fortress to defend me: H. is emended to give this sense by comparison with Ps. 31: 3, cf. R.P. Unaltered H. is hardly intelligible (? lit. 'to come continually thou hast ordained' > C. 'whereunto I may always resort: thou hast promised'). N.E.B.'s 'where 1 may ever find safety at thy call' attempts to render H. as received but is somewhat dubious.

Verse 6 *I leaned:* A literal rendering of H., cf. N.E.B. and contrast C.'s 'I have been holden up'. (So R.P.)

Verse 13 *and put to shame:* A variant H. reading is adopted to give this sense, and it is supported by one of the ancient versions (Peshitta), cf. Psalm 35: 4. The other reading seems to mean 'waste away' (> C. 'perish') which is less satisfactory in the context.

Verse 16 *I will begin:* The H. word which usually means 'to go/come' (> C. 'I will go forth') is thought to have here this particular meaning which nicely fits the context, cf. R.P. and N.E.B.

Verse 21 *Bless me beyond my former greatness:* H. lit. 'Do thou increase my greatness' is expanded in English *ad sensum.* C.'s 'thou hast brought me to great honour' is less satisfactory.

PSALM 72

Verse 3 *be laden with:* H. lit. 'lift up, carry' (> *be laden with),* cf. C.'s 'bring'.

Verse 5 *May he live:* H. is emended on the authority of the LXX to mean (lit.) 'Let him prolong (his days)', cf. R.P. and N.E.B. Unaltered H. has 'they shall fear thee' (so C.).

gives light: is added in English *ad sensum.* H. lit. 'and like the moon'.

Verse 6 *upon the new-mown fields:* The meaning of the H. word is not certain, but the root is connected with the notion of 'cutting'; C. 'into a fleece of wool'; R.P. 'upon grass before it is cut' ('before' is here dubious); N.E.B. 'early crops'.

that water: One consonant of H. is emended (with consequent change to the pointing) to give this sense, cf. R.P. and N.E.B. H. unaltered is unintelligible. C. has 'that water' but the (probably correct) translation is derived from the Vulgate rather than from H.

Verse 9 *his adversaries:* One H. word is emended to give this meaning which restores parallelism and an intelligible translation. H. unaltered may mean 'desert dweller', cf. C. 'they that dwell in the wilderness'. N.E.B.'s 'Ethiopians' is dubious.

Verse 10 *Sheba:* A close transliteration of the H. name, cf. R.P. and N.E.B. C. has 'Arabia'. Cf. Verse 15.

Verse 15 *Sheba:* As in Verse 10 above.

for him: i.e. the king, the subject of the psalm, cf. R.P. and N.E.B. C. understands the preposition to mean 'unto him' which is less likely.

Verse 16 *abundance:* The meaning of the H. word is not certainly known and the translation is based on the context, cf. R.P. and N.E.B. C. 'heap'.

let it flourish: The H. word is, on philological grounds, thought to have this meaning, cf. R.P. and N.E.B. C. has 'high' (upon the hills).

Verse 17 *Let its ears grow fat like the grain of Lebanon:* The H. verb is emended by the omission of two letters to allow it to be predicated of 'its ears' (< lit. 'its fruit'). H., then, means lit. 'Let its fruit flourish like Lebanon', cf. R.P. and N.E.B. C.'s '(his fruit) shall shake' is dubious. *its sheaves thicken:* The H. noun is emended to give the sense *its sheaves,* cf. R.P. and N.E.B. The verb 'thicken' is supplied in English ad *sensum.* H. unaltered has 'from a city' which in the context is hardly capable of translation. (> C. 'shall be green in the city like grass').

Verse 18 *endure as long as the sun:* The probable meaning of H., cf. R.P. and N.E.B. C.'s 'remain under the sun among the posterities' is dubious.

PSALM 73

Verse 6 *put on ... as a necklace:* A fairly literal translation of H., cf. R.P. and N.E.B. C.'s 'they are so holden with' is dubious.

clothe themselves ... as in a garment: A fairly lit. rendering of H., cf. R.P. and N.E.B. C.'s '(are) overwhelmed with' is dubious.

Verse 8 *slanders:* The H. word is given this meaning here as in a number of places in the O.T., cf. N.E.B. C.'s 'blasphemy' is impossible.

from on high: A literal rendering of H., cf. N.E.B.'s freer 'scornfully' and R.P.'s even freer 'they have proud looks'. C.'s 'against the most High' is dubious.

Verse 10 *my people turn to them:*

a) *my people:* H. 'his people' is emended on the authority of three of the ancient versions.

b) *turn:* An ancient Jewish tradition understood H.'s 'he shall restore' as '(my people) *turn*' and the ancient versions support this tradition.

c) *to them:* H. is emended to give this sense. H. unaltered means 'hither'.

The three changes are adopted by R.P. and N.E.B. C., because it substantially follows the Latin tradition (and LXX), is substantially the same 'therefore fall the people unto them'.

and find in them no fault: H. is corrected to give this sense, cf. R.P. and N.E.B. H. unaltered seems to mean 'and the waters of fulness will be drained out for them', which makes little sense. A number of the ancient versions support the emendation of the verb.

Verse 15 *thus:* The pointing (but not the consonants) of one H. word is emended to give this sense, cf. N.E.B. H. as pointed means 'behold' (C. 'lo'). R.P. 'even as they' requires emendation of the consonants of H.

Verse 18 *from their treacherous footholds:* The H. preposition is given here the meaning 'from'. *treacherous footholds* < H. (lit.) 'deceptions'. C.'s 'come to a fearful end' is dubious.

Verse 20 *when you rouse yourself:* The H. word is here understood to have this meaning, cf. N.E.B. 'on waking'. (R.P.'s emendation of the last word is not accepted here, as reasonable sense is achieved without it).

Verse 24 *lead me:* The H. verb is capable of this meaning (cf. R.P.) as well as 'receive' (so C. and N.E.B.).

Verse 26 *O God:* H., as received, has additionally the words 'strength of my heart' which are here omitted as a dittograph. C. and R.P. took 'God' to be a subject (rather than a vocative) and 'strength of my heart' as a predicate: 'God is the strength of my heart'.

Verse 28 C. adds 'in the gates of the daughter of Zion' to this verse. The words are not present in H., and are derived from the LXX and Vulgate.

PSALM 74

Verse 3 *Rouse yourself and go:* The H. expression means lit. 'pick up your steps (i.e. bestir yourself) and go', cf. C. 'Lift up thy feet' and R.P.'s (rather dubious) 'draw near and behold'. N.E.B.'s emendation is unnecessary.

utter ruins: The pointing of this H. noun (but not the consonants) is changed. C.'s 'that thou mayest utterly destroy' is dubious.

Verse 4 *their standards in triumph:* H., as received, has 'their standards as standards' (C. > 'their banners as tokens'). The repetition of the word 'standard' is here regarded as a dittograph and the word is consequently deleted. *in triumph* is added in English *ad sensum.*

Verse 5 *they have destroyed:* The H. verb is emended on the basis of comparison with verse 3. R.P. and N.E.B. also emend the word but in a different way. H., as received, appears to have a form of the verb 'to know' which is unintelligible in the context. C.'s 'was known to bring it to an excellent work' is highly dubious.

Verse 6 *they have broken down:* The meaning of what is assumed to be a verb in H. is not certainly known and the translation is based on the context, cf. C. ('they break down') and R.P.

Verse 11 *do you keep:* The H. verb is a form of that meaning 'to enclose, keep' and not of that meaning 'to destroy', cf. R.P. and N.E.B. (no consonantal emendation is necessary). Contrast C. which has 'to consume'.

in your bosom: A small correction to H. is made on the authority of one of the ancient versions (Jerome). An alternative reading is also adopted (and it is supported by the ancient versions). H. unaltered has 'from (thy bosom)', cf. C., who has to introduce a negative *ad sensum:* 'why pluckest thou not thy right hand out of thy bosom'.

Verse 14 *creatures of the waste:* H. is emended by the omission of an intrusive preposition to give this sense. C.'s 'gave him as food to the people in the wilderness' is dubious. R.P.'s (cf. N.E.B.) 'the creatures of the deep' is another solution which was considered but thought wrong on the grounds that a word is invented for which there is no evidence.

Verse 19 *wild beasts:* The pointing (but not the consonants) of the H. word is emended on the authority of three of the ancient versions (LXX, Jerome and Targum), to give this sense, cf. R.P. and N.E.B. H. unaltered has 'life'. C.'s 'multitude of the enemies' is dubious.

that praises you: A variant reading is adopted to give this sense, with the support of two of the ancient versions (LXX and Peshitta), cf. R.P. and N.E.B. C.'s 'of thy turtle dove' follows the other H. reading.

life of your afflicted: A literal rendering of H., cf. R.P. and N.E.B. C.'s 'congregation of the poor' is dubious.

Verse 20 *all that you have made:* The H. noun is emended to give this sense (lit. 'thy creations'), cf. R.P. and N.E.B. H. unaltered has 'thy covenant because' (cf. C. 'the covenant: for').

darkness: The H. word is emended slightly so that it is taken with *all that you have made* rather than with 'the earth' as in H., cf. C.

violence inhabits the earth: One word of H. is emended by the omission of one letter (and consequent repointing) to give lit. 'and (the) land (is) a habitation of violence', cf. N.E.B. C. has 'the earth is full of darkness and cruel habitations', which, though it follows H. as received, does not make so balanced a line.

Verse 23 *ascends:* The H. word is capable of meaning 'go up' or 'increase' (so C. and R.P.). The former meaning was judged more appropriate here. N.E.B., though rather free, nicely renders 'the mounting clamour'.

PSALM 75

Verse 1 *we call upon your name:* The H. verb is emended on the authority of two of the ancient versions (LXX and Peshitta) to give lit. '(with) a calling upon your name' > *we call upon your name.* Unaltered H. has 'and thy name is near' (cf. C. 'thy name also is so nigh', and N.E.B.), which is less likely. R.P.'s similar emendation is less satisfactory because it makes a more substantial change to H.: 'they that call upon thy name'.

and tell of all the wonders: The H. verb is emended (with some support from the versions cited) in a similar way to 'call upon' above, to give a lit.: 'and (with) a telling of all thy wondrous works' > *and tell of all the wonders you have done.* H. unaltered has 'they tell' > C. 'and that thy wondrous works declare'.

Verse 2 *appoint* a *time:* So H. lit., cf. R.P. and N.E.B. C.'s 'when I receive the congregation' is dubious.

Verse 3 *have founded:* The word is thought to bear this meaning, cf. R.P. and N.E.B. C.'s 'bear up' is dubious.

Verse 6 *who can raise up:* The H. word is identified as a verb (cf. N.E.B.) rather than as a verbal noun 'promotion' (so C.).

from the wilderness: A variant reading is adopted to give this sense, cf. N.E.B. R.P.'s 'from the wilderness nor yet from the mountains' is achieved by emendation, which is unnecessary.

Verse 8 *foams:* The meaning of the H. word is uncertain and the translation represents a plausible guess, cf. R.P. and N.E.B. C. has 'red'.

Verse 9 *in turn to each:* H. is emended by the addition of 'to this one' in the resulting phrase, (lit.) 'he pours out from this one to this one' > *he gives it in turn to each,* cf. N.E.B. The change has, perhaps, some support from two of the ancient versions (LXX and Peshitta). C. and R.P. have the somewhat dubious 'He poureth out of the same' < 'from this *(sc.* cup)'.

PSALM 76

Verse 3 *weapons of battle:* The H. word usually translated 'battle, war' probably has here the concrete sense *weapons of battle,* cf. R.P. and N.E.B. C. has 'the battle'.

Verse 4 *Radiant in light:* H. means lit. 'thou art illuminated' > *radiant in light are you.* N.E.B. and R.P. emend H. on the authority of one of the minor Greek versions (Theod.) which is unnecessary.

the eternal hills: H. is emended on the authority of one of the ancient versions (LXX), cf. R.P. It is assumed that H.'s (unaltered) 'prey' (> C. 'the robbers') arose because a scribe mistook the H. word meaning 'eternal' for a homonym meaning 'prey' and then substituted a more common word for 'prey' to strengthen his interpretation.

Verse 5 *valiant:* Such is the meaning of the H. expression (cf. R.P. and N.E.B.) rather than C.'s 'proud'.

were dumbfounded: The H. verb is thought, on philological grounds, to have this meaning, cf. N.E.B. C.'s 'were robbed' (cf. R.P.'s 'were made spoil') is less likely.

have lost their strength: The H. word often translated 'hand' has also the meaning 'force, strength'. The phrase then means lit. 'the men of war have not found their strength'. R.P.'s translation is in agreement with this understanding of the phrase. N.E.B. is freer. C.'s 'all the men whose hands were mighty have found nothing' is dubious.

Verse 6 *blast of your voice:* See on Ps. 106: 10.

Verse 10 *you crushed:* The pointing of H. (but not the consonants) is emended to give this sense. Unaltered it seems to mean 'the wrath of man shall praise you', cf. C. 'the fierceness of man shall turn to thy praise'.

you bridled: The H. word is thought, on philological grounds, to have this meaning and C.'s 'shalt thou refrain' is not too far removed from it. R.P.'s 'shall keep feast' is achieved by emendation. R.P.'s and N.E.B.'s references to Edom and Hamath (achieved by emendation of the pointing) are dubious for they scarcely fit the context.

PSALM 77

Verse 2 *I stretch out my hands:* By comparison with Ps. 143: 6, H. is emended by the addition of the H. word for 'I spread out', cf. R.P. (though there is no notice of emendation) and N.E.B.

my hands: the pointing (but not the consonants) of the H. word is emended. C.'s 'my sore ran' is dubious.

Verse 4 *eyelids:* This understanding of the H. phrase is that of the Targum, cf. N.E.B. C. has 'thou holdest mine eyes waking' which is less likely.

Verse 4 *I cannot flee:* The pointing (but not the consonants) of H. is emended to give a form of a verb which, on philological grounds, can bear this meaning. H. unaltered means 'I cannot speak' which is not likely in the context (for what then is the psalmist doing in the psalm?) although it is the translation adopted by C., R.P. and N.E.B.

Verse 5 *I remember:* The H. verb is taken with this verse, rather than with the verse that follows (so H.), on the authority of at least two of the ancient versions (Symm., Peshitta) cf. R.P. and N.E.B.

Verse 6 *I am grieved:* H. is emended to give a verb which, on philological grounds, is held to have this meaning. Unaltered H. has 'my song'. C., taking the verb with this verse (see on the verse above), renders 'I call to remembrance my song' which is less satisfactory, though it keeps more closely to H. as received.

my spirit makes search: A literal rendering of H. R.P. emends on the authority of some of the ancient versions to give '(I) search out my spirit'. C., too, translates in this way, following the Vulgate (and LXX) rather than H. N.E.B., on philological grounds, takes a different view of the meaning of the verb: 'my spirit was sunk (in despair)'.

Verse 10 *lost its strength:* H. is emended by the omission of two vowel letters (with subsequent change of pointing) to give the lit. sense 'become weak, sick', cf. R.P. and N.E.B. H. unaltered has 'I have pierced'. C. appears to confuse H. (unaltered) with the verb 'to be weak, sick' (> 'It is mine own infirmity') but this is not what H. (unaltered) has and his particular translation is hardly satisfactory.

changed: H. is emended by the omission of one vowel letter (with subsequent change of pointing) to give this sense, cf. R.P. and N.E.B. H. unaltered has 'years of', cf. C.'s 'I will remember the years of the right hand' where 'I will remember' has to be supplied.

Verse 18 *in the whirlwind:* A literal translation of H., cf. R.P. and N.E.B. C.'s 'round about' is a mistranslation.

PSALM 78

Verse 9 *armed with:* H. adds 'shooting' which is here deleted as an explanatory gloss, cf. R.P. C.'s 'carrying' is a dubious translation of the word.

Verse 25 *south east:* According to H. poetic idiom the two cardinal points are mentioned in parallelism in each part of the verse. In translation the two points are brought together. C. dubiously mentions both the 'East' and the 'South-West' winds.

Verse 40 *Again and again:* Such is the meaning of H., cf. R.P. and N.E.B. C.'s 'they turned back' is less satisfactory.

Verse 41 *power:* The H. word usually translated 'hand' (so C.) often, as here, means 'power', cf. R.P. and N.E.B.

Verse 50 *the first fruits of their manhood:* A literal rendering of H., cf. R.P. and N.E.B. C.'s 'the principal and mightiest' is dubious.

Verse 56 *slack as an unstrung bow:* Such is the meaning of the H. phrase, cf. R.P. and N.E.B. C.'s 'starting aside like a broken bow' is dubious.

Verse 59 *the ark of his might:* The H. expression 'his might' is probably elliptical for 'the ark of his might', cf. N.E.B. and Psalm 132: 7. C. has 'their power'.

Verse 61 *to bewail:* Cf. N.E.B. H. lit. 'his maidens were not lamented'. C. and R.P. assume that the H. verb is a form of 'to praise' (in a marriage feast) > C: 'their maidens were not given to marriage'. R.P. 'for their maidens no marriage songs were heard'.

Verse 62 *there was none to mourn for:* The pointing (but not the consonants) of the H. verb is changed to give this meaning. H. as received means 'his widows did not weep' and this sense is followed by C., R.P. and N.E.B., though it is less satisfactory.

Verse 63 *overcome with:* A literal rendering of H., cf. R.P. and N.E.B. C.'s 'refreshed with' is dubious.

Verse 69 *the ewes:* C. adds 'great with young ones' which mistranslates H. The H. word means 'ewes giving suck'.

Verse 70 *and guided them with skilful hand:* Such is the meaning of H., cf. R.P. and N.E.B. C.'s 'ruled them prudently with all his power' is dubious.

PSALM 80

Verse 6 *the victim:* The H. word 'strife, contention' here means 'the object of contention' > (here) *victim.* C. has 'very strife'. R.P.'s 'derision' is achieved by (unnecessary) emendation.

(laugh) us: A variant reading is adopted and it is supported by three of the ancient versions (LXX, Jer., Pesh.). The other reading has 'them'. C.'s 'us' is derived from the Vulgate (and LXX) rather than from H.

Verse 13 *locusts from the wild places:*

a) *locusts:* The H. word is thought to have this meaning, cf. N.E.B. C.'s (and R.P.'s) 'wild beasts' is dubious.

b) *from the wild places:* The H. word traditionally translated 'field' means 'open, wild country'.

Verse 15 *bestow your care upon this vine:* These words are taken with this verse rather than with the preceding one (as in H., cf. C.).

planted: H. adds 'upon the son of man thou hast made strong for thyself' which is here deleted as a variant of verse 17b, cf. R.P. and N.E.B.

Verse 16 *those that burn it and cut it down:* The two H. verbs are slightly emended to give this sense, cf. R.P. and N.E.B. H. unaltered has passive participles (cf. C.'s 'It is burnt ... and cut down') which fits the context less satisfactorily.

Verse 17 *power:* See on Ps. lxxviii: 41 above.

PSALM 81

Verse 6 *I heard a voice that I had not known:* A fairly literal translation of H. R.P. and N.E.B. omit the words as a gloss. C.'s 'and had heard a strange language' is dubious and misleading.

from the load: The H. word probably means a 'basket for carrying bricks', cf. N.E.B. It can mean 'jars' (cf. C.'s 'pots') but this does not fit this particular context.

Verse 7 *secret place of my thunder:* A fairly literal rendering of H., cf. R.P. and N.E.B. C.'s 'what time as the storm fell upon thee' is dubious.

cringe before him: Cf. R.P. and N.E.B. and contrast C.'s 'been found liars'. See on Ps. 18: 46.

Verse 15 *punishment:* The H. word probably has this meaning, cf. N.E.B. Otherwise H. seems to mean 'their time' (so C.), which in the phrase 'their time should have endured for ever' is less than satisfactory.

PSALM 82

Verse 1 *council of heaven:* H. lit. 'council of God'. The reference is to God's heavenly court. C.'s 'princes' goes back to an old Jewish interpretation of the phrase, *viz.* that God is the judge of human rulers.

PSALM 83

Verse 6 *The tribes of:* The H. word which often means 'tents' can also mean 'tribes', cf. N.E.B. C. and R.P. have 'tabernacles' which is less satisfactory here.

Verse 12 *pastures:* Such is the meaning of H., cf. R.P. and N.E.B.; contrast C.'s 'houses'.

Verse 13 *thistledown:* Such rather than 'wheel' (so C.) is the likely meaning of the H. word, cf. R.P. and N.E.B.

PSALM 84

Verse 5 *the highways to Zion:* H. means lit. 'in their hearts are the highways'. 'To Zion' is added in English *ad sensum,* cf. R.P. and N.E.B.

Verse 6 *dryness:* H. (lit.) means 'balsam trees' which grow in very dry land. *Dryness* here seeks to convey the essential meaning of H., cf. R.P. and N.E.B. C.'s 'misery' is dubious.

finds there a *spring from which to drink:* H. means lit. 'they make it a spring' > *find* a *spring from which to drink,* cf. R.P. and N.E.B. C. 'use it for a well'.

till the autumn rain shall clothe it with blessings: A fairly literal rendering of H., cf. R.P. C. understands the word translated 'blessings' as 'pools' which implies a different pointing of H. N.E.B., too, understands the word as 'pools', but also emends H. fairly substantially.

Verse 10 *stand at the threshold:* A fairly literal rendering of the H. word, cf. N.E.B. C.'s (cf. R.P.'s) 'door keeper' implies an official function rather than that the psalmist is merely lingering at the threshold of the temple.

Verse 11 *rampart:* The H. word, usually rendered 'sun' (cf. C.'s 'light'), here means 'a pinnacle, battlement', cf. N.E.B. R.P.'s 'defence' is somewhat colourless as a translation.

PSALM 85

Verse 8 *whose hearts are turned to him:* H. is emended on the authority of one of the ancient versions (LXX) to give this meaning, cf. N.E.B. H. unaltered means 'that they turn not again to folly', cf. C. 'that they turn not again'. R.P.'s 'even to the upright of heart' depends upon a more substantial emendation of H.

Verse 13 *and tread:* The pointing of H. (but not the consonants) is emended to give this sense. R.P.'s and N.E.B.'s more substantial emendation is unnecessary ('where he walketh, there shall be peace'). C. has 'he shall direct his going in the way' which is somewhat dubious.

PSALM 86

Verse 11 *let my heart delight:* The pointing (but not the consonants) of H. is emended on the authority of two of the ancient versions (LXX and Pesh.) to give this meaning, cf. R.P. H. unaltered has 'unite my heart' > C. 'O knit my heart unto thee', which is dubious because C. has to supply 'unto thee' which is not present in H.

PSALM 87

This is an extremely difficult psalm and both text and meaning are very uncertain. The panel have endeavoured to contrive a meaningful translation with the minimum of change to H.

Verse 1 *holy hill:* The H. plural is a plural of local extension. Contrast C.'s (and R.P.'s) 'holy hills'.

Verse 3 *kinsmen in Egypt:* H. has lit. 'I (might) speak of Rahab', where Rahab is a name for Egypt. *kinsmen in* is an interpretation of the H. word rendered 'them that know me' in C., cf. R.P. and N.E.B.

Verse 4 *many were born in her:* H. lit. 'a man and a man was born in her' > *many were born in her.*

Verse 5 *where every man was born:* H. means lit. 'this (man) was born there' > 'where this man (i.e. each man) was born'> *where every man was born.* There was no emendation of H. in this verse, contrast R.P. and N.E.B. which do so on the authority of a dubious LXX text.

Verse 6 *the dancers:* A literal rendering of H., cf. R.P. and N.E.B. C.'s 'trumpeters' is dubious.

shall make their song to your name: The division of consonants into words is emended in H. to give this sense, cf. R.P. and N.E.B. H. unaltered has lit. 'all my springs in thee' > C. 'all my fresh springs shall be in thee' which is scarcely intelligible.

PSALM 88

Verse 1 *my God, I call for help:* The pointing of H. is emended and one consonant omitted to give this sense, cf. verse 14 below, R.P. and N.E.B. H. unaltered has 'God of my salvation' (so C.) which is less satisfactory in that it fails to achieve the balance and parallelism of H. poetry.

Verse 5 *I lie among the dead:* The H. word is emended by the omission of one letter (also taking the letter *sin* for *shin).* By reference to an Arabic cognate the word is then given the meaning 'to lie, be prostrate', cf. N.E.B. Unaltered H. seems to mean 'free', cf. C.'s 'free among the dead' which makes no sense. R.P. emends more radically to allow 'I am become like unto the dead' which is not necessary.

Verse 7 *are brought against me:* The H. verb is, by reference to an Arabic cognate, and with the support of two of the ancient versions (LXX and Pesh.), given the lit. meaning 'thou hast brought against me', cf. N.E.B. The word is normally rendered 'afflict'. (> C. 'thou hast vexed me' cf. R.P.).

Verse 9 *I am so fast in prison:* H. is emended by the addition of the word 'I' to give this sense which is supported by two of the ancient versions (LXX and Pesh.). C., following the Vulgate (and LXX), is correct although probably not a translation of H. as received.

Verse 15 *rejected me:* See general note on *nephesh.*

Verse 16 *wearied:* The H. verb is thought here to have this meaning, preferable in the context and particularly in association with the words 'from my youth upward'. Contrast R.P. and N.E.B. (where the psalmist takes a long time to die). C., unlike H., takes 'from my youth up' with the second half of the verse.

I am tossed high and low: Two words are slightly emended (with the support of the LXX and Pesh.) to give these passive meanings (the first by emendation of pointing, the second by omission of one letter and emendation of the pointing) > lit. 'I am lifted up, 1 am brought low' > *I am tossed high and low.* H. unaltered has lit. 'I lift up thy terrors'; > C. 'thy terrors have I suffered' (cf. R.P. and N.E.B.), which is less satisfactory if not dubious.

I cease to be: The H. verb is emended to give a form of the verb usually translated 'to turn'; here, however, it is thought to bear the further meaning (cf. the Arabic cognate) 'to depart', 'to perish'. H. unaltered is unintelligible (cf. N.E.B.) and C.'s 'I have suffered' is likely to be a guess. R.P. and N.E.B. emend (in different ways).

Verse 17 *put me to silence:* a variant H. reading is here adopted, cf. N.E.B. C. has 'hath undone me'.

Verse 19 *and kept:* H. is emended to give this sense, cf. R.P. and N.E.B. H. unaltered has 'dark place' which is unintelligible. C. has 'and hid' which, as a translation of H., is dubious.

PSALM 89

Verse 6 *sons of heaven:* H. has lit. 'sons of gods'. C. and R.P. have 'among the gods'. N.E.B. 'in the court of heaven'. Cf. on Psalm 29: 1.

Verse 7 *great and terrible:* H. is emended to give this sense and the phrase is taken with the second half of the verse as in LXX, cf. R.P. and N.E.B. H. unaltered is obscure. C. renders 'very greatly' which is dubious.

Verse 8 *your power:* The pointing of H. (but not the consonants) is emended to give this sense, cf. N.E.B. H. unaltered appears to be an adjective 'strong' > C.'s (dubious) 'most mighty Lord' cf. R.P. (which also emends the pointing).

Verse 10 *Rahab like a carcase:* A fairly literal rendering of H., cf. N.E.B. (footnote). C.'s '(Egypt) and destroyed it' is dubious. Rahab, which in places means Egypt (cf. Ps. 87: 6) here refers to the primaeval chaos-monster, cf. Isa. 51: 9.

Verse 15 *who know the triumphal shout:* A fairly literal rendering of H., cf. (the freer) R.P. and N.E.B. C. has 'that can rejoice in thee'.

Verse 17 *our heads:* H. lit. 'horns'. The image is of a wild animal whose horns are exalted when it is fit and healthy.

Verse 18 *our king belongs to the Lord:* The H. word often translated 'shield' also in places (as here) can mean 'ruler, king'. H. means lit. 'to the Lord is our king'. R.P. and N.E.B. interpret the preposition 'to' as an emphatic particle which, though possible, seemed to the panel less likely in the context, for the Psalm goes on to refer to David as (human) king. C. has 'the Lord is our defence'.

he that rules over us to: H. lit. 'our king'. As *king* has already been used in this verse, we have adopted a synonymous expression here. For the preposition 'to', see on the phrase above.

Verse 19 *to your faithful one:* A variant H. reading is here adopted; the reference is to David. The other reading has 'your faithful ones' (> C. 'thy saints').

Verse 20 *I have set a youth above a warrior:*

youth The H. word is thus explained with the help of Ugaritic, cf. N.E.B. The translation of the rest of the phrase is fairly literal. C.'s 'I have laid help upon one that is mighty' is less satisfactory in the context, though it follows the usual interpretation in giving to the noun the meaning 'help'. R.P.'s 'I have set the crown upon one that is mighty' depends upon an emendation which, the panel judged, is unnecessary.

Verse 25 *head:* See on verse 17 above.

Verse 26 *Western Sea ... the streams of Mesopotamia:* The H. terms (lit. 'the Sea ... the rivers') are thought here to denote the ideal limits of the land of Canaan. Cf. Gen. 15: 18, Exod. 23: 31, Ps. 72: 8, 80: 11, etc.

Verse 38 *stands ... for evermore:* The pointing of one word in H. is emended to give this meaning. R.P. and N.E.B. emend in a different and more drastic way. H. as pointed means a 'witness in the skies' which is dubious in the context.

Verse 44 *bright sword:* One H. word is emended by the omission of one letter and the word is given the lit. meaning 'flash' with the help of Akkadian, cf. N.E.B. (free). H. unaltered has 'rock' which is unintelligible in the context. C.'s 'edge of his sword' (cf. R.P.) is not far from the truth (if not for the right reason).

Verse 45 *his lustre:* A H. variant reading is here adopted with the further support of a number of the ancient versions (Pesh., Jerome, Aq., Symm.). C.'s 'his glory' is substantially correct. R.P.'s 'royal sceptre' (cf. N.E.B.) involves an emendation of H. which is not necessary.

Verse 47 *so utterly:* The H. word, traditionally rendered 'for ever' (so C.), probably means 'to a pre-eminent degree', cf. R.P. and N.E.B.

Verse 48 *Remember how I draw to my eternal end:* H. is emended by rearrangement of the words, by repointing and by the omission of one consonant to give this reading. Comparison should be made with a similar phrase in Psalm 39: 5, cf. R.P. and N.E.B. C. has 'remember how short my time is', which does not quite get it right.

Verse 51 *your servant:* A variant reading attested by a number of H. Mss. is here adopted, cf. N.E.B. The other reading has 'thy servants', cf. C., R.P.

the onslaught of the peoples: The division of the H. consonants into words is emended (with consequent change to the pointing) to give this literal sense: 'strifes from (the) peoples'. The change has the support of two of the ancient versions (Jer. and Pesh.), and is adopted by N.E.B. R.P.'s emendation gives the same meaning but is more drastic.

PSALM 90

Verse 4 *passing:* The verb is taken with 'yesterday' (cf. R.P.) rather than with 'watch' (so C. and N.E.B.). This interpretation is preferable in that it conforms to the traditional punctuation.

Verse 5 *cut short:* Two H. homonyms are now recognised: the one means 'to flood, sweep away' (> C. and R.P. 'scatterest'); the other means 'cause to cease, stop' (> here *cut short*).

dream: The word usually translated 'sleep' (so C.) can also mean 'dream', cf. Jer., R.P. and N.E.B.

of the morning: The order of two H. words is inverted to give this meaning, cf. R.P.

Verse 7 *cease to be:* This meaning can be detected in the H. word (cf. the Pesh.) as well as 'to be afraid' (so C. and R.P.). *cease to be* fits the context better, cf. N.E.B.

Verse 9 *sigh:* This is what H. means, cf. R.P. and N.E.B. C.'s 'tale that is told' derives from Jerome's 'quasi sermonem loquens', a free paraphrase of the H. word which can mean 'meditation' as well as 'sigh'.

Verse 11 *Like those who fear you:* Such is the meaning of H. (abstract for concrete) cf. N.E.B. C. is dubious, if indeed it is intelligible. R.P. emends the text.

Verse 13 *will you be angry:* is supplied to indicate the meaning of H. which has simply 'How long?' cf. Ps. 6: 3.

PSALM 91

Verse 2 *He will say:* A change of the pointing (but not of the consonants) gives this sense, cf. R.P. and N.E.B. H. reads (as pointed) 'I will say' (so C.) The change is supported by two of the ancient versions (LXX and Jer.).

Verse 3 *curse:* A change of the pointing (but not of the consonants) gives this meaning as opposed to H. (as pointed) 'pestilence' (so C.) This alternative tradition is an old one (it is present in the LXX) and better fits a psalm which invokes God's protection against curses and spells.

Verse 9 *your refuge:* One consonant of H. is emended to give (lit.) 'As for thee, the Lord is thy refuge', cf. N.E.B. R.P. emends more drastically. H. unaltered has 'Thou, O Lord, art my refuge' (so C.) which does not fit the context.
Most high: H. refers to God (cf. R.P. and N.E.B.) and is not an adverb 'very high' (so C.).

Verse 16 *fill him:* The H. words 'fill' and 'cause to see' (> C. 'shew') are sometimes impossible to distinguish. 'Fill' is the more likely here, cf. R.P. and N.E.B.

PSALM 92

Verse 2 *faithfulness:* is correct rather than 'truth' (so C.).

Verse 9 *scattered:* Such is the meaning of the H. word (cf. R.P. and N.E.B.) rather than 'destroyed' (so C.).

Verse 10 *my head:* H. (lit.) 'my horn'. The metaphor is that of the proud carriage of an ox whose head is held high, and the present translation attempts to bring out the meaning for modern readers. The figure of speech is not abandoned because 'horns' are referred to in the next line of the translation.
wild oxen: Such is the meaning of the word which indicates a familiar animal and not a mythological one, cf. R.P. and N.E.B.

Verse 14 *sturdy and laden with branches:* The H. words here denote the sturdy and luxuriant growth of trees rather than healthy and well-fed human beings, cf. R.P. and N.E.B. and contrast C. 's 'fat and well-liking'.

PSALM 93

Verse 4 *pounding:* The reference is to waves crashing down, cf. English 'breakers'.

Verse 5 *than the mighty ... sea:* Cf. R.P. and N.E.B. C.'s 'mighty and rage horribly' is highly dubious as a translation of H.

PSALM 94

Verse 10 *disciplines:* The H. word has this meaning rather than 'nurtureth', cf. R.P. and N.E.B. and contrast C.

Verse 15 *righteous man:* A variant H. reading (supported by Symm. and Pesh.) is adopted to give this sense. H. (as pointed) has 'righteousness'; C. and R.P. take 'righteousness' as the subject, which is less likely, and N.E.B. emends the consonantal text.

with him: H. 'after him' (> C., R.P. and N.E.B. 'follows it') can also mean 'with him'. The panel took the view that the 'true of heart' were the recipients of justice rather than followers of it.

Verse 20 *court:* H. (lit.) 'seat' (C. 'stool' and R.P. 'council'). N.E.B.'s 'sanctimonious calumny' is very free if not dubious.

by means of: Such is likely to be the meaning of the H. preposition, cf. R.P. and N.E.B. C.'s 'as' is unlikely.

Verse 21 *life:* See separate note on *nephesh*.

PSALM 95

Verse 4 *depths:* Such is the likely meaning of the H. word (cf. R.P.) rather than 'corners' (so C.) which goes back to LXX and probably a corrupt H. N.E.B. has 'farthest places'.

Verse 4b *peaks:* So H., cf. R.P. C.'s 'strength' is very dubious.

Verse 5 *moulded:* Such is the meaning of the H. word, cf. N.E.B. ('fashioned'). Contrast C. (so R.P.) 'prepared'.

Verse 7 *his people and the sheep of his pasture:* So one H. manuscript (supported by Pesh.) cf. Pss. 79: 13 and 100: 2. The word 'his hand' is probably a corrupt addition to H. R.P.'s and N.E.B.'s emendation of H. (> 'ye shall know his power') is unnecessary and fails to note that the H. Ms. referred to above does not have the word 'his power' (lit. 'his hand').

Verse 8 *Meribah* and *Massah:* are the place-names mentioned in the story of the wanderings of the Israelites in the desert (see Ex. 17: 7, Nu. 20: 13, Deut. 33: 8, Deut. 6: 16 and 9: 22). In English translation it is necessary to decide whether to reproduce the names of the places (which is primary) or to try to bring out the meanings of the place-names (i.e. 'Strife' and 'Testing'). The panel preferred the former alternative.

Verse 10 *loathed:* Such is the meaning of the H. word, cf. R.P. C.'s 'grieved with' is less satisfactory.

PSALM 97

Verse 10 *The Lord loves those that hate evil:* Two small changes to H. and a repointing of the words in question gives this meaning which fits the context better than the vocative and imperative of H. (unaltered). (> C.'s 'O ye that love the Lord, see that ye hate evil'). Some manuscripts support part of this restoration. R.P. and N.E.B.'s treatment of the text is the same as that adopted here.

PSALM 99

Verse 1 *tremble:* A literal rendering of the H. word, cf. R.P. and N.E.B. C.'s 'be the people never so impatient' is misleading.

Verse 4 *The Mighty One is King:* A slight change of pointing (but not of the consonantal text) gives this meaning. C.'s 'the King's power loveth judgement' reflects accurately H. as it stands, but it makes little sense.

This translation avoids the rearrangement of the H. verse division undertaken by R.P. and N.E.B.

Verse 8 *pardoned:* This meaning, which clearly suits the context better than 'punishedst' (so C. and R.P.) is obtained by changing the pointing (but not the consonants) of the H. word in question, cf. N.E.B. The H. words 'punish' and 'forgive' (lit. 'make or declare innocent, clean') are very similar.

PSALM 100

Verse 2 *we are his:* So many H. manuscripts, cf. RP. and N.E.B. This reading reflects an ancient tradition and is preferable to 'not we ourselves' which, although also an old reading, is erroneous and constitutes an absurd statement of the obvious.

Verse 4 *faithfulness:* this rather than 'truth' (C.) is the meaning of the H. word, cf. R.P. and N.E.B.

PSALM 101

Verse 5 *wickedness:* rather than 'wicked person' (C.). No change to H. is required.

Verse 9 *morning by morning:* the probable meaning of H., cf. R.P. and N.E.B. C.'s 'soon' is dubious.

PSALM 102

Verse 3 *furnace:* The H. word probably denotes a place of burning rather than what is burnt (> C. 'firebrand'). The latter interpretation derives from the LXX and Vulgate.

Verse 4 *scorched:* The H. word is used of the blighting of a plant as well as of the wounding (> C. and R.P. 'smitten down') of a person. *'scorched'* is therefore more appropriate to the simile.

Verse 5 *I am weary:* It is assumed, for reasons concerned with metre as well as with sense, that a verb has dropped out here and it is consequently restored by conjecture, cf. R.P. C.'s 'For the voice of my groaning; my bones scarce cleave' represents an attempt to achieve sense without a verb; but it is hardly successful and indeed the addition of the word 'scarce' leads to a reversal of the meaning of H.

Verse 7 *Flit to and fro:* This reading (attested by manuscripts as well as by versional evidence) is preferred to H.'s 'sitteth alone'.

Verse 16 *shows himself in his glory:* More accurately renders H. than C.'s 'his glory shall appear'.

Verse 19 *height of his holiness:* a more literal rendering than C.'s 'sanctuary'.

Verse 23 *before my time:* Lit. H. 'in the way', i.e. 'in mid-course'. (> C. 'in my journey' which might be misleading).

PSALM 103

Verse 5 *being:* It was thought probable on philological grounds that the H. word (which has long been a puzzle to scholars) bears some such meaning, and this is supported by the 10th century Rabbinic authority Saadya. 'Desire' (LXX and Vulgate), 'mouth' (C. and A.V.) are likely to be guesses, for they cannot be supported by the evidence of philology. R.P.'s 'all thy life long' represents a conjectural emendation. N.E.B.'s 'prime of life' rests on philological considerations less likely to be correct than those upon which *being* rests.

PSALM 104

Verse 1 *how great you are:* Such is the meaning of H., cf. R.P. and N.E.B. C.'s 'exceeding glorious' is dubious.

Verse 7 *The deep covered it as with a mantle:* Some doubt attaches to H.'s 'thou hast covered it' (so C. and R.P.); for why should God be said to cover the earth with water, only (v.8) to uncover it again? Furthermore, there is some variation in the way the word is treated in the ancient versions. A change of two consonants (and consequent repointing) makes the 'deep' the subject of the verb, cf. N.E.B. The next verse then adverts to God's 'rebuke' of the deep.

Verse 12 *they give drink:* So H. C.'s (so R.P. and N.E.B.) 'All beasts of the field drink thereof' is a paraphrase (cf. R.P. and N.E.B.), for the 'beasts' are properly the object of the verb.

Verse 15 *servants:* The abstract H. word 'service' (so C. and R.P.) is here used to denote the domestic animals, *the servants of mankind*, cf. N.E.B.

Verse 26 *your creatures:* The cognate H. verb is now known to bear the meaning 'create' (here the noun means 'creatures'), cf. R.P. and N.E.B. The verb can also mean 'get', 'acquire' (hence a noun: 'things got, acquired', so C.'s 'riches').

PSALM 105

Verse 18 *neck:* lit. 'throat' (see general note on *nephesh* 'soul'). H. means lit. 'his throat came into iron', cf. R.P. and N.E.B. C.'s 'the iron entered into his soul' is impossible because *nephesh* is the subject of the verb.

Verse 22 *to rebuke:* At first sight the verb seems to mean 'to bind'; but it is now recognised that we have here a spelling slightly at variance with the normal. The verb in question then has the range of meanings 'to discipline, rebuke, instruct', cf. N.E.B. C.'s 'that he might inform' is in fact correct in principle because the tradition of the LXX (and Vulgate), on which C. was dependent, preserved the correct understanding of H. (The change to the text suggested by R.P. is not necessary.)

Verse 31 *gnats:* Such is the meaning of the H. word rather than C.'s 'lice', cf. R.P. N.E.B. has 'maggots'.

borders: Such is the meaning of the H. word rather than C.'s 'quarters', cf. R.P. and N.E.B.

Verse 37 *seen to stumble:* Such is the meaning of H. (*'seen to'* being supplied in English) rather than C.'s 'was not one feeble person', cf. R.P. and N.E.B.

Verse 38 *dread of Israel had fallen upon them:* This is a more literal translation (*'Israel'* being supplied in English for H.'s 'them' in the interests of clarity) than C.'s rather bald 'they were afraid of them', cf. R.P. and N.E.B.

PSALM 106

Verse 1 *Praise the Lord:* In H. the psalm begins with this exclamation which is omitted in C. It is present in R.P. and N.E.B. See also Pss. 111:1, 112: l.

Verse 10 *He commanded:* The word properly denotes the stentorian roar of God's command, rather than a (moral) 'rebuke' (so C., R.P. and N.E.B.).

Verse 17 *grew envious:* The H. word denotes 'display jealousy, jealous anger' as well as 'to excite to jealous anger'. The former meaning was thought more likely here (cf. R.P. and N.E.B.) rather than the latter (> C. 'they angered Moses').

Verse 21 *Glory of God:* H. has 'their glory' which represents a correction to the text made by the scribes in ancient times in order to avoid the unseemly statement that God's glory had been diminished. The original meaning as intended by the psalmist has been restored, cf. R.P. and N.E.B.

Verse 27 *to swear an oath against them:* H. has literally 'he lifted up his hand in regard to them'. The expression implies the taking of an oath rather than the lifting of the arm for the delivery of a blow (so apparently C.). The words *'an oath'* are supplied to make this clear, cf. R.P. and N.E.B.

Verse 33 *suffered:* H. (as pointed) means lit. 'and it went badly for Moses because of them', cf. N.E.B. C.'s and R.P.'s 'he *(sc.* God) punished Moses' follows a variant tradition which implies a different pointing of the consonants from that of H.

Verse 41 *after strange gods:* This phrase is added in English in order to bring out the force of the verb *'whored'*.

PSALM 107

Verse 2 *say (so):* So H. lit., cf. R.P. and N.E.B. C.'s 'give thanks' is probably supplied from the context.

Verse 4 *in the wilderness and in the desert:* Two words for desert are in fact present in H. (C. has but one word 'wilderness').

path: is taken with the *inhabited city* rather than with the *desert* (cf. R.P. and N.E.B.) despite H. (as accented) which takes the reverse view. C. which follows H. (as accented) is, however, dubious, for the words 'out of (the way)' have to be supplied and are not present in (or implied by) H.

Verse 5 *heart:* (cf. C. 'soul') i.e. the inner personality. See note on *nephesh.*

Verse 9 *thirsty and hungry:* Again, see note on *nephesh.* The probable literal meanings here are 'thirsty throat (appetite)' and 'hungry throat (appetite)'.

Verse 10 *deadly shadow:* The expression 'shadow of death' (so C.) in H. is an intensive and is comparable to modern English 'a deadly dull sermon'. But the expression may retain some suggestion of death and this is allowed for in the translation. See also Ps. 23: 4.

Verse 12 *tripped headlong:* The H. verb denotes 'stumbling and falling to the ground' rather than simply 'falling', cf. N.E.B. C. (so R.P.) has 'they fell down'.

Verse 14 *deadly shadow:* Cf. on verse 10 above.

Verse 17 H. lit. 'because of their way of transgression', an idiom which suggests that they are well into sin, not merely beginners. It is unnecessary to emend (as does R.S.V.) 'sick' for 'fools'.

Verse 18 *They:* See general note on *nephesh.*

Verse 20 *their life:* H. lit. 'them'.

Verse 29 *He calmed the storm to a silence:* H. (lit.) 'He established the storm to (i.e. so that it was) a silence', cf. N.E.B. C. (so R.P.) has 'he maketh the storm to cease', which is less satisfactory.

Verse 32 *Council:* The H. word means 'assembly' as well as 'seat' (so C.). The former meaning is here preferable, cf. R.P. and N.E.B.

Verses 39, 40 The order of these verses in H. is here inverted because the subject of (H.) verse 39 is unlikely to be the people mentioned in the preceding verses - their fortunes are not reversed again. It is probable that the people mentioned in (H.) verse 40 are the subject. The order of the verses in H. is probably due to scribal error.

Verse 39 *pours contempt upon princes:* Such is the obvious meaning of H. C.'s 'though he suffer them to be evil intreated through tyrants' ('princes')' is a highly dubious attempt to accommodate the meaning to fit the H. order of verses 39 and 40. It is more likely, however, that it is the princes who are the object of God's contempt and, as a consequence, *they are weakened and brought low.*

PSALM 108

Verse 2 *I will awaken the morning:* The verb is transitive and 'morning' is its object, cf. R.P. and N.E.B. (note). 'I will awake right early' (C.) is dubious.

Verse 4 *reaches to:* This variant reading (cf. R.P.) is preferable to the reading (lit.) 'from upon' (> C. 'greater than', cf. N.E.B.'s 'wider than').
faithfulness: rather than 'truth' (C.). See general note.

Verse 6 *us:* There is no pronominal object in H. cf. N.E.B. *'us'* is supplied *ad sensum,* cf. R.P. C. supplies 'them'.

Verse 7 *holy places:* The H. abstract noun has this concrete meaning here, cf. R.P. and N.E.B. Contrast C.'s 'holiness'.

Verse 8 *rod of command:* A commander's staff is here intended (cf. R.P. and N.E.B.) rather than a giver of laws (so C.) cf. Gen. 49: 10 (N.E.B.).

PSALM 109

Verse 3 *and that for no fault of mine:* The inversion of two consonants and a slight change of pointing gives this admirable sense, cf. N.E.B. H. has (lit.) 'and I am a prayer' which is nonsense. C.'s (so R.P.) 'I give myself to prayer' is a dubious interpretation.

Verse 5 *to stand against him:* H. has (lit.) 'upon/against him'. The words *'to stand'* are supplied *ad sensum,* cf. R.P. and N.E.B. C.'s 'to be ruler over' ('upon') is also supplied but is less likely in view of what follows in the second half of the verse.

adversary: Such is the meaning of the H. word *(stn)* which in later times became 'The Adversary' *par excellence*, i.e. Satan. Here a human enemy simply is intended.

Verse 7 *what he has hoarded:* is more likely here than C.'s highly dubious 'office', cf. R.P. and N.E.B.

Verse 12 *one (generation):* One letter of H. is corrected on the evidence of the LXX. So apparently N.E.B. (though there is no note). As it stands H. has 'another' (> C. and R.P. 'next').

Verse 17 *body:* H. lit. 'inside him' (> C. 'His bowels').

Verse 19 *me:* See general note on *nephesh.*

Verse 21 *writhes:* A change of the pointing (but not of the consonants) gives this meaning, cf. R.P. and N.E.B. H. (as pointed) has 'one has bored my heart' (> C. 'my heart is wounded within me') which is dubious.

Verse 30 *those that would condemn him:* Cf. R.P. and N.E.B. H. lit. 'the judges of his *nephesh'* (> C. 'soul'). For *nephesh* see general note. C.'s 'to save his soul from unrighteous judges' is very dubious for it fails to construe *nephesh* with 'judges' and this H. requires; furthermore 'unrighteous' in C. corresponds to nothing in H.

PSALM 110

Verse 2 *reign from Zion:* H.'s accentuation has been changed slightly (with consequent improvement to metre) so that 'from Zion' is taken with 'reign' rather than with the 'sceptre of power' (so H., as accented, which C., R.P. and N.E.B. follow).

Verse 3 *Noble are you from the day of your birth:* A change of pointing (but not of the consonants) of three H. words gives this sense, (lit. 'with you is nobility from the day of your birth'), cf. N.E.B. R.P.'s solution is similar but less satisfactory. It is scarcely possible to translate H. (as pointed), cf. C.'s dubious 'In the day of thy power shall the people offer free-will offerings with an holy worship. '

radiant: a change has been made to the accentuation (but not of the consonants). The resulting noun is assumed to have here the related meanings 'dawn' and 'radiance'. H. then means (lit.) 'radiance to you' > *radiant are you.* The same meaning is posited by the N.E.B. but it is achieved by inverting the order of two consonants and thereafter on grounds of comparative philology. R.P. also emends the text but with a less satisfactory meaning. H. (unaltered) seems to mean 'from dawn' which, with the preposition 'from', gives little sense; cf. C.'s 'of the morning'.

Verse 5 *the king:* The word 'king' is added in this translation to make clear who is the subject of the verb.

Verse 6 *Glorious in majesty:* A slight change to the consonants of one word and to the pointing of another gives, lit. 'full of majesty' >*glorious in majesty,* cf. N.E.B. H. has lit. 'he will fill the corpses' (> C.'s and R.P.'s dubious 'he will fill the places with the dead bodies').

wide land: H. has a singular noun 'large land'. Cf. and contrast C.'s 'divers countries'.

PSALM 111

Verse 1 *O praise the Lord:* see note on Ps. 106: 1.

company: Such is here the meaning of the H. word (cf. R.P. and N.E.B.) which has the range 'familiar converse, intimacy, council, counsel'. C.'s 'secretly' is misleading.

Verse 8 *faithfulness:* C. 'truth'. See general note on *emeth.*

Verse 10 *keep his commandments:* H. lit. 'keep them' (> C. 'do thereafter'). The word *'commandments'* is added for clarity.

PSALM 112

Verse 1 *O praise the Lord:* See note on Ps. 106: l.

Verse 5 *It goes well with:* is preferable (cf. R.P. and N.E.B.) to C.'s 'A good man', which is very doubtful.

affairs: The H. word can mean 'word' (so C. 'word') or 'affairs, business'. The latter meaning was thought to be better here, cf. R.P. and N.E.B.

Verse 9 *head:* H. lit. 'his horn' (so C.). See note on Psalm xcii: 10.

PSALM 113

Verses 5, 6 The H. order of the phrases has been rearranged in English so that the meaning is expressed more clearly.

PSALM 115

Verse 1 *faithfulness:* C. 'truth'. See general note on *emeth.*

Verses 8, 9, 10 *shield:* so H. literally. C. 'defence'.

Verse 14 *The blessing of the Lord be upon you:* H. lit. 'Blessed be (or 'are') you by the Lord' (> C. 'ye are the blessed of the Lord'). The words are more likely to represent a prayer than a statement, cf. R.P. and contrast N.E.B.

PSALM 116

Verse 1 *I love the Lord:* The divine name ('The Lord') is moved to this position in H. so that it becomes the object of the verb, cf. R.P. and N.E.B. 'I love' is what the H. verb means rather than '1 am well pleased' (C.).

Verse 2 *in the day:* A change of pointing (but not of consonants) gives this meaning, cf. R.P. H. (as pointed) 'in my days' (> C. 'as long as 1 live').

Verse 10 *I would perish:* The H. word is likely on philological and contextual grounds to carry here this meaning (cf. N.E.B.) rather than 'speak' (so C. and R.P.).

Verse 14 *grievous:* A possible meaning for the H. word (so ibn Ezra), which fits the context better than 'right dear' (so C., R.P. and N.E.B.).

PSALM 117

Verse 2 *great:* The H. word means, lit. 'is strong'.

faithfulness: see general note on *emeth.*

PSALM 118

Verse 2 *now proclaim:* C. adds 'that he is gracious': these words derive from the LXX and they are not present in H.

Verse 5 *set me free:* H. (lit.) 'he answered me with broadness' i.e. with freedom. So here *set me free.* (C. 'heard me at large'.)

Verses 10, 11, 12 *drove them back:* No change to H. The meaning, to which one of the ancient versions (LXX) bears witness, is posited on grounds of comparison with an Arabic cognate, cf. R.P. and N.E.B. C.'s 'destroyed them' is dubious.

Verse 12 *blazed:* Two consonants are changed to give this meaning for which there is support in the LXX, cf. R.P. H. (unaltered) seems to mean 'are extinguished', (> C. 'are extinct') which makes poor sense in the context. N.E.B.'s 'attack' is dubious.

Verse 26 *From the house ... bless you:* A fairly literal rendering of H., cf. R.P. and N.E.B. C.'s 'wished you good luck, ye that are of the house of the Lord' is dubious.

Verse 27 *guide the festal throng:* No change is made to H. It is very doubtful whether the H. word, here rendered *festal throng,* could mean 'sacrificial animal' (cf. C.'s 'sacrifice') and equally doubtful is the idea that such an animal should be tied to the horns of an altar. H. was taken to mean (lit.) 'bind the pilgrimage with ropes'. The phrase is recognised to constitute one of the major problems of the psalter, and a number of possible interpretations have been proposed. (N.E.B.'s treatment is similar to the present one, though it adopts a variant reading from a Dead Sea Scroll fragment.)

PSALM 119

Verse 14 *than:* One consonant of H. has been changed, cf. R.P. and N.E.B. C.'s 'I have had *as* great delight ... *as* in all manner' is dubious as a translation of H.

Verse 18 *take away the veil:* H. lit. 'uncover my eyes' (cf. C.'s 'open thou mine eyes').

Verse 24 *counsellors in my defence:* lit. 'men of my counsel' i.e. those giving me advice, cf. C. 'my counsellors'.

Verse 25 *I:* See general note on *nephesh.*

Verse 26 *examine:* H. lit. 'recounted', cf. C. 'acknowledged'.

Verse 28 *raise* me *up:* So H. lit. Contrast C.'s 'comfort'.

Verse 29 *grace:* H. lit. 'be gracious to me in (giving) your law'. C.'s 'cause thou me to make much of thy law' is dubious.

Verse 38 *for all who fear you:* H. lit. 'for your fear' where the abstract 'fear' means 'those who fear you.' C.'s 'that I may fear for you' is dubious.

Verse 48 *worship you with outstretched hands:* Three words from H. are deleted (in C. 'thy commandments which I have loved'), for with them the verse is too long; and nowhere else in the psalm are there two words for the law in the same verse. Two consonants are added to the word translated 'unto' in C. to allow the translation *(worship) you,* cf. R.P.

Verse 53 *I am seized with indignation:* H. lit. 'raging heat has seized me', cf. R.P. and N.E.B. C.'s 'I am horribly afraid' is dubious.

Verse 61 *the snares ... encompassed me:* H. lit. 'the ropes of the wicked surround me', cf. R.P. C.'s 'congregations ... have robbed me' (cf. N.E.B.) is less likely to be correct.

Verse 69 *smeared:* H. lit. 'the proud have plastered falsehood over me'. Cf. C. 'imagined a lie against me'.

Verse 78 *steal my rights through lies:* So H. lit. C.'s 'go about wickedly to destroy me' is very dubious.

Verse 79 The word order is closer to H. than is C.'s.

Verse 81 *languishes:* So H. lit. Contrast C.'s (so R.P. and N.E.B.) 'long for'.

Verse 90 *faithfulness:* C. 'truth'. See general note on *emeth.*

you have made: H. lit. 'you have made firm' (> C. 'thou hast laid the foundation').

Verse 91 as *for your judgements:* So lit. H. C.'s 'they continue ... according to thine ordinance' is dubious, for, amongst other things, it is not clear what is the antecedent to which the pronoun 'they' refers.

Verse 96 *perfection:* The H. word means lit. 'completeness/perfection', cf. C. 'all things'.

Verse 103 *tongue:* The H. word means lit. 'palate/roof of the mouth', cf. C.'s 'throat'.

Verse 113 *double-minded:* Cf. R.P. and N.E.B. The H. word, which occurs only here in the sense of moral imperfection, denotes what is divided. C.'s 'that imagine evil things' is dubious.

Verse 117 *delight in:* C.'s interpretation, though it owes probably more to the LXX than to H., is now, on philological grounds, vindicated, cf. R.P. and N.E.B.

Verse 118 *You scorn:* So H. lit. C.'s 'trodden down' is wrong.

calumnies against me: H. lit. 'for their calumny (against me) is a lie' cf. R.P. and N.E.B. C.'s 'for they imagine but deceit' is hardly satisfactory.

Verse 122 *stand surety:* So H. lit., cf. R.P. and N.E.B. C.'s 'make (your servant) to delight' is wrong.

Verse 123 *for the fulfilment:* supplied in English *ad sensum.*

Verse 126 *for the Lord:* A straightforward rendering of H. The fact that there is a switch from a third person reference to God to a second person reference need not tell against the rendering, though it causes R.P. to adopt a variant reading.

to act: So H. lit., cf. C.'s 'to lay to thine hand'.

Verse 127 *finest gold:* H. lit. 'gold'. *'finest'* is added in English for variety; cf. C.'s 'precious stone'.

Verse 128 *by all your precepts:* A change to H. (which appears to be corrupt) by reference to the LXX and Jer., makes possible this translation, cf. R.P. and N.E.B. C.'s 'I hold straight all thy commandments' is dubious.

Verse 139 *zeal and indignation:* Two words are supplied in English in order to make clear the meaning of the one H. word.

Choked my mouth: H. lit. 'reduced me to silence', cf. C.'s 'consumed me'.

Verse 140 *in the fire:* is supplied in English *ad sensum.*

Verse 147 *Before the morning light I rise:* H. lit. 'I forestall the morning light,' cf. C.'s 'early in the morning'.

Verse 149 *according to your judgements:* This variant reading is attested by a number of H. Mss. C.'s (so R.P.) 'as thou art wont' is a possible rendering of the other H. reading, but it is more likely that the verse would contain at least one reference to the law cf. on Verse 48.

Verse 156 *Numberless:* H. lit. has 'many'. C., R.P. and N.E.B. render 'great'.

Verse 160 *The sum:* so H. lit., cf. R.P. C.'s 'from everlasting' is dubious.

Verse 165 *nothing shall make them stumble:* H. lit. 'There is no stumbling-block for them', cf. C.'s 'they are not offended at it'.

PSALM 120

Verse 1 *That he may answer:* a slight change of the pointing (but not of the consonants) gives this preferable sense. H. (as pointed) has 'and he answered' (so C., R.P. and N.E.B.) But the rest of the Psalm suggests that God's answer has not yet come.

what will he do: ... what more will he do: Cf. R.P. and N.E.B. A common H. idiom which C. has failed to understand.

Verse 3 *you are sharp . . . juniper:* H. seems to mean lit. 'a warrior's arrows sharpened with coals of juniper', cf. C.'s (dubious) 'even mighty and sharp arrows with hot burning coals'.

PSALM 121

Verse 7 *life:* See general note on *nephesh.*

PSALM 122

Verse 3 *where the pilgrims gather in unity:* Cf. N.E.B. The word 'pilgrims' is added in English *ad sensum.* H. is taken to mean (lit.) 'where there is a gathering in unity'. C.'s 'that is at unity in itself' is dubious, as is

R.P.'s 'where houses stand close together' which in any case does not fit
verse 4 as well.

Verse 4 *as he commanded Israel:* H. lit. 'a testimony (i.e. law) for Israel'.
(> C. 'to testify unto Israel'). What is meant is that Israel receives a
command to 'go up'.

Verse 5 *thrones:* The H. word is plural, cf. C.'s 'seat'.

PSALM 123

Verse 5 *those at ease:* The H. word denotes 'those at ease', 'the secure'.
The connotations are those of arrogance (cf. R.P.) not of material wealth.
C.'s (cf. N.E.B.) 'wealthy' is a mistranslation.

PSALM 124

Verse 3 *raging:* Cf. R.P. and N.E.B. The H. word means 'boil, seethe'
and also act insolently' (> C.'s 'the waters of the proud'); the more
concrete meaning is preferable here.

us: See general note on *nephesh.*

Verse 6 *We:* see general note on *nephesh.*

PSALM 125

Verse 3 *have no sway:* Cf. R.P. and N.E.B. The H. word means (lit.) 'to
rest, remain upon', so here *have no sway.* Contrast C.s cometh not into'.

land: Cf. R.P. and N.E.B. The H. word means lit. 'lot' and 'land
apportioned by lot' (> here *land,* cf. C.'s 'lot'.)

PSALM 126

Verses 1, 5 *turn(ed) again the fortunes:* See note on xiv: 7.

restored to life: The H. word here means lit. 'healthy, strong', cf. Job 39:
4, and Isa. 38: 16, R.P. and N.E.B. C.'s 'dream' arises because a
homonym in H. has this meaning.

PSALM 127

Verse 2 *the watchmen watch:* Cf. N.E.B. The H. word means 'be watchful, wakeful over', cf. C.'s (so R.P.) 'waketh'.

Verse 3 *for:* This variant reading is attested by some H. Mss. and the LXX. The other reading has 'so'. C.'s 'for so' seems to preserve both traditions.

honour: The H. word is, on philological grounds, likely to have this meaning here. C.'s 'sleep' is unlikely in the context and there are very considerable objections to R.P.'s interpretation of the phrase as sexual union ('he blesseth ... in their beds'); N.E.B. regarded the word as unintelligible, but since then our understanding of the problem has improved.

Verse 5 *warrior:* such is the meaning of H. rather than 'giant' (C.).

sons of a man's youth: H. lit. 'sons of youth'. Contrast C.'s 'young children' which is dubious as a translation of H.

PSALM 128

Verse 3 *within your house:* H. lit. 'in the sides of your house'. It is the wife who is referred to, not the vine, cf. R.P. and N.E.B. C. has 'vine: upon the walls of thine house', which is dubious.

PSALM 129

Verse 4 *he has cut me free:* The words *'me free'* are supplied in English *ad sensum.* H. lit. 'has cut off the thongs' (cf. C.'s 'snares'.)

Verse 6 *comes to any good:* The H. word is on philological grounds thought to have the meaning 'shot up', 'put forth a stalk', cf. R.P. and N.E.B. The word is also attested with the meaning 'pluck', 'draw out', cf. C.'s 'afore it be plucked up'; but here the former meaning is preferable.

PSALM 130

Verse 6 *more than watchmen:* So lit. H. C.'s 'before the morning watch' is wrong.

PSALM 131

Verse 1 *my eyes:* So lit. H., cf. C.'s 'I have no proud looks'.

Verse 3 *calmed:* Cf. R.P. H. lit. 'smoothed'. C.'s 'refrain my soul' is dubious.

breast: supplied in English *ad sensum.*

PSALM 132

Verse 2 *comfort of my bed:* <H. lit. 'couch of my bed'.

Verse 3 C.'s 'neither the temples of my head to take any rest' is not present in H., but derives from the LXX.

Verse 4 *ark:* The word is supplied *ad sensum* from the context, cf. C.'s (so R.P.) 'temple of the Lord'. H. has 'Lord' simply.

Verse 5 *Ja-ar:* A proper name which should not be translated, cf. R.P. and N.E.B. Contrast C.'s 'in the wood'.

PSALM 133

Verse 1 *brothers:* is here not a vocative (so C.) but is part of the construction (lit.) 'the living together of brothers is good ...', cf. R.P. and N.E.B.

Verse 2 *fragrant as oil:* (2nd time). The words are supplied in English *ad sensum.*

Verse 3 *like the dew:* (2nd line). The words are supplied in English *ad sensum.* H. does not mean that the dew of Hermon falls on Zion.

PSALM 136

Verse 5 *wisdom:* so H. C. 'excellent wisdom'.

Verse 26 Verse 3 is repeated after this verse in the LXX, in the Vulgate and in C. but not in H.

PSALM 137

Verse 3 *despoiled us:* The H. word is obscure and on philological grounds this meaning is the most likely, cf. N.E.B. On this view, it is not necessary to emend the text (as does R.P.) by changing one consonant. C.'s 'our heaviness' is dubious.

Verse 5 *forget its mastery:* The meaning of the H. word is uncertain and the translation is based on the context here and in Psalm cii: 4.

Verse 8 *you that lay waste:* The pointing (but not the consonantal text) is emended to give this active meaning on the basis of comparison of H. with Symm., cf. R.P. and N.E.B. The passive meaning of H. (as pointed) (cf. C.'s 'wasted with misery') is unlikely in this context, because Babylon is not yet 'wasted with misery'.

PSALM 138

Verse 3 *put new strength:* The H. verb is emended on the authority of one of the ancient versions (Pesh.). C. follows the Vulgate (and LXX) and offers much the same meaning. The meaning of the H. word (as received) is not certain.

Verse 6 *he humbles:* One consonant of the H. verb is emended (with consequent change of pointing) and given this meaning which fits the context well; cf. R.P. and N.E.B. C.'s 'he beholdeth' is dubious.

Verse 7 *preserve* my *life:* A fairly literal rendering of H., cf. R.P. and N.E.B. C.'s 'yet shalt thou refresh me' is dubious.

PSALM 139

Verse 2 *you discern:* Such is probably the meaning of the H. verb here (cf. N.E.B.) rather than C.'s (cf. R.P.'s) 'thou art about'.

Verse 4 *encompassed me:* A fairly literal rendering of the H. verb, cf. R.P. and N.E.B. C.'s 'fashioned me' is dubious.

Verse 7 *make* my *bed:* A fairly literal rendering of H., cf. R.P. and N.E.B. and contrast C.'s 'go down to'.

Verse 8 *spread out my wings towards the morning:* A more likely interpretation of the H. phrase (cf. N.E.B.) than C.'s (cf. R.P.'s) 'take the wings of the morning'.

Verse 10 *will enclose me:* A reading from the Dead Sea Scrolls is here adopted to give this more likely meaning, cf. N.E.B. H., unaltered, has 'and the day around me turn to night.' > C.'s 'then shall my night be turned to day'.

Verse 12 *knit me together:* A fairly literal rendering of H., cf. N.E.B. and contrast C.'s 'thou hast covered me'. R.P. has 'fashioned me'.

Verse 13 *you are to be feared:* H. is emended to give this sense, cf. R.P. *fearful are your acts:* H. is emended on the authority of one of the ancient versions (LXX - some Mss.) to give lit. 'you are fearful'. *your acts* is supplied *ad sensum,* cf. R.P. and N.E.B. C.'s 'I am fearfully and wonderfully made' is dubious.

Verse 14 *you knew my soul:* The words are taken with this verse rather than with the previous as in H. The pointing (but not the consonants) of the H. verb is emended to give this meaning, cf. N.E.B. H. unaltered gives the less satisfactory meaning 'my soul knows well' (cf. C. and R.P.).

Verse 16 *and not one was late in growing:* H. is emended by adding one word (assumed to have been omitted by haplography) on the authority of one ancient version (Symm.), cf. N.E.B. H. unaltered has (lit.) 'and not one amongst them'. > C. (so R.P.) 'when as yet there was none of them'.

Verse 18 *were I to come to the end:* A variant H. reading is adopted to give this sense, cf. R.P. and N.E.B. The other reading has 'were I to wake up' > C.'s 'when 1 wake up' which is less likely to be correct.

Verse 20 *they affront you:* H. is emended (with the authority of Quinta) to give this sense, cf. N.E.B. H. as received has 'they speak' > C.'s (cf. R.P.) 'they speak unrighteously' which is less likely.

exalt themselves: A reading from the Dead Sea Scrolls (with support from Symm. and Jerome) is adopted to give this meaning, cf. N.E.B. H. as received is obscure. C. (cf. R.P.) has 'take thy name in vain' which is dubious.

PSALM 140

Verse 5 *rogues:* The pointing of the H. word (but not the consonants) is emended to give this meaning, cf. N.E.B. H. as pointed seems to mean 'cords' > C. (so R.P.) 'and spread a net abroad with cords' which is less satisfactory.

Verse 9 *Let not those that beset me lift up their heads:* H. is emended by the addition of a negative, and a variant reading is adopted for the verb giving this meaning. The words *Let not those ... lift up* are taken with this verse rather than with the previous verse as in H. This treatment restores satisfactorily parallelism and meaning, cf. R.P. and (in part) N.E.B.

Verse 11 *the evil, the violent man – let him be hunted to the end:* The H. adjective 'evil' is taken to refer, as another description, to the 'violent man' and, like it, to be the subject of the passive verb in English. H. then literally means 'An evil, violent man one will hunt with thrusts' (i.e. *to the end*). The impersonal 'one will hunt' is more naturally expressed by a passive construction in English. This solution was preferred to understanding 'evil' as the subject of the active H. verb (so C. and R.P.).

PSALM 141

Verse 5 *the faithful man rebukes me:* H. is emended to give this sense, cf. N.E.B. H. unaltered is somewhat obscure and C.'s 'smite me friendly: and rebuke me' is dubious.

Verse 6 *(oil) of the wicked:* H. is emended on the authority of two of the ancient versions (LXX and Pesh.) to give this sense, cf. R.P. and N.E.B. H. unaltered has 'head' which is probably a corrupt assimilation to 'my head' which follows.

anoint: The H. verb is slightly emended, cf. R.P. and N.E.B. C.'s 'break (my head)' is dubious.

Verses 7, 8 These verses are extremely difficult.

Verse 7 *They shall be cast down by that Mighty One who is their judge:* lit. 'They shall be cast down at the hands of the Rock who is their judge'. C.'s 'Let their judges be overthrown in stony places' (cf. R.P.) is dubious.

Verse 8 *As when a farmer breaks the ground:* One H. word is emended on the authority of two of the ancient versions (Symm. and Jerome, cf. LXX and Pesh.) so that the phrase means lit. 'Like a cleaver *(sc.* ploughman) who breaks up on the land', cf. R.P. Unaltered H. has two participles > C. 'as when one breaketh and heweth wood'. 'Wood' is supplied by C. and is not present in H. N.E.B.'s solution to the problem is different and involves more substantial changes to the pointing.

their bones: The H. word is emended with the authority of one of the ancient versions (LXX), cf. R.P. and N.E.B. Unaltered H. has 'our bones' (so C.).

Verse 9 *my life:* See general note on *nephesh.*

PSALM 142
Verse 4 *I look ... and see:* A variant reading from the Dead Sea Scrolls is adopted here.

Verse 5 *for me:* See general note on *nephesh.*
Verse 8 *Bring me:* See general note on *nephesh.*

PSALM 143
Verse 2 *Bring not:* A variant H. reading, supported also by one of the ancient versions (Pesh.), is here adopted giving this sense. The other reading has 'do not come' > C. 'Enter not ... with' which is less likely.

Verse 9 *for I run to you for shelter:* A variant H. reading is here adopted giving this sense, cf. N.E.B. The majority reading has 'I cover'.

R.P. emends (as opposed to accepting a variant H. reading). C.'s 'I flee unto thee to hide me' is not unreasonable.

Verse 10 *in an even path:* A variant H. reading is adopted giving this sense, cf. R.P. and N.E.B. The other reading has 'land' > C. 'land of righteousness', which is less likely.

Verse 12 *against me:* See general note on *nephesh.*

PSALM 144

Verse 2 *my strength:* H. is emended by comparison with Psalm xviii: 2. As received, it has 'my loving-kindness' > C. 'my hope'; > R.P. 'my refuge': > N.E.B. 'my help that never fails', which is less satisfactory.

peoples: A variant H. reading with this meaning is adopted, cf. R.P. and N.E.B. The other reading has 'my people' (cf. C.).

Verse 6 *scatter them on every side:* The reference of the H. phrase is to the lightning flashes and not to (God's) enemies, cf. R.P. and N.E.B. and contrast C.'s dubious 'and tear them' *(sc.* enemies); see on Ps. xviii:15.

with the roar of the thunderbolt: H. has lit. 'and make them roar' (i.e. his arrows, a figure for the lightning flashes).

Verses 10, 11 *from the peril of the sword:* This phrase is taken with verse 11 rather than with the previous verse as in H. (cf. C).

Verse 15 *no miscarriage or untimely birth:* A fairly literal rendering of H., cf. R.P. and N.E.B. C.'s 'no decay; no leading into captivity' is dubious and misleading.

PSALM 145

Verse 7 *Their lips shall flow:* A fairly literal rendering of H. *(their lips* added *ad sensum),* cf. R.P. and N.E.B. Contrast C.'s passive verb 'shall be shewed'.

Verse 16 *your bounteous gift:* The H. phrase is ambiguous, having the literal force 'what pleases'. It could mean 'with what pleases them' (i.e.

321

what they want) > N.E.B. 'what they desire' or 'what pleases you' > here *your bounteous gift.*

PSALM 147

Verse 3 *binds up their wounds:* A literal rendering of H., cf. R.P. and N.E.B. Contrast C.'s 'giveth medicine to heal their sickness'.

Verse 17 *the waters harden:* H. is emended to give the lit. sense 'the waters stand', cf. R.P. and N.E.B. Unaltered H. means 'who can stand' (> C. 'who is able to abide') which is dubious.

Verse 20 *Praise the Lord:* H. concludes the Ps. with this exclamation which is omitted in C. It is present in R.P. and N.E.B., cf. also Ps. 149: 9.

PSALM 148

Verse 3 *stars of light:* A literal rendering of H., cf. R.P. and N.E.B. C.'s 'stars and light' is dubious.

Verse 5 *for he commanded:* C. adds before these words 'he spake the word and they were made'. The words are, however, not in H. but are derived ultimately from the LXX.

Verse 7 *from the earth:* A literal rendering of H., cf. N.E.B. C. (and R.P.) have 'upon the earth'.

PSALM 149

Verse 9 *the judgement that is decreed:* H. means lit: 'to do to them the judgement that is written'. C.'s 'that they may be avenged of them, as it is written' is rather free as a translation of H.
Praise the Lord: See on Ps. 147: 20 above.

PSALM 150

Verse 1 *in his sanctuary:* The H. abstract noun (C. 'holiness') here denotes (God's) *sanctuary,* cf. R.P. and N.E.B.

20789818R00182

Made in the USA
Charleston, SC
28 July 2013